# Transforming Your STEM Career Through Leadership and Innovation: Inspiration and Strategies for Women

D1467904

**Transforming Your STEM Career Through Leadership and Innovation: Inspiration and Strategies for Women** is accompanied by a website featuring:

- Women's leadership success stories
- Additional innovation resources
- Best practices for women interested in developing leadership skills in the STEM industries

To access these companion resources, please visit Booksite.elsevier.com/9780123969934

# Transforming Your STEM Career Through Leadership and Innovation: Inspiration and Strategies for Women

*Written and Edited by*

**Pamela McCauley Bush**
Orlando, FL, USA

**ELSEVIER**

AMSTERDAM • BOSTON • HEIDELBERG • LONDON
NEW YORK • OXFORD • PARIS • SAN DIEGO
SAN FRANCISCO • SINGAPORE • SYDNEY • TOKYO

Academic Press is an imprint of Elsevier

Academic Press is an imprint of Elsevier
32 Jamestown Road, London NW1 7BY, UK
225 Wyman Street, Waltham, MA 02451, USA
525 B Street, Suite 1800, San Diego, CA 92101-4495, USA

**Notice**
No responsibility is assumed by the publisher for any injury and/or damage to persons or
property as a matter of products liability, negligence or otherwise, or from any use or operation
of any methods, products, instructions or ideas contained in the material herein. Because of rapid
advances in the medical sciences, in particular, independent verification of diagnoses and drug
dosages should be made

**British Library Cataloguing-in-Publication Data**
A catalogue record for this book is available from the British Library

**Library of Congress Cataloging-in-Publication Data**
A catalog record for this book is available from the Library of Congress

ISBN : 978-0-12-396993-4

For information on all Academic Press publications visit our
website at www.elsevierdirect.com

Printed and bound in United States of America

12 13 14 15   10 9 8 7 6 5 4 3 2 1

Working together to grow
libraries in developing countries

www.elsevier.com | www.bookaid.org | www.sabre.org

ELSEVIER   BOOK AID International   Sabre Foundation

To my husband, Michael Antone Bush

Thank you for challenging me to put my experiences into words as I seek to empower and encourage women, girls, and anyone with a dream. I am eternally grateful for your love, encouragement, and faith in me.

# Contents

**4.    Leadership and Innovation Characteristics**

**5.    Developing the Leader in You**

# How to Get the Most Out of this Book

This book can be used in a classroom setting, professional groups, in small groups or as an individual over a 2-, 4-, 8- or 16-week period. To get the most out of the book, finding another person (or group) to share this experience with can be useful. The group interaction creates the opportunity for discussion, interaction and accountability as you define and move toward the attainment of your leadership and innovation goals.

The following steps can be followed:

1. Complete reading assignments and review Key Points from the Chapter
   a. Complete actions suggested in the chapter
   b. Write your results down and save them for group interaction (you don't have to share everything with the group; only what you're comfortable with sharing)
2. Individually review and analyze your responses to make sure they are consistent with your goals
3. Meet for a weekly or monthly discussion session (in person, via social media, internet, Skype, etc.)
   a. Discuss the Key Points from the Chapter as a group
   b. Share your responses to the chapter assignments
   c. Identify an accountability partner that you hold "accountable" for attaining what you've identified in your responses
4. Individually review your responses to see if the group discussion has impacted or enhanced your responses
5. Document all of your responses and review each chapter's responses of the previous week as you prepare your chapter assignment for the current week
6. At the completion of the reading, compile a "Leadership and Innovation" Summary Notebook and Log

## COMMITMENT PAGE

As I read this book, I make a commitment to myself to seek a fulfilling career and lifestyle every day. I will use the resources provided to me in this book, my community and globally to achieve my dreams. I agree to do what is necessary throughout my career to lead, change, transform and grow as I seek to fully attain my greatest ambitions as a leader and innovator. I will not quit until I have achieved my goals.

_____

Signed by Reader

_____

Date

# Acknowledgments

The publication of this manuscript is the culmination of support from many people in my professional and personal life. I want to thank Elsevier Publishers for the opportunity to be a part of your publishing family: specifically Senior Acquisitions Editor Ms. Kristine Jones and Editorial Project Manager Mr. Andy Albrecht. Special appreciation is extended to Dr. Christine Grant for your outstanding National Science Foundation, PURPOSE Institute workshop series which focuses on female faculty in engineering. As a result of the PURPOSE Institute, I had the opportunity to meet fellow Elsevier author Ms. Peggy Pritchard. Peggy, thank you for the introduction to our wonderful editor Ms. Kristine Jones. I would also like to thank my mentors and collaborators: Dr. Deborah Reinhart, Dr. Mary Ann Bauman and Ms. Beverly Seay, Dr. Lesia Crumpton-Young and Ms. Gail Evans, for your persistent support, guidance, and for serving as outstanding examples of successful leadership.

I am forever grateful to the many wonderful students I have had the opportunity to teach over the last 20 years at the University of Central Florida, the Massachusetts Institute of Technology and in numerous workshops around world. You have been a great source of inspiration for me. A special acknowledgement goes to my brilliant industrial engineering undergraduate research students Bianca Garcia and Alexandra Villalobos Rolandi. Alex and Bianca, thank you for your commitment and exemplary support in the final stages of this project – I can't begin to thank you enough for all of the time, research, editing and support you eagerly offered. I would also like to thank Rachel Borrelli for your support in the early stages of the research, organization and data collection. To my former assistant, Angela Shirley, I say thank you for your outstanding organizational skills and commitment. To my current research assistants, Thayer El-Dajanni and Jessica Hooper, thank you from the bottom of my heart for the many hours of effort you put into assisting me with the details of this project. Dr. Charlotte Brammer, thank you for taking the time to help me understand how (and why) women in engineering communicate differently from others – your insights were very valuable. Finally, I would like to thank Gail Evans for being a constant source of inspiration through your published works and friendship. I am genuinely grateful for the support that each of you has offered to me in this process.

On a personal note, I want to thank my loving and supportive family. My daughter and son-in-law, Annette and Nathan Hemphill, thank you for the constant words of encouragement and Sunday brunch when I desperately needed it! I want to thank my sisters, Princess Hill, LaWanna Porter and Pipina Figaro

Smith, for always believing in me. To my big brother, Maurice McCauley, Jr., thanks for the quiet encouragement and inspiration only you always give. To my wonderful Prayer Partner, Sandra Jeter and dear friends, Veronica Nealy, Susan Rowe and Darlynda Bogle – thank you for the encouragement, insights and feedback. To my parents, Maurice and LaFrance McCauley, thanks for giving me the vision to lead and help others pursue their vision to become leaders, innovators and better global citizens.

Finally, to my wonderful husband, Michael Bush, thank you for encouraging me to finish *and publish* this important book, as you know how near this topic is to my heart. I will always be thankful that you see gifts in me that I may not see in myself. Your love, strength, encouragement and support are priceless gifts.

Sincerely,
Pamela McCauley Bush, PhD, CPE

As I travel the United States and globally to discuss engineering, leadership, and innovation, it has become apparent to me that there is a dearth of encouragement and support for individuals in the STEM fields seeking to lead, innovate, and attain stellar careers. This issue is even more significant for women in STEM carreers. This is unfortunate because the opportunities for us to excel are ever present but we are often sidelined due to lack of positive reinforcement or because of the challenges we face in our professional and/or personal environment. As a result, we often become withdrawn, disillusioned, and fail to achieve all that we're fully capable of achieving. As a woman in engineering, I have found these experiences to be disheartening when I see women who are not being encouraged, supported, or moved in the direction of leadership and innovation. This is because I can clearly see the power, potential, and opportunity for amazing outcomes in these women and their organizations. Thus, I embarked on a "mission" to reach these women. This mission has taken me to various venues to share my experiences, message of empowerment, and basic processes that I and others have used to achieve our dreams. However, physically traveling to locations around the globe is not an efficient process to reach the masses of women that need to hear this message. Thus, I embarked upon the development of a book that would speak to the needs of these individuals from a person who has been through a similar situation.

I am a natural optimist and have had many exciting experiences that have produced a good measure of success in my career. Despite this optimism, as an African American, female engineer in the professional setting, I have often times felt isolated, misunderstood, not supported, and even unwelcomed. My natural optimism, support system, faith, and engineering problem-solving skills have always allowed me to deal with these situations and come out stronger. However, I've seen situations where this was not the case for other women. In many instances, they quit, they left the profession, or they withdrew and accepted mediocre roles rather than the stellar roles they were called to fulfill. This is a problem – but it is a problem with a solution. None of this had to happen if they had been given the guidance, encouragement, support, and knowledge to achieve their career goals. I hope this book will be a part of the solution for countless women seeking to realize their leadership and innovation dreams.

Finally, it is important to stress that this book is not a social science or theoretically based approach to leadership, self-improvement, or career success. I am a STEM professional speaking to other STEM professionals, and while I share details of research studies, the objective is on sharing practical knowledge, experiences, and encouragement from the "trenches." The objective is to reach every reader in a way that provides insight into common experiences of other women that will stir your creative energies, empower you, and set fire to your focus on accomplishing your greatest dreams. I like to think of the chapters that follow as letters; letters to a dear friend who is bursting with potential and on the verge of walking into greatness as a STEM professional. This friend and I share a common bond. This bond that ties us together is a beautiful tapestry that consists of exciting career and personal aspirations, a desire to impact the world, and a willingness to put in the work to "make it happen." As you read the pages of these letters, it is my intention that you will experience a sense of connection and know that you are not alone in your experiences and there are people who have succeeded in comparable situations. For me it is powerful to know that there are others who have had similar experiences, common challenges, and personal fears but yet still achieved great things. If they did it – I'm encouraged that I can do it, too! Likewise, I trust that you will find value in the stories, guidelines, resources, and conversations shared in the pages of this book and on the companion website. Let the "letters" that follow empower, inspire, encourage, and uplift you in the pursuit of your innovation and leadership dreams. You can certainly make it happen!

With great confidence in you,

Pamela McCauley Bush

## Chapter 1

# A Call to Leadership

*Our deepest fear is not that we are inadequate. Our deepest fear is that we are powerful beyond measure. It is our light, not our darkness, that frightens us. We ask ourselves, who am I to be brilliant, gorgeous, talented and fabulous? Actually, who are you not to be?*

**Marianne Williamson**

## YOU MADE IT!

You have succeeded in fostering a vision and achieving a STEM career, something that far differentiates you from most men and women. Many of the women I talk to and interact with around the world are leaders in their STEM fields, and yet so many of them don't realize what an important contribution they are making to their communities and the world. Given the challenges you've overcome to secure a career in a STEM field, it is imperative that you realize the significance of your achievements to date, and use this as fuel to propel you to the next level, and carry others with you. The world needs innovators to address global challenges like environmental destruction, economic crisis, and health issues, and those of us with knowledge and experience in STEM careers must do our part to help develop solutions to these challenges.

Your days are probably already incredibly full with various responsibilities from career, family, and the community. For most of us, we manage to do this well but it is difficult in the scarce remaining time to find time for your many other interests. Somehow, we find a way to juggle the various roles we are required to play. So how do we begin to think about adding something else to our lives in the

Transforming your STEM Career through Leadership and Innovation.
http://dx.doi.org/10.1016/B978-0-12-396993-4.00001-1

**1**

midst of all we have going on today? It's actually a management action. In many ways, you are a manager each day – managing tasks at hand, at home, or at the workplace and managing people and relationships around you. But there is a difference between *managing* and *leading*. A manager is one who functions within defined parameters and works toward a definite goal. A person's intelligence, inherent skills, knowledge, creativity, and personality contribute toward this end result. However, it is *passion* that makes a leader out of a manager. A manager with a passion to make a difference, sculpt change, or create something new, goes beyond managing to leading. In a company, the CEO who achieves targets is likely a good manager, but the shift supervisor, who instills in people the desire to be the best in the company, may actually be the true leader. So for our careers, we must be managers as well as leaders. In other words, we must engage in the activities on a day to day basis (manager role) that will result in achieving the long-term vision we have for our career and life impact (leadership role). Yes, it takes effort to do this but it can be accomplished and the results are well worth the effort.

So, recognize the fact that you are a success as a professional, student, or aspiring STEM educator, innovator, or leader. Truly take time to celebrate yourself and where you are today. In my experience, this celebration and appreciation of our achievements can be powerful in restoring and maintaining the confidence we need to move forward. You made it! And let this moment be a celebration of your success, vision, and ambition today as well as the launch-party for your plan to go to the next level! It's time to transform your STEM career as a leader and an innovator.

## YOU MATTER

You matter when it comes to making a difference in your community, country, and the world. There is a broad consensus that the long-term key to continued U.S. competitiveness in an increasingly global economic environment lies in the quality of our STEM workforce. According to a survey taken in 2004, by that time scientific innovation had already produced roughly half of all U.S. economic growth in the previous 50 years [1]. The STEM fields and those who work in them are critical engines of innovation and growth. According to one recent estimate, about 6% of the U.S. workforce is employed in STEM fields [2], while the STEM workforce accounts for more than 50% of the nation's sustained economic growth.

While you were growing up there were undoubtedly people who mattered to you. Perhaps you looked up to a grandparent who took care of you and your siblings while your parents worked, or the professor who spent extra time helping you with your thesis. As we get older we tend to forget just how much each of us matters and the effect we have on individuals in our community. You matter. You matter to someone and to a "cause" today. Someone is looking up to you – whether it's a co-worker, a student, or the kid next door – it's important to recognize that because you've made it, people admire and respect you, and as a socially conscious individual you should take this as a leadership challenge. As we considered women in STEM this becomes even more important. It is critical that we, as women, inspire and encourage other women to maintain and develop their STEM careers as this has a ripple effect when we don't; not only do we waste talent that has taken years to grow and develop but we deter other women from pursuing and staying in the profession. Your example impacts society and young women's perceptions of their opportunities in STEM careers. In order to serve the world to the best of our ability, we as STEM leaders must encourage other women from all walks of life to join us in our mission. We are not monolithic – and that is great! STEM careers demand diversity in problem solving among their team members, and diversity among women not only allows us to work in various environments but also encourages diversity in thoughts and ideas. The result is a solution resource that represents perspectives, experience and ultimately produces better outcomes. Remember, the value you bring today and in the future – you matter.

## WHERE WE ARE TODAY

There seems to be a universal sigh of reluctance among women when it comes to taking on leadership roles in our careers. The National Science Foundation estimates that between 4.8 and 6.4 million people work directly in science, engineering, and technology – just over 4% of the U.S. workforce. However, while women comprise about half of the global population, we made up about 27% of the STEM professionals in the latest 2008 survey. While sex disparities vary among STEM occupations, the most extreme disparities are in engineering, where women make up a meager 13% of the workforce according to the most recent estimates [3]. Unfortunately, our presence hasn't always translated into leadership or innovation opportunities. And, in cases where it has, there is often a feeling of dissatisfaction, isolation, and lack of acceptance. So why are so many of us unhappy, leading and innovating in our careers? An American Association of University Women (AAUW) study designated eight factors that depress the numbers of women in STEM professions:

- mistaken beliefs about our intelligence
- gender stereotypes
- self-assessment
- spatial skills
- the college student experience
- university and college faculty
- implicit bias
- workplace bias

The truth of the matter is one or two of these factors would be enough to discourage women from pursuing, maintaining, and excelling in a STEM related career, much less the synergistic impact of multiple factors. However, despite these known factors that inhibit our growth – we are succeeding. Certainly, not on the level we'd desire but it's important to note that there are many who've managed to navigate this environment and have satisfying and rewarding careers. The objective now is to learn from them, do what we can to change the environment, and move forward as individuals and leaders ourselves as this will move us all forward as women.

In an article published in the Harvard Business Review, Dr Anna Fels examines why (and if) women lack ambition [4]. In her study, Dr Fels identifies two main causes for this perceived lack of drive – social conditioning and sexual stereotyping. In the past, society has expected women to be self-sacrificing and not to demand or expect recognition. Traditionally they have been the lynchpins around which the family revolves and today they often play the same role in the workplace. They are team players, not leaders. A woman who seeks recognition for herself is deemed selfish and outside the norms historically imposed on her. Men, on the other hand, who stand alone and demand recognition, are accepted as playing one of the roles that history has not only given them but, in fact, expects of them. Men who are both part of a team, and simultaneously break away from group thinking so as to don the leadership mantle, are admired and given the recognition they seek. Women who attempt to emulate this type of behavior are often considered masculine or viewed as having stepped away from femininity. Social conditioning seems to state that femininity, which is a woman's birthright, cannot exist simultaneously with power or leadership.

Although remnants of this social conditioning exist today, our society is in constant flux and we are moving towards a culture – albeit, glacially – that allows women to take advantage of leadership opportunities. As I watched Senator Mary Landrieu on the *Sunday Morning News* share her insights on the importance of spreading awareness about the impact of breast cancer in our country, I was impressed not only by her intellect and ambition but also by the compassion and sincerity with which she spoke. She spoke of women "reaching across the aisle" to make a difference for the real cause. I was reminded of the power that one individual – and allow me to say the power that one *woman* – can have on society. One determined woman can change a community, a region, a state, and a nation. Let's commit to making a difference!

Today, women in STEM leadership positions have adopted new cultural attitudes that celebrate what women have achieved in corporate America, small business, technology, and politics. According to The Center for Women's Business Research, their most recent survey in 2009 showed 75% of all women-owned businesses, representing a total of 7.2 million firms, employed 7.3 million people, and generated $1.1 trillion in sales [5]. The number of women in presidential cabinet positions has risen from no more than one during President Roosevelt's term in 1933 and during Nixon's second term in 1974, to seven in Obama's cabinet today. According to Rutger's Center for American Women and Politics, women hold 90 of the 535 seats in the 112th US Congress (16.8%) – 17 of the 100 seats in the Senate and 73 of the 435 seats in the House of Representatives. Furthermore, three women serve as Delegates to the House from Guam, the Virgin Islands, and Washington, D.C [6]. Like it or not, be it nature or nurture, in most countries women are "socialized" to be caretakers.

As a result, women often devise solutions that benefit many, and applying this mindset to innovation and leadership can bring about powerful and broadly beneficial outcomes.

I have come across remarkably inspiring stories of female achievers, both historic and current. In the course of this book we will look at a few of them, from all over the world and from different eras. These stories strengthen my belief that women can excel in any role they wish to take on. I have included these stories in this book because the history of successful women leaders is the bedrock upon which we must build. Throughout history, women have persisted against all odds and often have had to work much harder than their male colleagues, breaking away from gender stereotypes and teaching many of us that we can succeed. These trailblazers provide leadership examples of women who fought against the norms of society, who proved that their goals were achievable, and who set benchmarks for other women to follow.

A study conducted in 2005 by Aurora, an organization that works to uplift women, and Caliper, a management consultancy firm, found that "women leaders mainly possess the following qualities: they are highly assertive, urgent, persuasive, collaborative, and intelligent risk-takers." Interestingly, women leaders do feel the sting of rejection more than their male counterparts but they rapidly develop an "I'll show you" attitude. The study also noted that female leaders possess an inclusive, team-oriented style of problem solving and decision making, and are more likely than their male counterparts to ignore rules and take risks [7]. This study should be encouraging, and even empowering, to women. A willingness to take risks is an essential element in leadership and innovation, and usually we eagerly apply this sentiment to personal environments. We may not be so willing to do this in our professional environments, however, but that is exactly what we need to do: confidently and eagerly take risks to achieve our objectives in professional settings. We clearly know how to do it. It's just a matter of recognizing that it's acceptable, expected, and even encouraged for us to do so on a daily basis in our careers.

## PERSPECTIVES FROM OTHER WOMEN

### Women in Industry

For many STEM professionals, the ideal career path leads to corporate leadership at the highest levels of a company. An example of this pattern is seen in the historic appointment of Virginia Rometty, CEO of IBM. A STEM professional, Rometty holds a Bachelor of Science degree with high honors in computer science and electrical engineering from Northwestern University. In a *New York Times* article Ms Rometty shares a story of how her husband's, Mr Mark Rometty's, input has been of value to her in her career ascension. Ms Rometty credits her husband with a crucial insight that helped to shape her corporate ambitions at important decision-making points.

According to the article, the following quote by Ms. Rometty is taken from a *Fortune magazine* conference on women and careers:

*Early in my career, I can remember being offered a big job. I right away said, "You know what? I'm not ready for this job. I need more time, I need more experience and then I could really do it well." And so I said to him, "I need to go home and think about it." … And my husband at the time, as usual, I'm blah-blah-blahing, and he's just sitting there. And as I'm telling him about this, I told him I would get back to them tomorrow. And he said to me, he looked at me, and he just looked at me and he said, "Do you think a man would have ever answered that question that way?" And I sort of sat there – and it taught me a lesson [8].*

This was indeed an opportunity for a powerful lesson and Ms Rometty learned it well. Mr Rometty's question, "… do you think a man would ever answer the question that way?" highlights an important difference between men and women; while we are in no way trying to "be" men, we can learn a lot from how they approach many situations. This is one of those situations. In other words, be eager to accept new opportunities and, if a leadership position has been presented to you, strongly consider the reasons that you *can* do the job and do it well, rather than immediately questioning your ability.

As the CEO of IBM, Virginia Rometty has broken a major glass ceiling in this outstanding leadership role. Unfortunately, she seems to be a rare case, as we don't see many female leaders like her in the highest levels of the largest corporations. Various CEOs have voiced their thoughts and concerns on the struggles women face to get to the top and the ensuing fight to stay on top.

Dr Glenda Stone, CEO of Aurora says,

*There is still a lack of critical mass regarding women leaders at the top of corporations, so to get there, women need to be highly visible and quite persuasive about their ability. The collaborative leadership style of women leaders is valuable for retaining employees and widely considering issues and business decisions so the best economic results can be obtained [9].*

Similarly, Herb Greenberg, CEO of Caliper, says,

*Women in senior positions have usually been very determined about getting where they are. Their persuasiveness, flexibility and assertiveness enable them to listen, learn, reflect, and then implement a plan that incorporates the best of everyone's ideas. This approach ideally positions them for great leadership in today's business environment [10].*

It is highly reassuring to know that the struggles women face on a day-to-day basis are noticed and acknowledged. Our efforts are not going to waste. However, considering that the corporate world is becoming increasingly competitive, companies need to use the best management talent available not only to stay ahead but for basic survival. Unfortunately, the "glass ceiling" precludes the utilization of a large and highly talented pool of management expertise. The glass ceiling does exist, and, even though cracks have begun to appear in it, it is a reality in the lives of many female corporate leaders. Women must be allowed to exercise their leadership capabilities, not just for their own benefit, but to ensure the ongoing growth and development of commerce and industry. In an excellent treatise in her book, *The Difference 'Difference' Makes*, Deborah Rhode says:

*As management experts have increasingly recognized, the business case for diversity is clear. A wide array of research indicates that the representation of women in leadership positions has a positive correlation with economic performance, measured in tangible terms such as organizational growth, increased market share, and return on investment [11].*

Everyone recognizes the importance of integrating people from different social, cultural, and ethnic backgrounds to enable business to function with a broader and more effective focus. This is no doubt essential; but what about gender diversity? Are we not overlooking the "complete" integration acceptance of 50% of the population? If the integration of minority segments of the population can re-energize business management, what about the integration of the talented female population, among whose ranks are highly capable future leaders?

The integration of women into leadership positions is not a new concept; it is as old as the Bible. In her book, *Jesus CEO* [12], Laurie Beth Jones says, "Jesus said to both women and men 'The kingdom is within you.' He delegated equal power and authority to anyone who asked. He said that in heaven there is neither male nor female, and he came to see that things were done 'on earth, as it is in heaven.'" Fast forward two thousand years and "diversity" has become a buzzword in business circles, people have come to accept it as a fact of life and are willing to assimilate it into their lives – both corporate and at home. By doing this studies have consistently shown that they bring in more varied talent and thus increase opportunities for organizational success.

The story of Linda Alvarado is a story of one woman determined to succeed, having made an unconventional choice early in her career. She was a woman trying to establish herself in the American construction industry – traditionally a male domain with women numbering less than 1% of the workforce. In addition, she came from a minority community, hailing from a traditional Hispanic background, with great ambition but few examples of female leadership in male-dominated professions.

Her initial days in the construction industry were marked by considerable hostility from her male colleagues. She experienced this in the form of graffiti on the walls and pictures of her in "various stages of undress." Undeterred by these conditions, Linda knew that she liked buildings and construction sites. Construction was to her a sense of the creative process that ended up with this structure of great permanence and beauty [13]. Linda worked her way to project engineering, after initial roles in accounting and project management support. She gradually worked on building her skills by taking classes in survey, estimation, and construction supervision.

Determined to show that women could succeed in the field, Linda started her own construction management company. While seeking for funding for this venture, Linda's proposal was rejected by as many as six banks. Despite the consistent rejection and challenges, she persisted. Her parents supported her by mortgaging their house, in order to provide her with the initial capital. Today, Linda's construction contracting firm, Alvarado Construction in Denver, Colorado, is a fast-growing multimillion-dollar company.

Not only is Linda a successful entrepreneur, but also a corporate director of three Fortune 150 companies, a recipient of numerous awards for her business achievements, and the first Hispanic owner of a major league baseball franchise. The examples of success in male dominated industries should be a source of encouragement, inspiration and hope for women presently in these positions. We have done it - succeeded in these fields. We can do it and you can do it.

## Women in Politics

We need women not just in business, but also in politics; and not just any women – we need women with backgrounds in STEM professions, women who are educated to solve problems, answer difficult questions, and seek new ways to address issues. A woman with this kind of education and experience has a lot to offer in a political environment. However, there is an old adage coloring the perspective of women as political leaders in some environments. This old adage is that female political leaders will bring an end to war since no woman would allow her son to go to war. While this phrase may seem heartwarming, this perspective can negatively impact opportunities for female leaders in governance, despite the fact that female leaders all over the world have disproven this prediction time and again. This puerile image, which ignores the many "iron women" in the history of women leaders, is still prevalent today.

However, times do seem to be changing. There was a time when Golda Meir, the prime minister of Israel and the world's first elected female head of government, was considered an oddity. Then came India's Indira Gandhi, who was considered an accident of history. Perhaps it was the long and successful tenure of England's first female prime minister, Margaret Thatcher, which changed the world's perceptions of what a woman could achieve. This Iron Lady, who was paid the dubious compliment of being called the only man in her cabinet, was one of the country's most successful leaders. Today, there are more women in positions of political leadership than ever before. Currently, Chile, the Philippines, Liberia, and Sri Lanka have female presidents. Germany, New Zealand, and Bangladesh have women as heads of government. Although few in number, these are welcomed developments.

One of the reasons for this growing acceptance of women in positions of political leadership is that women are perceived by voters to be, by and large, less prone to corruption and more open and willing to listen compared to male leaders. A *Voice of America* report on Women Leaders in February 2006 [14] talks about the changing perceptions among voters and in the world of politics. In this report, Colombian women's rights activist Luz Piedad Calceido commented on the fact that voters around the world are increasingly turning to women because of their ability to reach agreements and find common ground.

*"If we don't have women in this process, we cannot reconstruct our countries," she says. "Why? For a simple reason, because women are more educated for the care of people. [...] while some see this stereotype as a strength, others see it as a weakness, arguing that women tend to be strong on domestic issues but weak on military and foreign policy decisions."*

Samra Filipovic-Hadziabdic, the director of the Gender Equality Agency of Bosnia and Herzegovina, isn't buying that argument. It has been said that "Women can be tough you know – just remember your mother."

Studies have shown that politically, when women lead, legislation tends to be more nonpartisan, as well as both family- and child-friendly. The female perspective allows us to come up with solutions that impact our families in a more positive way, and thus our country. This is not to say that all women lead the same way; this generalization is based on a historical review of women leading in the U.S.

The Administrator of the Environmental Protection Agency (EPA), Lisa P. Jackson, is an example of STEM leadership applied to politics. Jackson leads EPA's efforts to protect the health and environment of America. She and a staff of more than 17,000 professionals are working across the nation. Her background in engineering began as a Tulane University student where she graduated *summa cum laude* with a degree in chemical engineering. She later earned a master's degree in chemical engineering from Princeton University.

Jackson is the first African-American to serve as EPA Administrator. In her time as the leader of this organization she has made it a priority to focus on vulnerable groups including children, the elderly, and low-income communities that are particularly susceptible to environmental and health threats [15]. This example is consistent with historic examples of women leaders in politics who tend to place a stronger emphasis on issues that impact the community and family.

## Technology: Grace Hopper

There are many famous names in the history of computers and computing. Often, that of Grace Hopper is overlooked. Born in 1906, she was a mechanically minded child who often helped her surveyor grandfather plan the streets of New York. While studying at Vassar, she became a member of Phi Beta Kappa and won a fellowship that financed her further studies. After graduating, she joined her alma mater as a math instructor, where she was known for her unusual teaching techniques. Her students learned to play card and dice games and predict the probable outcomes. She would give out the final examination at the beginning of the semester so her students knew what they were expected to learn and understand.

At the outbreak of World War II, Grace tried to join the Navy but was rejected because, at 36, she was too old. However, she did not give up, and, after a long struggle, she convinced the Navy to accept her. Grace graduated at the top of her officers' training class. She was assigned to the ordnance services and sent to Harvard to work on computers for calculating firing ranges for Naval Artillery. It was laborious and, by today's standards, primitive work, but it produced results. At the end of the war, Grace published a book on her work. She continued to work with computers during the post-war years and hoped one day to write computer programs that would allow laymen to use computers. She was mocked for her ideas, as the establishment believed that computers were far too complex for anyone but a scientist to use. In the 1950s, the Navy promoted her to Lt Commander and she began working on a program that could be used in a business environment. In 1955 Grace completed her work on a program that she later helped develop into COBOL. COBOL, which stands for **CO**mmon **B**usiness-**O**riented **L**anguage, is a third-generation programing language and one of the oldest programing languages still in active use today. Its primary domain is in business, finance, and administrative systems for companies and governments.

Grace continued working with computers until she reached retirement age in 1966. Six months later, after realizing their computer development programs could not continue without her, the Navy called Grace back to duty. Known among her fellow workers as "Amazing Grace," she decorated her office with a clock that ran backwards and a skull and crossbones ensign to remind her staff to always be unconventional and flexible in their thinking. She retired again in 1986 with the rank of Rear Admiral. At the time of her retirement she was the oldest actively serving military officer.

The recipient of many honors for her groundbreaking work on computers, Grace Hopper died in 1992. She was posthumously inducted into the National Women's Hall of Fame in 1994. In the same year, the Navy announced that a new ship would be named after her. Admiral Hopper was truly a passionate leader willing to face challenges and difficulties to make her dreams come true, and, in doing so, she enlightened the world with technology [16].

While women are driven by many of the same motivations that drive men, other factors contribute to the diversity that women bring to the leadership stage. It is often an emotional trial or an important cause that drives women. For instance, a woman's drive could stem from losing a friend to breast cancer and thereby becoming an advocate for the cause, or pursuing a position on a school board in order to improve her children's educational environment. Sometimes, a woman keeps the family business alive after the death of a spouse or parent even though her focus might have been elsewhere under normal circumstances.

## Environment: Wangari Maathai

The primary motivating factor in your life may be a strong passion for a cause, as was the case with Wangari Maathai. Wangari was born in Kenya in 1940. A good student, she was able to pursue her studies until she obtained her Doctorate in Anatomy at the age of 36, becoming the first woman in that part of Africa to earn a PhD [17].

But this is not her claim to fame. Having spent much of her youth studying away from her country, Wangari was heartbroken when she returned to discover that the beautiful green countryside in which she had spent her early childhood was beginning to disappear. Mining, logging, and other developmental activities had eaten into the lush forests of her homeland. Examining the problem further, she found that this devastation was not limited to Kenya, but was spreading across Africa. Industrialization of the continent required raw materials to feed these industries, which was, in turn, destroying Africa's forests. There was no organized awareness of the ecological disaster that was facing the continent at the time and thus there was no action to contain the deforestation.

Wangari realized that she could not sit idly by and watch the looming ecological disaster ruin her homeland. As one of the few women from her part of the world to have achieved so much academic distinction, and the prestigious Chair of Veterinary Anatomy at Nairobi University, she felt compelled to do something. She started the Green Belt movement, employing the economically weakest section of African society – women from the poorest families. The Green Belt movement has created a renewable source of lumber by planting over 30 million trees. It has also enabled women employed by the organization to earn a livelihood [18].

Today, Wangari is known as "the Tree Woman of Africa" [18]. Besides her environmental activism, she is also an advocate for democracy and human rights and has addressed the United Nations several times on these issues. In 2002, Wangari entered politics and was elected to parliament. In 2003, she was appointed as Assistant Minister for Environment & Natural Resources. In 2004, she was awarded the Nobel Peace Prize. Wangari had the means to live a comfortable life in the higher echelons of society, but her conscience urged her to step outside of her cocoon and make a difference in the lives of not just the women of her country but the entire continent of Africa.

## WHAT CAN YOU DO TODAY?

While it can take years and hard work to rise to a leadership position in your company, you might be wondering what you can do now, *today*, to nurture the leadership qualities that you already possess. Leadership is not a mystery; it is a process of acquiring skills and knowledge. Everything you do in support of a candidate, in support of community issues, and in your work in public office is part of the learning curve. Use what you learn today to commit to learning more tomorrow. The more you know, the stronger you are. As Francis Bacon once said, "Knowledge is power." If you know more than your opponents you have the power to overcome their opposition.

Leadership is in some ways like building a house. The actual construction requires material, equipment, and specific skills. The builder must be competent and knowledgeable, but without the architect who had the vision and competence to design the house he would have nothing to do. The world is full of builders – women with the skills and competence – and architects – visionaries who have the idea for construction in the first place.

If you're thinking to yourself, *I'm not sure where to lead*, ask yourself this question: Is there anything that you feel passionately about? What are you doing about it? Many women are either confused about the answer or altogether avoid the question for a multitude of reasons. We normally suppress our "inconvenient" passions, lest they disrupt our everyday lives. By doing this, we are denying our-selves many avenues of fulfillment and achievement. When women succeed as leaders, the realization that their leadership – driven by their passion – has con-tributed to something tangible creates a rare but intense feeling of satisfaction.

Leadership is about creation: creating something better than what currently exists, or creating something that did not exist before. As French novelist Victor Hugo once said, "There is nothing like a dream to create the future" [19].

Maybe there's a small project at work or in your community that you care about; identify that opportunity, and ASK for it – don't wait for someone to offer it to you. Once you have chosen a leadership role to pursue, take one step further and find another woman who you can support in her leadership endeav-ors. For example, if your roommate is the Editor in Chief of a campus magazine, offer to submit an article in your field of expertise. If you know someone who is putting on a fundraiser for cancer awareness, offer to help her with the event or make a donation. The support you offer to another woman in her leadership role is sure to come back your way. When women are discouraged from taking lead-ership positions, the world is missing out on a giant demographic that it could otherwise tap into and utilize the unique talents of. Inspiration is not always an immediate event – inspiration can be generated. We must generate inspiration by supporting each other's passions and setting an example when we pursue our own. In case I haven't stressed this enough, professionals, in the area of STEM careers in particular, are critically needed as leaders and innovators.

I welcome my sisters all over the world to join me in this cause that I feel most passionate about: the call to female leadership in the fields where they are most misrepresented and where I feel the world needs us the most. I have never believed that I had all of the answers. It's not about *me*, and, with all due respect, it's not about *you*. It's about *us*. It's about women using what we have; using our collective gifts, education, experiences, wisdom, and talent in a way that has never before been afforded to humankind. We now have the ability to innovate, lead, reach out, and make a difference for each other, our communities, our coun-try, and our world – to inspire those that we've never met and may never meet. It is our time to change the world and "our responsibility" make it a better place.

## THE CHALLENGES WE FACE

The challenges we face in the engineering, medicine, environmental, and infor-mation management fields are many. We are on our way to making solar energy affordable, providing energy from fusion, developing carbon sequestration methods, managing the nitrogen cycle, providing access to clean water, and restoring and improving urban infrastructure. These are challenges that I am confident STEM professionals working with each other and various professionals can solve. Some other challenges on the global to-do list are listed as follows: advance health informatics, engineer better medicines, reverse-engineer the brain, prevent nuclear terror, secure cyberspace, enhance virtual reality, advance personalized learning, and engineer the tools for scientific discovery. These puzzles aren't going to solve themselves, and I invite you to take part in the exciting possibilities that await our future STEM professionals.

In order to take full advantage of the opportunities before us, we must change the way leadership and business are done. We need to think globally and collaboratively. Modern-day technology allows us access to considerably more information, and we can utilize this to reach out to our increasingly global community. The global economy is struggling and in need of innovation in every nation. In order to alleviate the technological, economic, and innovative problems of the world, national and international STEM professionals must establish research efforts that are focused not on "individual reputation" but on addressing global needs. People are suffering in many parts of the world – women, men, and children alike – and I truly believe with all my heart that this suffering can be ameliorated or eliminated through collaborative leadership and innovation.

## LEAD TODAY

Leading is about believing and being passionate in what you believe. In our own personal lives we have seen how our likes and dislikes influence our behavior and our actions. In the same manner, our passion and our belief in something will determine the extent to which we are willing to commit ourselves to working for it. Working towards changing "what is" to "what should be" requires decisive action and an ability to step forward and take control. This is the beginning of leadership.

Start now. Take it one day at a time but start today. Understand that leading is a long-term process, and there is no age limit for starting on the leadership path; however, we must start now. Sure, the younger you are the more time you have, but you can acquire knowledge at any age and this knowledge can open many doors for you, including those to leadership. If you have doubts about this consider the story of Nola Ochs, as reported in *USA Today* [20]:

*Like most students at Fort Hays State University, Nola Ochs plans to spend some time reading and studying during this week's fall break. But she'll take time out on Wednesday to celebrate her 95th birthday.*

*Ochs is living at Wooster Hall on campus while pursuing her general studies degree at the university. She has about 15 hours of classes left to get her degree. If she gets it, Ochs will be the Guinness Book of World Records' oldest college graduate.*

*But it will also be the culmination of a lifetime of learning. She started at Fort Hays in 1930, when it was known as Kansas State Teacher's College. In the 1970s, she took classes part time at a community college and completed a few virtual classes on the Internet before deciding to attend classes this semester.*

*Though Nola is amused by her potential status as the world's oldest graduate, she said she's more excited about getting to walk at the graduation ceremony with her granddaughter.*

Developing leadership skills is an ongoing process. There is no cut-off point at which you can say to yourself "Now I'm ready." There will never be a time when you can say that you're 100% knowledgeable, experienced and prepared to become a leader. Just do it. If you know yourself and your cause, you will be able to judge when the time is ripe for you to stand up and declare yourself a leader. Do not wait for someone to call you, as we have been saying all along. The initiative has to come from within: from you and me. This book will provide some easy-to-follow guidelines to becoming a leader and also demonstrate why it is important for you to lead people. Not only will you need to be passionate about your own beliefs, but you must also inspire others to lead. You need to move out of the comfortable cocoon of your world, be strong at heart, and be sure in the knowledge that whatever you are doing will be beneficial for all those within your realm of influence. That's what leadership is all about – achieving something for others that would not have been possible without you! A leader's passion embraces much more than her immediate surroundings. It's about doing what's best for those who are "following" you.

It is probably not going to be easy to realize your leadership ambitions. There will be times when you are compelled to do things you do not want to do, times when you will have to stand alone, and, of course, times when you will lose. You must be prepared to cope with these eventualities. If you are persistent, your victories will outweigh your losses and you will be a success. Even if you do not ultimately experience the big victories, it does not mean you have not succeeded.

## SUMMARY

After reading this book you will probably recognize that you already have all of the equipment necessary to propel you towards your leadership goals and inspire others as well. To summarize what this first chapter is all about, I've broken down and listed a few key points to take away from it below.

To become effective leaders there are four things you have to do:

**1.** See yourself as a leader.
   Recognize the potential in yourself. There is so much you can do. The problem is that you probably never sat down to seriously think about your strengths in relation to issues you feel strongly about. Do it now. You will be surprised at how much you can contribute. Later in this book we will

examine how you can define your strengths. However, you can make a start now by keeping just one thing in mind – don't be modest, be honest!

2. **Make a commitment.**

It is not easy being a leader and it can be very demanding - your life is probably already very full and to make this step toward leading is a definite commitment. You may feel that you can't afford to get involved. If you feel strongly enough about something, you will be able to find a way to rearrange your life a little so that you do not have to give up on other things that are important to you. Sure, it means extra effort, but you will find the personal rewards you derive worthwhile. Being a leader is never going to be easy. Success requires that you juggle different roles and manage time well. Don't let it put you off. The struggle is worth it and the fruit at the top of the tree is always the sweetest.

3. **Choose the issue you want to get involved in.**

Find an area where your unique contribution will make a real difference. It may be as small a matter as getting the street around your home repaired, or getting extra streetlights in your neighborhood, but your contribution here is of great importance. You see, the issue itself is not of importance; what is important is your commitment to it. Don't compromise on the level of commitment. If you compromise on your involvement, you compromise your chances of success. Make a list of these issues that matter to you.

4. **Understand that leadership is a learning process.**

Be willing to take time to know about leadership. Read, observe, take a note of the leaders around you and in the areas that matter to you. The best way to learn is to observe. Find a female leader championing a cause you care about and support her. When you shadow someone, you come to understand the finer nuances of leadership.

5. **Understand what it means to be an innovator.**

Understand what innovation involves, as well as the type of environments where your innovative skills will be nurtured. This should also include taking time to develop strategies that focus on innovative approaches or innovation development as a method to refocus your career. Additionally, you will learn how to evaluate the merit of your ideas from an innovation perspective as well as gaining an appreciation for the relationship you will need to be a successful innovator.

Believe you can be an innovator and leader.

You can do it, but you have to stand up for yourself. Recognition of your efforts and for your achievements is a tool that will empower you as a leader. You have a right to demand recognition for what you have achieved. It benefits not just you, but your cause, and also our collective cause of seeing women advance in all walks of life. Recognition gives you the respect of others and endorses you with the authority to take more responsibility.

A woman ready to play hardball has her motives and sexuality questioned at every step. Young women of today, especially those in college, are ready to fight for their dues and are ready to demand recognition for themselves and their achievements. However, after a few years of joining the work-force, the pressures of marriage and family, coupled with the perception that a career leads to the disintegration of family, begin to set in. Although the propaganda states that devoting one's life solely to the family is noble, rewarding, and feminine in nature, it tends to demotivate some women from pursuing their ambitions and also places innumerable barriers in their path to success outside the family.

Ayn Rand created the phrase "the virtue of selfishness." Her bestselling novel, *The Fountainhead* [21], defined and popularized greatness as being true to one's own abilities, intellect, and ambitions. Don't stop halfway down the road – follow your passion through to the end.

## REFERENCES

[1] Science and Engineering Indicators 2004. www.nsf.gov/statistics/seind04/c3/c3h.htm (accessed March 21, 2012).

[2] Cover B, Jones JI, Watson A. Science, technology, engineering, and mathematics (STEM) occupations: a visual essay. Monthly Labor Review 2011:134.

[3] nsf.gov, S&E Indicators 2012, Chapter 3. Science and Engineering Labor Force, Highlights, US National Science Foundation (NSF). www.nsf.gov/statistics/seind12/c3/c3h.htm (accessed March 21, 2012).

[4] Fels A. Do Women Lack Ambition? Harvard Business Review. 2005. http://hbr.org/product/do-women-lack-ambition-hbr-onpoint-enhanced-editio/an/9424-PDF-ENG?Ntt=Anna+Fels (accessed March 21, 2012).

[5] Center for Women's Business Research, Key Facts. www.womensbusinessresearchcenter.org/research/keyfacts/ (accessed April 26, 2012).

[6] Facts, Information by Level of Office, Executive, Center for American Women and Politics. www.cawp.rutgers.edu/fast_facts/levels_of_office/executive.php (accessed April 26, 2012).

[7] 2005. www.auroravoice.com/dna.pdf (accessed March 21, 2012).

[8] Stewart JB. A C.E.O.'s Support System, a k a Husband, NYTimes.com. 2011. www.nytimes.com/2011/11/05/business/a-ceos-support-system-a-k-a-husband.html?_r=1&pagewanted=all (accessed April 26, 2012).

[9] Senior businesswomen 'more assertive' than male counterparts, Manchester Evening News, menmedia.co.uk.http://menmedia.co.uk/manchestereveningnews/news/s/155/155752_senior_businesswomen_more_assertie_than_male_counterparts.html (accessed March 21, 2012).

[10] Women Business Leaders More Persuasive Than Men. 2005. www.auroravoice.com/pressarticle.asp?articleid=403 (accessed March 21, 2012).

[11] Rhode DL. The Difference 'Difference' Makes: Women and Leadership. Stanford: Stanford Law and Politics; 2003.

[12] Jones LB. Jesus, CEO: Using Ancient Wisdom for Visionary Leadership. New York, NY: Hyperion; 1995.

[13] Martin D, Martin R. The Risk Takers: 16 Women and Men Who Built Great Businesses Share Their Entrepreneurial Strategies for Success. New York, NY: Vanguard Press; 2010.

[14] Voters Demonstrate More Acceptance of Women Leaders, News, English. 2006. www.voanews.com/english/news/a-13-2006-02-08-voa76.html (accessed March 21, 2012).

[15] About the EPA Administrator, About EPA, US EPA. www.epa.gov/aboutepa/administrator.html (accessed April 26, 2012).

[16] Beyer KW. Grace Hopper and the Invention of the Information Age. Cambridge, MA: MIT Press; 2009.

[17] Maathai W. Unbowed. London: Random House; 2007.

[18] Maathai W. Unbowed. London: Random House; 2007.

[19] Utah Education Network, UEN Website http://www.uen.org/utahlink/activities/view_activity. cgi?activity_id=8982 (accessed September 6, 2012).

[20] Student set to become world's oldest graduate, USATODAY.com. www.usatoday.com/news/ offbeat/2006-11-21-lifelong-learner_x.htm (accessed March 21, 2012).

[21] Rand A. The Fountainhead. Indianapolis, Indiana: The Bobbs-Merrill Company; 1943.

## Chapter 2

# Why Innovation Matters Even More Today

*Innovation and Women*

*When innovations are examined with a gender lens to determine implications on women's well-being, empowerment and gender equality, a powerful, untapped strategy emerges to transform women's lives and gender relations.*

**Malhotra A. et al. (2009)**

The innovation needs of both the United States and the global community have generated a public plea for STEM professionals to turn their ideas, research, and knowledge into innovative products and services like never before. In fact, the current innovation crisis may be the most exciting thing that ever happened to STEM careers. Exciting new innovations – like Apple products, the Nintendo Wii, new gas-saving, battery-using automobiles – have placed innovation in vogue alongside the floral prints of fashion week, low-cal FroYo, and the Kardashians. It's suddenly trendy for young people to be interested in what were previously considered geeky gadgets.

How does this need for innovation apply to you? How does it apply to students, educators, and current STEM professionals? Also, what does it mean

Transforming your STEM Career through Leadership and Innovation.
http://dx.doi.org/10.1016/B978-0-12-396993-4.00002-3

**19**

for women? These are all questions that need to be answered as the most likely innovators are those STEM professionals. Thus, the impact that enhancing innovation can have with this population affects the economic health of a community, nation, and the world. According to one recent estimate, while about 5% of the U.S. workforce is employed in STEM fields, the STEM workforce accounts for more than 50% of the nation's sustained economic growth [1]. The STEM fields and those who work in them are critical engines of innovation and growth. However, having the knowledge alone is not enough. The most probable innovators are those with the knowledge, access and resources, as well as the motivation coupled with inspiration to embark upon the path to discovery.

So what exactly do we mean by innovation? While the word is often thrown around pretentiously in the media, the term actually derives its meaning from the Latin word *innovatus*, which is the noun form of *innovare*, "to renew or change." Innovation generally refers to the creation of better or more effective products, processes, technologies, or ideas that are accepted by markets, governments, and society. Innovation differs from invention or renovation, in that innovation generally signifies a substantial positive change as opposed to incremental changes. Innovation is where skill and ability meet determination and passion. While we may already have the passion and determination to turn an idea into an innovation, often we don't know how to go about doing that. A large part of the process involves applying your unique skillset to make a difference in the world.

Suri Poulos is one such woman. Born in America, armed with a BA in Fine Arts and an MBA, Suri started out in the IT world before branching out on her own. In 1989, Poulos & Partners began as a management-consulting firm in the U.K., where Suri was a founding partner. Poulos & Partners provided expertise in organizational development, coaching, counseling, and team development to leading organizations.

After many years of consulting for corporations, working with adults, and with an MSc in Counseling & Psychotherapy, Suri came up with a lucrative creative business concept: teaching children through play. She saw an opportunity to make a social contribution while developing a unique business scheme. Suri knew that it was difficult to penetrate the mainstream school system and alter the rigid National Curriculum in the U.K. She therefore modified her model to an after-school activity funded by parents. This led to the birth of the MindLab after-school program for kids, which emphasizes the development of social and emotional skills in children through play.

Today, MindLab is well known not only in the U.K. but throughout Europe. The MindLab program has benefited over 1,000,000 students in 15 countries internationally. Suri applied the franchise system, providing a business opportunity to many. Suri's is an example of positive outcomes, as she merged business and creativity. Her ability to leverage her skills as well as her innovative concept, and her determined execution, stand testimony to the entrepreneurial drive she possesses. Suri's advice to women who wish to start their own business is to find something they are passionate about. She also suggests that aspiring women should speak to successful entrepreneurs who are usually more than willing to share their experiences.

## THE RELATIONSHIP BETWEEN LEADERSHIP AND INNOVATION

The implementation of an innovation requires leadership. Never before has the world experienced such dynamic change in technologies, economies, and societies as it is experiencing today. Innovation through new ideas, products, and practices is increasingly becoming a force for social change. Furthermore, scientists and technical professionals depend on the leaders of their organizations, who are often called upon to take the lead in transitioning an idea into a product.

Historically, innovators were seen as lone individuals or those working closely with one or two others (e.g., Albert Einstein, Marie Curie) but today we need a group of individuals to take that idea from theory to practice. We are in need of what I like to call *inspired engineering*: the focused and persistent use of engineering knowledge, research, education, and leadership to produce innovative outcomes, products, and services to meet local, national, and global needs. But engineering alone will not do it. We also need leaders. Having an understanding of what it is needed, how we can get there, and what our individual roles are can lead one into significant and valuable leadership activities.

But what type of leadership really makes a difference in innovation? According to a recent study, "transformational leadership has a definite impact on the level of innovation in an organization." [2] When considering the relationship between leadership and innovation Gumusluoğlu and Ilsev provide a research study that evaluates this relationship or more specifically the relationship between "transformational leadership" and innovation. The concept or theory of transformational leadership was introduced over 30 years ago [3] and further developed by Bass and Avolio [4]. Transformational leadership behaviors closely match the determinants of innovation and creativity at the workplace, some of which are vision, support for innovation, autonomy, encouragement, recognition, and challenge. According to Bass and Avolio, transformational leadership has four components: charismatic role modeling, individualized consideration, inspirational motivation, and intellectual stimulation. Using charisma (naturally occurring or cultivated), the leader inspires admiration, respect, and loyalty, while emphasizing the importance of having a common mission. By individualized consideration, the leader builds one-on-one relationships with his or her team members, as well as gaining an understanding of their differing needs, skills, and aspirations. Inspirational motivation takes place when the leader articulates an exciting vision of the future around the mission, while showing the followers how to achieve the goals. The leader clearly expresses his or her belief that the individual team member can be successful at his or her core area of focus. Finally, intellectual stimulation is integrated into this leadership style when the leader broadens and elevates the interest or thinking of his or her employees and stimulates followers to think about old problems in new ways [5]. The result is a sense of purpose, empowerment, and creative thinking toward the attainment of the team's mission.

Who wouldn't want to be a transformational leader? What organization wouldn't want to hire these types of individuals to lead teams and encourage an entire team to innovate? Well, the good news is that we can cultivate our skills and become transformational leaders. This is particularly important if we want to see innovation realized in our organizations.

## What Innovation Is Not

Innovation is not a random event; it is a process used to transform ideas into commercial value. You might come up with great ideas and inventions in your sleep, but innovation doesn't generally happen overnight. Transforming an idea into an innovation often involves the knowledge and efforts of multiple individuals in various functional areas of an organization. This can be difficult for STEM professionals because often we are taught to work alone; however, that is changing as organizations and academic institutions are promoting collaboration and interdisciplinary teams. To make the transition from the research laboratory (concept, theory, or preliminary results) to practice (innovation) can be challenging, but, with careful planning, this can be done. For the individual innovator, this may mean joining select organizations so that you can identify individuals to collaborate with on your ideas. For those in corporations or institutions that are promoting innovation, the process may be easier. In innovative organizations, the leadership tends to seek participation from a variety of individuals. If you desire to innovate, the ultimate goal should be to identify the area where your creative tendencies will be valued and you will have an opportunity to see them realized. This may mean asking for a transfer to a different department, focus area, or geographic location. A careful evaluation of your organization and the types of innovation will be valuable as you seek to position yourself to see your innovative energies transferred into useful products or services.

For those who find it difficult to reach out, either geographically or personally, your dreams of being a part of an innovative team can still be attained. There are tremendous resources to support you, including professional societies, electronic communication, electronic mentoring and social media resources, to name a few. The value of establishing, nurturing, and maintaining these relationships cannot be overemphasized. A report by the National Academy of Engineering notes a trend, largely possible due to advancements in science and engineering, which has resulted in an "engulfing" of the globe [6]. This concept is referred to as "the death of distance" by Frances Cairncross of *The Economist*. This concept points to the interaction of people globally for services (e.g., help desk support), consumer purchases online, health care (e.g., surgery performed remotely with a remote-controlled robot), and comprehensive communication including economic communication via cell phone, e-mail, and resources such as Skype. To take advantage of global resources to support innovation we must apply these Internet and communication resources used for social interaction with the same intensity toward the attainment of our innovation goals.

Now the technology resources are identified, it's important for us to determine the "human resources" needed to support innovation. When it comes to innovating in your career, you need a trusted individual to act as your innovation soundboard and you need a support team. If you are in a position where you do not have this type of support, don't despair. Given the degree of connectivity in today's society, you can create a virtual team to support your innovation process in almost any environment. You can build that support and create your team. Remember, innovation is a team sport!

## PERSONAL INNOVATION VS ORGANIZATIONAL INNOVATION

Praveen Gupta, author of *Business Innovation in the 21ˢᵗ Century* [7], has found a way to quantify innovation using the following equation:

**Innovation value** $=$ (resources) (speed of thought)

The speed of thought is described by the following equation:

**Speed of thought** $=$ (function) (knowledge, play, imagination)

Gupta then created a new unit called *Einstein* (*Ei*), to represent the units of the innovation value. This new unit is given the maximum value of "1." Therefore, **Innovation value** (Ei) is equal to the **resources** (commitment) times **a function of knowledge, play, and imagination** (KPI). This equation not only identifies a numerical value but also sheds light on elements of innovation that can be used to maximize the innovation value. Gupta writes, "the innovation can be increased with more resources or faster generation and processing of ideas [and] can be accelerated with better utilization of intellectual resources rather than merely allocating more physical resources to innovation."

Gupta uses Table 2.1 to demonstrate quantification of innovation [8].

While it is not necessary to have a certain "Innovation Score" in order to initiate and grow your innovative abilities, it is important to understand where you are as innovator so that you can improve upon your skillset. This equation for calculating innovation levels will certainly appeal to many STEM professionals but the more important thing to understand is the elements or factors within the equation. Having access to resources, knowledge, an ability to experiment, and imagination create a foundation to see innovation realized. So, do not be overly concerned with the equation, instead understand that each of these items is needed in various portions for an individual to be a consistent innovator.

**TABLE 2.1** Matrix for Assessing Personal Innovation

|  | Description | Example |
|---|---|---|
| Resources (R) | Degree of resources or time committed | 50 percent (limited time and insufficient resources) and 50 percent (limited time and insufficient resources) |
| Knowledge (K) | Extent (%) of knowledge based on research and experience | 75 percent (significant knowledge and experience gained, some latest work is to be explored) |
| Play (P) | Percentage (%) of possible combinations of various variables explored | 40 percent (percentage of combination of variables explored mentally, experimentally or through simulation – work is in progress) |
| Imagination (I) | Dimension extrapolated as a percentage of ideal solution for breakthrough improvement | 66 percent (selected dimension is extrapolated such that improvement is expected to be about 30 percent, which is about 66 percent of the breakthrough improvement) |
| Innovation value (Iv) | Estimated innovation level | 0.182 (Long way to find an innovative solution due to lack of effort and play – to accelerate, one needs to improve all elements of innovation) |
| Comments | Initial estimation of the proposed model – further work is required | Innovation value $= 0.5 * ((0.75 + 0.4 + 0.66) / 3)^2 = \mathbf{0.182}$ <br> **Einstein** |

Source: Gupta P. "Assess Personal Innovation Levels." RealInnovation.com.

## Personal Innovation

Applying innovation principles can be effective in both the professional and personal environment. Personal innovation is a technique that has been used by many individuals to create opportunities for growth or change in areas of one's career or personal life. This is often found in the entertainment industry where we see individuals such as Madonna, Queen Latifah, and others "recreate" themselves. In the most simple terms, what they've actually done is identified opportunities which they then tailored their abilities and skills to meet. They are then able to put massive marketing efforts behind the convergence of these opportunities with their newfound abilities. There is absolutely no reason we shouldn't be applying these same principles to our STEM careers. While we may not have the marketing budget that these entertainment icons have to support our personal innovation there are considerable resources available via electronic communication, social networking, organizational membership, and relationship development to support and promote our personal innovation.

## Organizational Innovation

Organizational innovation can be applied in many forms to produce the creative, value-added, and profitable outcomes expected in the business environment. Generally, there are three different types of organizational innovation: product and service innovation, operational innovation, and business model innovation [9].

## Product and Service Innovation

Product and service innovation aims to improve a company's (you guessed it!) products and services. Innovation often begins with ideas about market opportunities made possible by new technologies. Product and service innovation focuses on bringing new capabilities to life that benefit both customers and the companies who provide for them. Organizations engaged in product or service innovation preoccupy themselves with listening to customers and differentiating their offerings and speed of execution. Some current examples are Nintendo's Wii gaming system (product innovation) and Virgin Atlantic and Southwest Airlines (service innovation). In a study performed in Australia [10], the test to evaluate a new product or service for innovation value is defined by assessing key factors (see Table 2.2).

## Operational Innovation

Operational, or process, innovation, focuses on making an internal business process a core strength, as Toyota has done through its lean automotive production process. Operational innovations can increase bottom-line profitability, improve efficiency and productivity, and increase employee job satisfaction. They also deliver enhanced product or service value to the customer. Operational innovations usually involve the implementation of a new or significantly improved production or delivery method. For example, Dell revolutionized the way computers were ordered and delivered through its direct order fulfillment model.

## Business Model Innovation

Business model innovation involves changing the way business is done in terms of capturing value. These innovators devise new formulas for the enterprise to make money. Google, for example, has reinvented the way companies make

**TABLE 2.2  Tests of a new product or service**

| Test | Meaning |
|------|---------|
| 1. Valuable benefits test | Does the new product, service, technology or process provide benefits in a manner that is clearly superior to existing services or methods? Can you articulate the "value proposition" of what is new and why it is better in value terms that customers or clients can appreciate? |
| 2. Scale-up test | Can the concept be mass-produced in volumes and with the consistent quality to its specification in order to satisfy the market need? There have been many ideas that made it to the prototype stage, but when it came time to scale up, they failed to be "mass-producible" or production proved to be prohibitive from a cost perspective. |
| 3. Marketing test | Have you determined or assessed demand, and do you have a channel to the client or consumer base? Many inventors end up with a garage or warehouse full of their products, because they did not do their homework on the marketing test. The whole marketing mix must be planned as part of the commercialisation process. This includes design, branding, pricing, distribution, sales, and other factors. |
| 4. Leadership (team) test | Do the key people involved in this initiative have the knowledge, skills, experience and courage to take it through to fruition? |
| 5. Intellectual property control test | You have to make decisions around your IP, and either buy, own or licence-in the core technologies and other elements of IP involved in the innovation. |
| 6. ROI (return on investment) test | This represents the financial bottom line of the innovation. Will it pay? The new concept must generate enough profit to make it worthwhile, including accounting for risk and the time discounted value of money. |
| 7. Corporate social responsibility test | This is also sometimes referred to as the sustainable development or sustainability test, and refers to the environmental sustainability of the initiative and also the social/community outcomes. Products, services and technologies must now at least not harm the environment and community, or do so minimally, and where possible are advantaged by producing positive bottom line outcomes on all these dimensions. Leading companies often find a way to make progress on all three dimensions of value creation outcomes (financial, environmental, and social), with their inventions and innovations. |
| 8. Strategic fit test | Is the new initiative (product, service, process, technology, business model) consistent and aligned with your firm's overall business strategy? |

Source: Samson D. (2010)

money by advertising on the Web, and Apple has forever changed the way music is sold and distributed. Business model innovation often involves a company shedding "non core" business functions and reconfiguring its value chain. It emphasizes external collaboration and partnerships. Proctor & Gamble, as well as Eli Lily, are contemporary examples of companies that employ open, collaborative innovation models.

## Personal Innovation

Personal innovation tailors career focus, personal capabilities, skills, and relationships to meet current and emerging needs in a given area of opportunity (Figure 2.1). Individuals who are successful at this know themselves, know the career landscape, and know how to take action [11].

To excel in personal innovation the following process can be applied and tailored to address our goals of "recreating" ourselves or personal innovation.

1. Determine your true passion:
   a. What ideas get you excited?
   b. What are the things you do that you lose track of time and can work on for hours without noticing the time passing?
   c. If there were no constraints, barriers, or limitations what would you "see" yourself doing in your ultimate career?

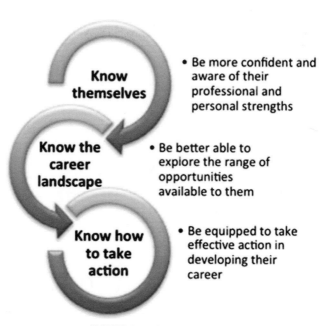

**FIGURE 2.1**   Career innovation.

2. Identify how this passion can be developed into useful skills, talents, or services that you can demonstrate.
3. Determine at least three environments where your personal innovation will be valued; in other words define the target audience and how they will benefit by your presence and the demonstration of your personal innovation through the application of your ideas, talents, and abilities.
4. Establish a plan to demonstrate this new skill, passion, or talent in an environment where it is valued and you are recognized. For example, will it be beneficial for you to take a new leadership role in your job, join a professional organization, or establish a collaboration with an international partner?
5. Determine the resources you will need to do the following:
   a. Develop your passion into a personal innovation that is represented in a new "you" whether in skills, career focus, or image (i.e., new personal technical abilities, interpersonal skills, image changes, etc.)
   b. Communicate your personal innovation outcomes to the community where it is valued
   c. Access the community or environment where your personal innovation is valued
   d. Sustain your personal innovation
6. Create a realistic (but aggressive) timeline to initiate the process.

In order to be successful in personal innovation, you need to know your strengths. If you are a perfectionist, as many of us are, and you tend to focus on your faults, you will waste time constantly trying to improve them. In her book, *Know Your Strengths Inventory: A Life Coaching Tool* [12], Phyllis E. Reardon teaches us that the better we know our strengths, the better decisions we make, and better decisions lead to more successful outcomes in life and work. Know your strengths, be confident in what you know, and don't get hung up on the imperfections. In order to develop our strengths into a fruitful product, we have to understand the landscape where the opportunities are: what matters and *to whom*. Take your personal strengths into an environment where they are valued.

According to David Nordfors, co-founder and executive director of the VINNOVA-Stanford Research Center of Innovation Journalism at Stanford University, "Innovation is today the most important driver of economic growth. It relies upon a social climate supporting entrepreneurship within a culture of economic and intellectual freedom [13]." That social climate is here, and these opportunities are yours for the taking!

### Who Are the Innovators?

Innovators are individuals with knowledge in specific areas. They are equipped with problem-solving skills, and background and expertise in their line of work, and they know not only how to turn ideas into products but how to motivate people to buy them. The innovators of the world cannot generally exist as one individual but as a collection – as denoted by models of innovation ecosystems. Innovation requires a specific environment (as discussed by David Nordfors above), as well as a network of symbiotic relationships among innovators. While individual innovation is possible, if you're going to be a lone innovator it can be very difficult, as you must assume many roles in order to maintain your own innovation ecosystem. Innovation ecosystems characterize the individuals or components of the innovation continuum such that the roles and the expected outcomes associated with each role are determined, and everyone's place in the innovation process is defined.

## Keys to Personal Innovation

When it comes to personal innovation, there are a few key points to keep in mind. Number one on my list is *passion*. Passion is the food that fuels your determination and, more importantly, encourages others to help you to their best ability. The second most important aspect of personal innovation is having a *vision*. If you don't have a vision, you will have little desire to plan or think ahead. Which leads me to planning: have a plan, and carry it out to its completion – these things don't happen overnight. Focusing on your ultimate goal will only get you so far without a plan to get you there. Lastly, know where you can add value, and be confident in what you know. Your confidence will breed the resilience and determination needed to see your project through. There will be times when you are frustrated, when people are unsupportive, and when you have to reorganize and adjust your plans. Your confidence is what helps you decide who to listen to and take advice from, and who to ignore. Determination and resilience will be your best weapons against the inevitable discouragements that come your way. Always remember, if you have a passion for something, it will be hard to put that fire out.

## How Do We Innovate?

1. Knowledge
   As I've mentioned before, it is important to use what you know. Know yourself, know the landscape, and know how to take action. If you don't know these things, find someone who does, or do your best to gather the necessary information.
2. Don't be afraid to think differently
   Think differently, and be confident in the way you think. Take a look at your résumé; your thoughts and ideas are not only valid, but valuable. If you see that your career reflects a different mindset than others that is a good thing! Yours is a career that celebrates diversity of thought and action, and people who think differently are the ones we need the most right now. As Andy Warhol put simply, "you have to do stuff that average people don't understand, because those are the only good things." Being different is what ultimately will make you a better innovator.

3. Find a need that's not being filled in your area of knowledge
   This can apply to career innovation, product development, or services. Ask yourself, "What is it about my career that needs to change in order to differentiate me or move me forward?" This can be your carrier technical area, services offered on a community or personal level. Start by finding this area that needs a "change". (Hint: I suggest you start small.) Then make that change! Find an area where your unique contribution will make a real difference. It may be as small a matter as getting the street around your home cleaned or repaired, or getting extra streetlights in your neighbourhood, but your contribution will be of great importance.

4. Create a brief but clear explanation of the innovation
   Write down why it matters and make sure it's not currently being done. Your brief explanation can be as short as a paragraph or a bulleted list, but write it down!

5. Determine who wants this innovation
   Who does it matter to? Who's willing to pay for it? Where does it add the most value? What are those environments and who are those individuals? Your consumer is ultimately the person who will benefit from your innovation, and you need to know whom you're helping in order to create the best product for them.

6. Protect your idea/innovation
   You are protecting not only your idea but also the manner in which you want to see it manifested. At this point you may want to seek legal counsel or research on how you can protect your idea.

7. Identify a trusted person who can be your "Innovation soundboard"
   Your innovation soundboard is a person you are comfortable talking about your career with, or the ideas you intend to develop.

8. Develop a "core team" of three to five supporters
   These are advocates with key areas of knowledge who you can trust to help you carry out your innovation.

9. Create a plan to develop the idea to at least a "proof of concept"
   Write down a more detailed plan in which you design a process to go from idea to development, or a "proof of concept" of your idea.

10. Decide if you want to take the innovation to the finish line or if you will partner with organizations/other individuals to see it realized
    If it is your career we're talking about, you're probably going to carry out that form of personal innovation on your own. However, if you're developing a product, letting others take over can be a smart thing to do because it allows you to keep your STEM "hat" on while others come in and do what they are educated or trained to do in order to see the innovation realized.

## INNOVATION AND WOMEN

Given the critical importance of innovation and the low percentage of women in the STEM workforce, it is clear that we need to come up with incentives to promote and encourage innovation among women in research, technology,

## Core Levers

1. Break boundaries for strategic partnerships
2. Engage women in design and diffusion
3. Cultivate champions
4. Create "buzz" to make it "stick"
5. Capitalize on opportune timing and context
6. Target efforts to reach poor women
7. Synergize top-down and bottom-up approaches

**FIGURE 2.2**   Core Levers. *Source: International Center for Research on Women (ICRW) (2009)*

education, and business. The two focus areas with respect to women and innovation include, first, the need to encourage women (particularly STEM professionals) to focus more on innovation, and, second, the impact that innovation can have on women in a community. When women innovate, they impact society in different ways than teams comprised of only men. This is often seen in developing countries, where the impact of innovations can be quickly realized.

A research study by the International Center for Research on Women (ICRW) examined innovation with a gender lens and identified seven core levers critical for innovation to catalyze meaningful change for women in developing countries (see Figure 2.2) [14]. This research is the first scholarly assessment of its kind to understand how innovations have improved women's well-being, empowered women, and advanced gender equality. The research reveals the significant impact innovation can have on women. Specifically, innovations can benefit women in many smaller nations simply by improving their well-being in terms of health, nutrition, income, and even life span. In addition, these sometimes small but vital improvements in well-being through innovation can lead to women's empowerment as well as securing freedom and needed resources for women in a community.

## MODELS OF INNOVATION

A basic model can be applied to innovation. In its simplest form, a **linear model of innovation** has been traditionally used in manufacturing organizations. This is where an agent (person or business) innovates in order to sell the innovation. In addition to linear models of innovation with the global thrust for increased innovation in our communities (primarily in the business environment), we have developed collaborative systems of innovation – which brings us back to **innovation ecosystems**, mentioned earlier in the chapter.

If we look at the European innovation ecosystem (Figure 2.3) [15], we can see the characteristics that many other countries have incorporated as well.

**Idea generation** can be performed by an individual in his or her garage, but it is a crucial component of the innovation ecosystem. **Product innovation** involves a design, and development of the idea into a product. **Talent**

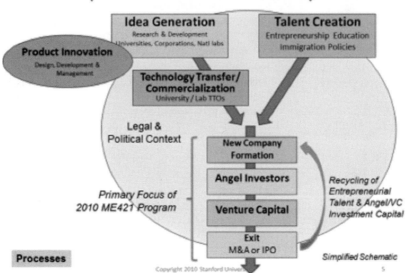

**FIGURE 2.3**  European innovation ecosystem. *Source: Dr. Burton H. Lee, Program Director Department of Mechanical Engineering (ME 421 European Entreprenuership & Innovation Program 2010). Copyright 2010 Stanford University.*

**creation** often means understanding what skills or knowledge you need to acquire personally before you can do product innovation. **Technology transfer** requires capital. This is the phase where you are marketing your new skill – finding a new job, volunteering somewhere you can demonstrate your skill, or selling the manifested innovation that is part of your new career portfolio. Within an ecosystem these four major components may occur sequentially or overlap.

## CREATING YOUR OWN MICRO-INNOVATION ECOSYSTEM

While personal innovation might mean we don't need the help of organizations or corporations, we can create a micro version of this system in our personal careers. Your micro-innovation system begins with the same step as any other innovation ecosystem:

- *Idea Generation* – your concept reduced to a useful product or service, documented, and details associated with the development of the innovation researched and confirmed.
- *Product Innovation* – the creation of your product or innovation can take on a variety of approaches including developing the initial idea as a computer simulation or a physical prototype.

- *Talent Creation* – for the individual innovator, the talent will generally begin with you. However, you will need to acquire talent that goes beyond you to see the idea fully realized. Individuals to consider include marketing professionals, legal support, and other technical individuals.
- *Technology Transfer* – the transfer of the idea from your personal laboratory, garage, or personal computer is the point at which you will begin to see (hopefully) the concept move into a value-added innovation. This is rarely done as an individual due to the various skills required at this point. Thus, it's often useful (once your idea has been protected) to seek additional collaborators at this point.

The next step for you, if you are truly seeking to be an innovator, is to carry out your mission. As I've said before, Please, write your idea down – seeing it on paper will be a powerful motivator. Next, write down at least a four-step plan to move toward the development of the idea. Create a schedule and then – *take the first step* in your plan. Perhaps you don't have the necessary skill or it will take years to fully develop your idea – don't despair – in this case you might find someone who does or who can help you. Then you can start the product innovation process, and plan for technology transfer or commercialization of your innovation. As an alternative to creating an idea on your own, your process may involve becoming an *intrapreneur – a person that innovates within an organization.* Many companies are now encouraging employees to create products and develop them in-house with certain appropriations. The last stage is to seek funding or support for your innovation, so you can transition the product into the hands of the users or those who value it.

As much as we tend to "love" our ideas love alone will not lead to innovation. If an idea is to mature into an innovation, it will require other people to recognize the value and be willing to support it in the development process. The "Tests of a New Product or Service" table, developed by Samson, can be a useful resource to begin the evaluation. For your idea or concept, consider summarizing a response to each of the areas identified in Table 2.2.

Once you have completed a similar table for your idea, you can begin to honestly look at the potential associated with your concept. As you look to refine your concept, consider assessing the areas the test did not produce strong or favorable outcomes in. For these areas, determine how you can refine the concept to achieve more positive results in the test. The evaluation of your idea will be an iterative process that should take place numerous times in order for you to have a comprehensive understanding of the potential role associated with your idea as well as the most appropriate strategy for developing the innovation.

## SUMMARY

The collaborative and connective nature of innovation today can be fostered greatly with the use of technology. Gaining an understanding of the importance, impact, and process for innovation can be valuable in moving you forward toward the realization of your innovations. The time to innovate is now – whether you do it as a part of your organization or as an individual. Remember, a marathon begins with a single step. Take that first step today toward attaining your dream.

## REFERENCES

[1] Babco E. Skills for the Innovation Economy: What the 21st Century Workforce Needs and How to Provide It. Commission on Professionals in Science and Technology 2004; Washington, DC.

[2] Gumusluoğlu L, Ilsev A. Transformational leadership and organizational innovation: the roles of internal and external support for innovation. Journal of Product Innovation Management 2009;26:264–77.

[3] Burns JM. Leadership. New York, NY: Harper & Row; 1978.

[4] Bass BM, Avolio BJ. Multifactor Leadership Questionnaire. Redwood City: Mind Garden; 1995.

[5] Bass BM. From transactional to transformational leadership: Learning to share the vision. Organizational Dynamics 1990;18(3):19–31.

[6] Augustine NR. Is America Falling Off the Flat Earth? Washington DC: The National Academies Press; 2007.

[7] Gupta P. Business Innovation in the 21st Century. Charleston, SC: BookSurge Publishing; 2007.

[8] Gupta P. Assess Personal Innovation Levels. RealInnovation.com www.realinnovation.com/content/c070423a.asp (accessed May 4, 2012).

[9] CIMS. http://cims.poole.ncsu.edu/ (accessed March 30, 2012).

[10] Samson D. Innovation for business success: Achieving a systematic innovation capability. Univ. of Melbourne; 2010.

[11] Career Innovation. www.careerinnovation.com/ (accessed March 30, 2012).

[12] Reardon PE. Know Your Strengths Inventory: A Life Coaching Tool. Charleston, SC: CreateSpace; 2011.

[13] Nordfors D. What Is Innovation?. IIP Digital 2009 http://iipdigital.usembassy.gov/st/english/publication/2009/11/20091109105608ebyessedo0.6893579.html (accessed March 30, 2012).

[14] Malhotra A, Schulte J, Patel P, Petesch P. Innovation for women's empowerment and gender equality. International Center for Research on Women 2009.

[15] The presentation of a network model for the development of innovation in R&D centers. Dr. Burton H. Lee, Program Director, Department of Mechanical Engineering (ME 421 European Entreprenuership & Innovation Program 2010), Stanford University. Copyright 2010 Stanford University.

## Chapter 3

# Why More Women Don't Lead and Innovate

*No person is your friend who demands your silence or denies your right to grow.*

*Alice Walker*

## Chapter Outline

The objective of this book is to enlighten, empower, and encourage you to achieve your goals no matter what age or stage you currently find yourself in from a career or personal perspective. The topics thus far have been designed to enlighten you to the need and call to us to lead. The focus of this chapter is to help us understand factors that have impeded the progress of women for generations and how to overcome these issues in your career. Specifically, the goal is to gain an understanding of the common factors that women face when seeking leadership opportunities, particularly in male-dominated careers such as STEM fields, and understand how you can mitigate the impact of these factors.

Given the number of qualified women in STEM professions and recognizing the tremendous opportunities for leadership, why don't more of us lead? Many

*Transforming your STEM Career through Leadership and Innovation.*
http://dx.doi.org/10.1016/B978-0-12-396993-4.00003-5

categories of challenges exist that inhibit the opportunities, perspective, and willingness of some women to step into leadership positions. I have characterized these categories of career perception factors as cultural, individual, and organizational (Figure 3.1). These categories have an individual and synergistic impact on our likelihood for pursuing and achieving leadership goals in a career. Additionally, the degree to which each factor will impact a woman's career varies from a societal, organizational, and individual perspective. The key is to recognize and manage these factors. This pyramid of career perception factors (see Figure 3.1) must be managed throughout the life of your career, and each will require varying levels of focus depending on the phase of your career path you find yourself in in a given season. These three categories can be further defined as follows:

- Cultural factors that influence our perspectives are feedback, relationships, and experiences in our environment (country, region, and home). This includes observations and our exposure to those factors that represent the cultural norms for the environment.
- Individual factors are a function of our personality, our responses to the cultural factors, experiences, and feedback we received for select behavior. This is the area where we have the most control if we recognize that our perceptions are not working to support the attainment of our goals.
- Organizational factors are a function of the career environment (e.g., academia) that we select and the career path within that environment (e.g., administration) to determine the organizational culture and how it will impact our career goals. To understand organizational factors, they should be studied with an in-depth view to fully understand the perception and align with opportunities that you will be seeking in your tenure within the organization.

While a vast body of knowledge exists to provide an understanding of how to mitigate the impact of the conditions created by the organizational, cultural, and individual categories, we will briefly discuss each and focus most of our energy on the category that we have the most control over – the individual factors.

**FIGURE 3.1**    Career perception factors

## CULTURAL CAREER PERCEPTION ISSUES

Most of us have heard of the glass ceiling, the invisible barrier to career advancement for many women. Evidence of some type of barrier can find support in the statistics. Specifically, although women constitute almost half of the American workforce and hold over 50% of the management and professional positions, they make up a mere 2% of the Fortune 500 CEOs [1]. The situation is even more dire for Women of Color, where in 2005 only 5% of all managers, professionals, and related occupations were African American women; Latina women constituted 3.3% and Asian women 2.6% [2]. In Europe, the numbers are a bit different but show a similar pattern. In 2005, women represented 44% of the workforce, 30% of the managerial positions, and 3% of the company CEOs [1]. For the numbers to be consistent across nations suggests that there are strong cultural norms at work in these environments. Could it be possible that something as simple as cultural "stereotyping" is standing in the way of the development and advancement of women in these environments?

*Stereotypes 101*

*Stereotypes can be defined as cognitive shortcuts or generalizations that we use to make sense of our complex social world. Gender stereotypes are widely shared within cultures and this can be problematic as the nature of stereotyping is to over-simplify reality. Gender stereotypes emphasize "natural differences" between women and men. However, the empirical literature suggests that gender differences are far from natural. Extensive research has shown that women and men are actually more similar than different and that there is more variation within women's leadership styles than there is between women and men. By creating false perceptions that women and men are "planets apart", stereotyping, however, results in women being overlooked for the top jobs – no matter how strong their actual credentials.*

**Source: Catalyst, 2007**

Research indicates that this is in fact what's happening. In the study "Women 'Take Care,' Men 'Take Charge'" [3] researchers surveyed 296 corporate leaders, 34% of whom were CEOs, and asked them to rate how effective men and women are at different essential leadership behaviors. Likewise, in "Different Cultures, Similar Perceptions: Stereotyping of Western European Business Leaders," researchers analyzed the responses of 935 leaders from 10 different countries, 42% of whom were top management [4]. Both of these studies found patterns of stereotypic judgments by men **and women** that limited their perceptions of women as effective leaders. These perceptions inhibit women's advancement because the "taking charge" skills and stereotypically masculine behaviors, such as assertiveness and competitiveness, are often seen as absent from women, yet they are prerequisites for leadership. The key here is to recognize when you are being stereotyped and confront it. It is equally important that we do not stereotype and recognize how our generalizations may be impacting the success of our career as well as those of other women.

Specific strategies that can be used to mitigate the dilemmas women leaders face from an organizational perspective when being stereotyped have been adapted from the Catalyst study and include the following: [1]

1. Recognize when you're being stereotyped or facing any type of organizational norm that's limiting your opportunity.
2. Talk about the issue! With your management, co-workers, and others.
3. Show them otherwise. Become visible and openly demonstrate your skills, knowledge, and accomplishments; seek high-level assignments, and speak up in meetings.
4. Ask for what you want! Use clear and effective communication.
5. Minimize the issue. Shift the attention away from gender and back to the task, mission, and vision of the organization.

The use of these strategies can be valuable in managing the impact that stereotyping can have on your career.

Let us also talk about the "unsaid things" that women deal with when aspiring to become leaders. Many of these "unsaid" things can have devastating impact when we're not aware or prepared for them. In addition to the organizational limitations, this can easily be translated into negative personal responses. When this happens, the result is often manifested in career-limiting insecurities. These insecurities can begin to manifest whenever we begin to walk the path to becoming leaders. These doubts are often not consciously perceived, but rather demonstrated as we rationalize why we can't or shouldn't do something. These thoughts ultimately lead us to doubt ourselves and our ability to lead, innovate, and widen our horizons.

## ORGANIZATIONAL CAREER PERCEPTION ISSUES

In order to attain career success and achieve your leadership goals it is critical to understand your organization. It is imperative to ask and get answers to questions such as: What are the organizational values? What are the priorities of top management? How is success rewarded? Are there opportunities available that are compatible with my career vision? Addressing these questions gives the likelihood of attaining your goals in an organization. Management is often asked to evaluate the developmental climate of an organization, but it is equally important for aspiring leaders to do similar assessments. When evaluating the developmental climate in your organization consider the elements of a developmental climate as defined in a chapter from the Center for Creative Leadership [5] (see Table 3.1).

You may not be able to get a definitive or holistic perspective of the organization for each of these elements. In those cases, start with your department or division of the organization and work your way up to create a hierarchical assessment of the development climate by levels. The confidence associated with the accuracy of your assessment may be higher in the lower levels of the organization as you will have more knowledge of the conditions in these levels; however, continue with your evaluation to assess the full organization. Assessment of these

**TABLE 3.1** Elements of a Developmental Climate in Organizations

| Element | Statements that Reflect Each Element |
|---|---|
| Priority of top management | Our CEO demonstrates a real commitment to the development of people<br>The development of people is a key part of our overall business strategy |
| Recognition and rewards | Good performance is recognized and rewarded<br>We reward people who develop the talents and skills needed for effectiveness in the organization |
| Communication | High-performing employees are highlighted in the organization's formal communication channels<br>People can readily access information about developmental strategies and opportunities in the organization |
| Efforts to track and measure | We have organizational metrics for tracking whether we are developing the leadership talent we need<br>Formal development initiatives are regularly evaluated as part of efforts to enhance their effectiveness<br>Bosses monitor employees' progress on developmental goals |
| Resources | We do not let short-term business pressure interfere with our development of people<br>We take a long-term perspective when planning for development – five or ten years out, not just tomorrow<br>We plan development activities for the key points in a career where they can have the most impact<br>Our human resources processes (compensation, benefits, and so forth) all work together to support people development |
| Employee skills | We attract people who are motivated to expand their capabilities<br>The ability to learn, grow, and adapt to new situations is valued among employees |

Source: Van Velsor, McCauley, and Ruderman (2010)

aspects of an organization can be a good starting point to determine the level of commitment to development of leaders and talent as well as providing insight into your future leadership development opportunities.

A Catalyst [6] study asked senior-level executives in the U.S. and Europe to independently rate the effectiveness of female and male leaders on a select list of key leadership characteristics [1]. In this study, both men and women rated women as better at stereotypically feminine "care-taking" skills such as supporting and encouraging others. Likewise, women and men rated the men as excelling more at conventionally masculine "taking charge" skills that are essential to leadership such as influencing superiors and problem solving. Additionally, the research shows that these perceptions are even more prominent when women are seeking leadership or advancement in traditionally male-dominated fields such as engineering and law. In these professions women are viewed as even more "out of place" and thus have to exert effort not only as leaders but to prove they belong. These are the types of cultural and organizational issues that we must be mindful of in our career management plans.

In recent decades, private organizations have developed programs to alleviate some of the known corporate challenges. The National Science Foundation's (NSF) ADVANCE Program began funding initiatives to increase the representation and advancement of women in academic science and engineering careers in 2001. The goal of the ADVANCE program is to increase the representation and advancement of women in academic science and engineering careers through research and developmental projects, thereby developing a more diverse science and engineering workforce. ADVANCE programs fund research and projects that focus on institutional and faculty-related barriers. These project focus areas include analysis of institutional structure, work-life support issues, equitable career support, and empowerment to address gender-equity barriers. The institutional issues are particularly important as research has shown that women's representation and advancement in academic STEM positions are affected by many external factors that are unrelated to their ability, interest, and technical skills, such as: [7]

- Organizational constraints of academic institutions
- Differential effects of work and family demands
- Implicit and explicit bias
- Underrepresentation of women in academic leadership and decision-making positions.

The cumulative effect of such diverse and significant factors in the workplace has resulted in the creation of barriers that impact the number of women entering and advancing in academic STEM careers.

While the goal of this book is to empower the reader as an individual, recognizing the importance of organizational or systemic issues is critical, as we can assist in leading our organizations to change. Participating in efforts that bring about organizational change can have long-term benefits on the careers of women, particularly for issues that directly impact career advancement. For instance, when a professor is seeking tenure at academic institutions there is a limited and standard time to demonstrate proficiency. The tenure clause at most institutions does not allow for extended leave after a pregnancy relative to the time toward tenure. Thus, in those institutions, when a woman takes time off to care for newborn children the "tenure clock" doesn't stop, thereby resulting in a reduced amount of time available to attain the indicators of success for an academic career. Some argue that the tenure clock should pause for a few years and continue when the female faculty member can drop her child off at preschool every day and return to work. If rearing a young child didn't interfere with the tenure clock more women might rise in academia. Keep in mind, the objective is not to give women an unfair advantage or lower the expectation. The goal of these types of initiatives is to develop and retain a pool of highly- qualified individuals to lead and innovate. If there are systemic issues that discourage women from pursuing and desiring to advance and lead in these environments, they need to be addressed because when they aren't, everyone loses.

Getting back to your assessment of our organizations, if we do not directly address the question of organizational culture and we find that we are not properly aligned in terms of our vision and the organization, this can become a daunting situation. If several years pass where we've consistently tried and have not been given developmental opportunities and our perception is that we're not accepted, this can lead to personal or professional despair, frustration, and a sense of hopelessness. A sad but realistic picture of this is captured in the excerpt from the book, *Smart Women, Smart Moves*: [8]

*Several years ago one of my friends called me in a panic. She had been interviewing women who had been in top executive positions for seven to ten years. She said it was as if they got suited up, got on the bus, and went to the game, but… they never got off the bench. At first they were hopeful, but after a few years they became resigned to the reality that they would never quite belong. She said that she found more alcoholism, clinical depression and anorexia-bulimia in this group of women than she had ever seen.*

These situations represent a waste of valuable resources and are an unfortunate reality that many women face. Rather than internalizing the frustration and disappointment, a healthier response is to take. Take action and recognize that this is an opportunity for you to take your talents, passion, and vision to another environment within your organizational or perhaps in another corporation, university or community. You should consider your options on a global level – perhaps it's time to work in another country. Yes, the difficult situation you find yourself in can be a signal that it's time for a change – a change to lead you to your true destiny and vision. But first you must realize that you *can* exit. This is an empowering first step. The next step is to plan an effective exit strategy and finally but most importantly take action and execute your exit strategy. This exit strategy can include physical (geographical) moves as well as a change in perspective. For example, realizing your goals may mean you leave your department, organization, community, state, or country. It may also require changes in professional or personal relationships and strategic alliances. However, the most important change will be in our perspective of what opportunities are available to us. You may have had some difficult, unfair, and blatantly biased situations come your way. Accept that it happened. Accept that it wasn't fair, and right now commit to putting it behind you, taking action and moving forward. The greatest news is you're still here and things can *and will* change. Suit up ladies! It's time to get back in the game!

## INDIVIDUAL CAREER PERCEPTION ISSUES

Perhaps the areas that impact us most are not global, national, cultural, or organizational but, rather, individual issues that are bound by our perceptions, expectations, and self-image. The powerful individual category of factors is at the core of our career potential and the career perception pyramid. Understanding ourselves and how to most effectively respond to the cultural and organizational challenges is critical in learning how to navigate the career path. Think about it: there are numerous situations where one person seems to manage comfortably in what appears to be a difficult situation while another person completely falls apart under the pressure. Much of this has to do with individuals' differences. The outcomes associated with confronting and addressing our individual challenges such as misperceptions, areas for professional development, and personal biases can pay great dividends in the path to our personal and career development.

Luckily, our individual perceptions are the category of challenges that we have the most control over in the career perception pyramid! I have created a list of some of the most common issues women face, based on my personal experiences, the literature, and observing many other women over the last 20 years. The individual career factors include the following:

- Because we don't believe we can
- Impact on family life
- Not recognizing our strengths
- Perception of limited opportunity or failure to recognize opportunities
- Lack of role models and mentors

These factors have consistently appeared as reasons for women not pursuing and excelling in leadership positions in STEM and non-STEM careers. However, with a clear understanding of the issues and a plan to overcome them, women can succeed and lead in their careers.

## Because We Don't Believe We Can

The "conditioning" of our expectations in leadership may have a basis as simple as stimulus-response theory. Stimulus-response (S-R) theories are core to the principles of conditioning and are based on the assumption that human behavior is learned. For example, if the stimulus is the recognition when in pursuit of a leadership opportunity and the resulting response is not favorable, this will eventually lead to a learning outcome. Theoretically speaking, when this learning "outcome" is negative we have essentially been "conditioned" not to pursue leadership opportunities. The negative response leads to interpretations that ultimately suggest to us that we cannot be successful in these opportunities. Simply put, when no positive reinforcement is offered, but rather negative reinforcement, this will lead to a change in behavior, in this case failure to consider or pursue leadership opportunities.

Additionally, women may be especially vulnerable to losing confidence when not rewarded in male-dominated careers such as STEM fields. This can lead to feelings of insecurity, "not belonging," and, ultimately, a lack of confidence. These feelings manifest when we begin to think about our leadership visions. Often, that "little negative voice" within us inhibits our desire to lead, questioning our own abilities to handle the new challenges that leadership entails. We do not believe we can do all that we would like to do and this result is a function of many factors including social conditioning as well as our perception of ourselves. It may be due to what others around us think regarding our abilities. The common thread here is that these are individual perception-based challenges that are manifested as a lack of self-knowledge and self-confidence. The key is to recognize when we're falling victim to negative conditions and to take an active role in the "reconditioning" of our expectations. To recondition we must alter our S-R relationship with new knowledge and experiences that demonstrate positive rewards for seeking leadership roles. I have found three useful approaches for changing my perceptions when reconditioning is necessary. These three approaches include:

- Mentally cataloging my past experiences that were successful.
- Identifying through the literature other experiences where individuals were successful in a similar endeavor.
- Developing a plan to recognize and eradicate the feelings, actions, and attitudes that I demonstrate when this negative conditioning is influencing my decision making or thought processes.

As we consider our perceptions they are impacted by our environment and, thus, we must evaluate the perceptions of others and the impact of these views on women's opportunities for leadership. Based on the results of a recent Catalyst study, the old adage "women 'take care,' men 'take charge'" persists and is impacting the modern workplace. The study indicated that gender stereotypes attribute traits such as sensitivity and being emotional to women, while attributing traits such as aggressiveness and rationality to men [3]. Top corporate leaders were asked to judge how effective female and male leaders are on 10 behaviors essential to leadership. Based on the common gender stereotypes from previous research, each of the behaviors was classified as either feminine or masculine (Table 3.2). Specifically, leadership behaviors that depend on the task-oriented "take charge" traits of men were categorized as masculine, while those that rely on the people-oriented "caretaker" traits of women were classified as feminine [3].

The judgment from male and female corporate managers did in fact match the patterns of stereotypical expectations in all areas, with the exception of a few categories. Female respondents ascribed to male leaders greater competency at networking, a stereotypic feminine behavior, and male respondents saw male leaders as better at inspiring, a behavior also classified as feminine. Additionally, problem solving was the only masculine behavior at which women perceived women leaders to be superior.

Although objective evidence tells us that they should not be, respondents' perceptions were generally aligned with gender stereotypes. Together, these facts give us some indication that respondents were likely not basing their perceptions on fact but rather on gender stereotypes. This does not suggest that respondents were not being honest when they reported their observations. Because people are generally unaware of how their thinking is automatically influenced by stereotypes they conclude that their perceptions come from objective observations,

**TABLE 3.2** How Leader Behaviors Connect to Feminine and Masculine Stereotypes

| Feminine Behaviors – Taking Care | Masculine Behaviors – Taking Charge |
|---|---|
| **Supporting** Encouraging, assisting, and providing resources for others | **Problem-Solving** Identifying, analyzing, and acting decisively to remove impediments to work performance |
| **Rewarding** Providing praise, recognition, and financial remuneration when appropriate | **Influencing Upward** Affecting others in positions of higher rank |
| **Mentoring** Facilitating the skill development and career advancement of subordinates | **Delegating** Authorizing others to have substantial responsibility and discretion |
| **Networking** Developing and maintaining relationships with others who may provide information or support resources | |
| **Consulting** Checking with others before making plans or decisions that affect them | |
| **Team-Building** Encouraging positive identification with the organization unit, cooperation, and constructive conflict resolution | |
| **Inspiring** Motivating others toward greater enthusiasm for, and commitment to, work objects by appealing to emotions, value, or personal example | |

Source: Women "Take Care," Men "Take Charge" ( 2005)

thus they have confidence in these thoughts and believe them to be true. It is this kind of perception that we must be mindful of and resist, as it can clearly interfere with our perceptions of ourselves and other women and reduce the opportunities for women to gain leadership positions.

## Impact on Family Life

Research on women in employment has highlighted work–family balance as a major concern [9, 9a]. Working mothers around the world are known to always be working a "second shift" after they finish a day at their hectic jobs [10]. Many countries across the world have conducted time-use surveys [11], and a common finding is that women in paid employment generally spend more hours per day on household duties than do their male counterparts [12]. In academia, public, and private industry both women and men identify family responsibilities as a possible barrier to advancement; however, women are affected differently than men by this "family penalty." [13] Although both women and men feel that having a family hinders their success at work, women are more likely than men to report foregoing marriage or children and delaying having children in the path to career advancement. As tradition would dictate, the study showed among women and men with families that women are more likely to report they are the primary caregivers as well as having a greater likelihood of having a partner that also works full time. As a result of this situation women can find themselves overwhelmed by career and family issues, thereby increasing the likelihood of leaving the STEM career and reducing the likelihood of pursuing leadership opportunities.

In their article "Women at the Top" researchers Cheung and Halpern [14] offer a cross-cultural model for women in leadership that is applicable to the current culture of gender with promise for creating environments where women can simultaneously thrive in career and family life. This model includes: (a) relationship-oriented leadership traits for women, (b) the importance of teamwork and consensus building at home and work, and (c) an effective work–family interface that women with "family care" responsibilities can create and use to break through the glass ceiling.

The support and cooperation of the immediate family members often determine the level of success a woman achieves as a leader. Will your family be neglected when you embark on your journey? Depending on what your definition of "neglect" is, they may be neglected or suffer less than "optimal" outcomes in some areas. You may not be able to go on class field trips, lead the Parent Teacher Association (PTA), or be home every evening for a sit-down dinner. However, with a supportive network, communication, and planning (short term and long term), it is possible to have a successful family life and career. Figure 3.2 provides an overview of this model that is proposed by Cheung and Halpern [14].

As you consider the impact of family on your career ambitions, this overview can be a useful resource to establish your plan – the essence here is to "plan." While we're usually equally happy to have a bundle of joy the moment it arrives, whether it's planned or not, a thoughtful, well-planned strategy goes a long way in reducing long-term family and work stress. Family planning is an intensely personal, value-based activity and there is no one way to do it. Obviously, it can work out well under a variety of circumstances. The objective in planning should be to fulfill the personal vision that you have for your life while sustaining the career vision. This strategy should take into consideration objective factors such as your biological clock, finances, resources and family support. Additionally, factors such as phase of your career, availability for downtime, and organizational climate should be evaluated. Finally, don't neglect to take into consideration the time that you will need to do all activities and stay healthy. The time you will need as a parent and leader to recover, refresh, and re-engage throughout your career.

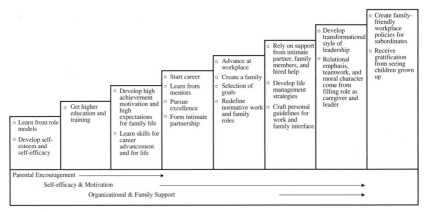

**FIGURE 3.2**    Step-by-Step model of leadership development incorporating work and family roles.
*Source: Cheung and Halpern (2010)*

As you plan your strategy for career success communicate with your family. Explain to your family what your aspirations are and why they are important to you. Share your short-term and long-term vision. Will they understand you and support you? The likely answer is yes (hopefully). Yes, they will understand and they will give you their support – maybe reluctantly in the beginning, but happily and full-heartedly later as the realization of your career vision benefits the entire family.

## Not Recognizing our Strengths

Be yourself. Your best abilities will shine through when you remain true to yourself and recognize how to utilize your strengths to attain your goals. The premise of the book *Now, Discover Your Strengths* [15] is that those achieving great results have learned to focus on and develop their strengths while not letting their weaknesses hold them back. The weaknesses can be mitigated through a number of strategies without impacting the focus on developing our strengths. Strategies for dealing with our weaknesses include seeking activities that will improve our abilities in this area, utilizing a support system, using one of our strengths to overwhelm a weakness, finding a complementary partner with the talent we're lacking, and simply giving up the activities that require this weakness. The most appropriate strategy will depend on the significance of the weakness, access to resources, and your personal desires. The point being made is that weaknesses must be addressed; however, we should not spend too much time focusing on them and trying to make them stronger, as this will detract from the recognition and development of our strengths and natural gifts. The manifestation of our strengths or the lack thereof, is seen in our daily decision making as we react instinctively to many situations throughout the day. We make small decisions very quickly as our brain is taking the most efficient paths, and these decisions aggregate to our performance for the day, week, month, and eventually over our career. Thus, knowing our strengths and seeking goals that are aligned with them will naturally lead to a higher level of performance.

So how do we "know" strengths? For a characteristic to be considered a "strength" it must be something that we can do consistently and predictably at optimal levels of performance. This strength is innate but also enhanced with effort as the authors describe it to be a function of talent, knowledge, and skills where each is described as follows: [16]

- Talent: naturally recurring patterns of thought, feeling or behavior that can be productively applied. Often talents will come so easily to us that we don't recognize them as talents and we believe everyone can do the same or similar things.
- Knowledge: facts and lessons learned from an information gathering and experiential perspective.
- Skills: the mechanics, structure, process, or steps to accomplish an activity.

The key to building strengths is to first identify your primary talents, then refine and enhance them with related knowledge and skill development activities. The question most of us ask is, "How do I know my strengths?" This book is a valuable resource in narrowing down your unique strengths as it is accompanied with a Strengths Finder Test. Using data collected over a 30-year period, the authors developed 34 "themes of human talent" (see Table 3.3). Take time to review this table and make note of attributes you believe to be your strengths.

### TABLE 3.3  Personal Themes for Strengths

| Attribute | Definition |
| --- | --- |
| Achiever | one with a constant drive for accomplishing tasks |
| Activator | one who acts to start things in motion |
| Adaptability | one who is especially adept at accommodating to changes in direction/plan |
| Analytical | one who requires data and/or proof to make sense of their circumstances |
| Arranger | one who enjoys orchestrating many tasks and variables to a successful outcome |
| Belief | one who strives to find some ultimate meaning behind everything they do |
| Command | one who steps up to positions of leadership without fear or confrontation |
| Communication | one who uses words to inspire action and education |
| Competition | one who thrives on comparison and competition to be successful |
| Connectedness | one who seeks to unite others through commonality |

*Continued*

**TABLE 3.3** Personal Themes for Strengths—*Cont'd*

| Attribute | Definition |
|---|---|
| **Consistency** | one who believes in treating everyone the same to avoid unfair advantage |
| **Context** | one who is able to use the past to make better decisions in the present |
| **Deliberative** | one who proceeds with caution, seeking to always have a plan and know all of the details |
| **Developer** | one who sees the untapped potential in others |
| **Discipline** | one who seeks to make sense of the world by imposition of order |
| **Empathy** | one who is especially in tune with the emotions of others |
| **Focus** | one who requires a clear sense of direction to be successful |
| **Futuristic** | one who has a keen sense of using an eye towards the future to drive today's success |
| **Harmony** | one who seeks to avoid conflict and achieve success through consensus |
| **Ideation** | one who is adept at seeing underlying concepts that unite disparate ideas |
| **Includer** | one who instinctively works to include everyone |
| **Individualization** | one who draws upon the uniqueness of individuals to create successful teams |
| **Input** | one who is constantly collecting information or objects for future use |
| **Intellection** | one who enjoys thinking and thought-provoking conversation often for its own sake, and also can data compress complex concepts into simplified models |
| **Learner** | one who must constantly be challenged and learning new things to feel successful |
| **Maximizer** | one who seeks to take people and projects from great to excellent |
| **Positivity** | one who has a knack for bringing the light-side to any situation |
| **Relator** | one who is most comfortable with fewer, deeper relationships |
| **Responsibility** | one who, inexplicably, must follow through on commitments |
| **Restorative** | one who thrives on solving difficult problems |
| **Self-Assurance** | one who stays true to their beliefs and judgments, and is confident of his/her ability |

**TABLE 3.3** Personal Themes for Strengths—*Cont'd*

| Attribute | Definition |
|---|---|
| **Significance** | one who seeks to be seen as significant by others |
| **Strategic** | one who is able to see a clear direction through the complexity of a situation |
| **Woo** | one who is able to easily persuade |

Source: Buckingham and Clifton (2001)

**TABLE 3.4** My Strength Identification Log

| | Spontaneous Thoughts | Yearning | Rapid Learning Experiences | Feeling of Satisfaction |
|---|---|---|---|---|
| Morning | | | | |
| Afternoon | | | | |
| Evening | | | | |

Source: Buckingham and Clifton (2001)

An empirical method to find your natural talents is to monitor your behavior and feelings over an extended period of time. To do this, create a Strengths Monitoring Notebook (on paper or using an electronic resource such as your smart phone or smart pad) and commit to seven to fourteen days to evaluate your responses to various situations. Take note and log the following throughout the day: [16]

1. Spontaneous thoughts: your instinctive thoughts, reactions, and perspectives to situations you encounter throughout the day
2. Yearnings: activities that you are drawn to naturally, even if you don't do these activities, as many times we're busy doing the "other things" that are expected and focused on "making income to live," not being able to pursue our yearnings
3. Rapid learning experiences: situations where you quickly acquire a skill or learn a new activity are an indication of natural talent
4. Feelings of satisfaction: when using our natural talent, it generates a positive feeling and a sense of satisfaction; this is also an indicator of natural talent

Using a table similar to the format shown in Table 3.4 [15], log your activities over the next week or two weeks.

After you have logged your behavior, thoughts, and emotions for at least a week, list the following based on the time, activities, and behaviors in your professional and personal environment:

1. My top three spontaneous thoughts for the week(s) occurred when and were about what topic?
2. My top three yearnings for the week(s) occurred when and were about what topics?
3. My top three rapid learning experiences happened when I was doing what?
4. My top three feelings of satisfaction took place when I was doing what activity?

Once you've answered these questions begin to assess how you can integrate more opportunities to experience these affirmative behaviors and feelings in your current task. Ask yourself what aspects of my job generate these positive feelings? More importantly, begin to assess how your next career move should be designed to integrate your strengths. It is important to also consider the personal environment because we may find our greatest strengths not being used in the work environment. In this case, we will need to evaluate how to identify tasks that we can engage in where our primary strengths can be utilized. Once you have identified your strengths, it is useful to create a plan to enhance these strengths and align your career goals with activities where your strengths add value. Know your strengths and build on them. We have spent enough time learning about our weaknesses and agonizing over how to change them. While we must address critical weaknesses that could be detrimental to us, we should spend much more time focusing on developing our natural abilities, as these represent our greatest areas of growth potential and career success.

## Perception of Limited Opportunity or Failure to Recognize Opportunities

Wherever there is a problem there is an opportunity. Gaining access to the problem and acquiring the permission to "lead" is the goal. Getting into a position to address the problem must be the top priority of every aspiring leader. Although the higher you climb the ladder, the fewer formal leadership opportunities, be comforted that an array of leadership opportunities exists throughout most organizations. In the book *Leaders*, the authors point out that "The truth is that leadership opportunities are plentiful and within reach of most people." [17] The key is to be able to recognize those opportunities. Simply put, wherever there is a challenge, problem, or pressing issue you can be sure there is an opportunity – an opportunity for a leader, an opportunity for leadership. Chanda Kochhar, ICICI Bank's joint managing director and chief financial officer, shared her ability to recognize how a challenge can become a leadership opportunity in her discussion with Wharton Professor Michael Useem at the World Economic Forum in Davos [18]. ICICI is India's largest privately owned bank with assets of nearly

$80 billion in 2007 and a growing global presence. Kochhar was running the corporate side of the bank and managing almost 50% of its business profits and assets when her CEO asked her to take over the consumer credit division. At that time the consumer credit division was less than 1% of the bank's business. She asked her CEO a very poignant question, "Why should I move from handling 50% of the bank to handling 1% of the bank?" His answer signaled an opportunity when he stated, "Because I want to make this business more than 50% of the bank." Kochhar recognized this opportunity and accepted it, ultimately achieving this extraordinary goal of making the consumer credit business more than 50% of the bank's business. What appeared to be a reduction in responsibilities was actually a challenge that produced a significant leadership opportunity. However, one key point here is that Kochhar asked the question and obtained clarity around the nature of the challenge. This allowed her to see that the offering of this opportunity was due to the recognition of her talents and was in fact a new opportunity for her to demonstrate her leadership capabilities.

In some cases, due to the shortages of female leaders in STEM fields, we may think, "They don't want a woman leader." Well, the truth is, maybe they don't. It is possible that they haven't had any women leaders as of yet and don't understand how much they would gain from a fresh perspective of a new leader, who just so happens to be a woman! Albeit, it is difficult to be the first woman to lead among men, but that doesn't mean that the opportunity does not exist or cannot be created. Stop thinking about what "they" want. It is what you want that is of sublime importance. Decide what you want and think positively – they may not want a woman leader – but they definitely want a leader. Take the steps to become that leader.

If you are thinking along the lines of "They've already got ONE woman leader," do we really want to be in the minority? A world equal in terms of gender representation is not one where there is at least one woman. It is one where there are women comparable in number to men. It is time we realize the potential within us and the opportunities that exist out there.

Create the opportunities for leadership for yourself and other women. Take up a cause or a challenge and become a leader. Perception of opportunity is embedded in Your mind and will ultimately become what is manifested in our world. Don't allow it to be influenced by that little negative voice inside your head. Remember, many of the obstacles you perceive are imaginary and the ones that are real can be overcome.

Defining the type of opportunity that you are looking for (i.e., the leadership position) will allow you to realize your leadership and innovation goals. Find someone who has done something similar and note the following about them:

- **How (H)** did they identify the opportunity? What resources did it require? How much time? Can I use technology to adapt my model of resources?
- **Where (W)** was the opportunity in relation to the person's professional position? Was it within or outside the company? In a professional organization? With a competitor? Within the company as a project?

- **What (W)** did they do to realize the opportunity? Did they go to their manager? Highlight their success on another project? What was it about the organization that supported the attainment of this goal?
- **When (W)** – at what point did they pursue the opportunity? When did they start to see it manifesting?

You can use this person or persons as a model for how to recognize, plan and ultimately pursue your desired opportunity. For your opportunity, identify your **H-W-W-W (HW³)** assessment approach.

## Lack of Role Models and Mentors

Research and practice have shown that mentoring can provide supporting and encouraging opportunities for retention and sustained advancement of women in STEM disciplines. Mentoring also combats the feelings of isolation, lack of insight, and feelings of belonging. A number of formal mentoring programs have been highlighted in STEM literature in the U.S. and can be used as models of successful mentoring strategies [19]. These programs include Mentor-Net, Mentoring in Medicine, the Executive Leadership in Academic Medicine (ELAM), Georgia Tech ADVANCE, the Building Interdisciplinary Research Center in Women's Health (BIRCWH) at the University of California-Davis, and Working on Women in Science (WOWS) at the University of North Carolina, to name a few. Isolation is a critical problem since it can be a major source of dissatisfaction among women and can influence their decision to leave an academic or industry position. Women report being excluded from informal social gatherings and more formal events, as well as from collaborating on research or teaching. Women are also less likely than their male colleagues to have role models or mentors and, therefore, get limited advice on navigating the workplace, professional and career development, and advancing in their careers [20, 20a].

The University of Michigan's Stephen M. Ross School of Business and the Center for Education of Women, and Catalyst, a research organization from New York, conducted a survey among 1,684 women students from the top 12 Business Schools in October 2005 [21]. They were trying to judge why the number of women joining a business school had not increased, compared to those in law or medical schools. Most of the women spoke about lack of role models, and 90% of them said that too few of the women business leaders were being showcased as mentors or as role models for the students. This scarcity of examples often inhibits us from taking that first stride forward.

This is not a new issue, however, and technology can help us mitigate it more quickly today. If you cannot relate to someone who you know personally, as a mentor, look around in your community or the global community via the Internet. You will be able to see many women and men who have been able to lead in ordinary as well as adverse circumstances. Look at the woman who stands out in a group;

watch how she behaves and how she deals with difficult situations. How does she handle a client? How does she react in a crisis situation? She could be your mentor or your role model, and you can strive to follow a similar path. She may not be famous or well known, but even in her limited field she is a first among equals.

Let me caution you here: although I am eager and glad to help other women, many women are not as available and willing to engage others. If you reach out to someone and she isn't receptive, do not take it personally. It may be any number of reasons including time, professional limitations, and personal preferences. In any event, do not make it about you, take it personally, or become discouraged if you don't get the response you desire.

Mentoring can be valuable to your career for many reasons, including increased confidence, an increased desire to pursue a career, feelings of support and understanding, and enhanced optimism about the choices you are making regarding your career. More specifically, you will receive guidance in decision making, minimize your mistakes, discover the path to success sooner, and find someone who believes in you – all of which will lead to fewer sleepless nights! And you're going to need your sleep as a future leader. Mentoring can also have direct benefits from a career standpoint, as a mentor can help guide your career, create opportunity, and allow you to benefit from their experiences. Make the decision to identify role models and/or mentors today. It will truly make a difference in your career.

## Mentoring Up Close and Personal

Most of us have known a few women or had mothers who were leaders in the professional and personal settings. These were often our first examples of female leadership whether they had the accompanying titles or not – they lead. This may have meant corralling a family, soccer team, or after-school crew for studying. In some cases, we watched our mothers succeed as exceptional working women who then came home and managed this second environment with enviable levels of ease that included cooking dinner, encouraging children, preparing for the next day, and creating an environment of comfort for everyone in the home.

It is also important to note that fathers have set leadership examples and mentored many young women. Although we may not have directly associated a father's success with our ability to be successful as women, their encouragement often provides the impetus for us to pursue and succeed in nontraditional careers. My father is certainly an example of this – requiring me to take countless math classes from the 7th grade through my high school graduation to make sure I maintained certain career options. Additionally, he set a wonderful example for me, with a powerful work ethic, integrity, and constant discussion about the importance of education. In fact, without his guidance I would never have considered a career in engineering as I would not have had the math background that gave me the confidence to even consider this career. He and my mother, though neither was college educated, made it clear to my siblings and me that we could accomplish anything we set our minds to achieve. However, it was still very different for me as a woman and a mother to figure out how to become a leader in my field and balance what I considered to be my duties at home. Additionally, as an undergraduate attending community college I had never met a female engineering professor. So although I was an "engineering major" I had a difficult time "seeing" myself as an engineer. To add more complexity (and uncertainty) to my equation, I was also a young single mother and had never met a successful single mom who was an engineer.

However, when I entered the University of Oklahoma this changed and so did my perception of what I could become. This happened as a result of good role models, confronting my perceptions about my abilities, and professional counseling. My confidence in what I could become became even more solid when I met African-American female engineers. While this experience allowed me to meet these individuals to be inspired, the state of technology today permits us to be exposed to role models thousands of miles away. Thus, there is no need for anyone that needs to be encouraged to be without the knowledge of a person who has succeeded in a similar endeavor.

Even today, it is rare to see a "group" of powerful woman in a corporate setting. It is often an isolated event, consisting of one lone woman who has somehow set herself apart from the rest. This is not how things should be! A memory that has stuck with me over the years occurred at a time when I was working on a project in a mixed group of men and women, and someone joked that the women were "taking over." There were only about five females among twenty or so faculty, but because in the engineering faculty environment having 25% female is unusual, (and we did have powerful personalities), we were perceived as taking over.

Each of us has leadership skills in some area. If you have a goal and the passion to achieve it, rest assured, you have the potential to become a leader and see this vision realized.

I have been fortunate enough to have many mentors from undergraduate and graduate school and as a professional. One of my earliest mentors, Dr Howard Adams, is a nationally recognized STEM mentor, and has spent years of his life mentoring STEM professionals. Without his inspiration, faith in me, and constant mentoring, I would never have received a single degree in engineering. I met Dr Howard Adams when he arrived at the University of Oklahoma to give a speech geared at encouraging minority students to consider graduate degrees in engineering. At the time, Dr Adams was Director of the GEM Foundation, and he was the most inspirational and impressive person I had ever heard speak. Moreover, he was telling me I could get a graduate degree in engineering – me, a young African-American woman who was also a single mother. I was convinced I was the most unlikely candidate for success in the entire room – that is, until I heard him speak. Immediately after his speech I went up and introduced myself. I explained my situation to him and asked if his comments *still* applied to me given my lack-luster academic performance, financial challenges, and the fact that I was a single mother. With complete confidence he totally assured me that I could in fact accomplish a goal of a graduate degree – and even a PhD in engineering. He also gave me his business card and made me promise him that I would stay in touch and share my plans of graduate school. Although Dr. Adams lived more than 1,000 miles from my university, his willingness to encourage me was the exact mentoring role model that I needed. That very moment he became one of the most influential people in my life and totally changed the course of my future [22].

I've had other priceless mentors including Dr Adedeji Badiru (graduate school), Dr Debra Reinhart (faculty career mentor), Ms Beverly Seay (business career mentor), and Ms Gail Evans (writing). Some of these mentors spent countless hours with me while others I spoke with intermittently over a period of years. Despite this, the impact they have had has been immeasurable. These relationships made such a difference in my life that they've encouraged me to be a mentor. Mentoring has become one of the most rewarding aspects of my career.

Many people have not had the benefit of a formal or informal mentor in the professional environment. Do you NEED a mentor? The answer to this question is overwhelmingly, yes. Many have succeeded without them, but in today's innovation culture an advisor, mentor, or coach is an indispensable resource. To begin the process of understanding your mentoring needs, make a list of the mentors that you could benefit from in your life: from a personal and professional perspective. Also, don't limit yourself to those in your city, region, or even country. For professional, include both internal members of your organization as well as external. Your regional list can include local, national, and international mentors. Again, start by creating a Personal Mentor List and Professional Mentor List. List the areas of guidance that you're seeking support in (i.e., career advancement, education, writing, etc.) Put at least three names on the page for each category. Plan to send an introductory note to the individual and, based on their level of accessibility, request a conversation or meeting to discuss their willingness to mentor you. Table 3.5 is an excellent resource for further understanding mentoring.

Professional and personal development through mentoring is an ongoing process, thus this table should be an evolving document and updated at least annually. The mentors that you need in year 3 of your career may not be the same mentors you need in year 10. It is important to recognize what our career

---

**TABLE 3.5  Mentoring Focus Areas**

|  | External / Internal | Primary Growth Needs | Priority | Deadline |
|---|---|---|---|---|
| Technical skills |  |  |  |  |
| Communication skills |  |  |  |  |
| Understanding organizational culture |  |  |  |  |

development needs are and to purposefully pursue the areas of support that we need at the appropriate times.

Now that you've clarified your mentoring needs, the resources to meet these needs should be identified (Table 3.6).

So suppose there are no candidates near you to provide mentoring. Don't despair – you can still achieve your goals through a concept known as Biblio-therapy. Biblio-therapy is the use of self-help and personal development materials for personal and professional growth. Even if you've been fortunate enough to have role models and mentors, it can be helpful to develop what I call a "Biblio-MEntor-Collage." This BMEC is comprised of three to five key books or resources (biblio) that you utilize to provide advice and guidance (mentor) in a particular area, and you combine these sources into one common resource (collage) for convenient use (Table 3.7).

**TABLE 3.6** Mentoring Resources

|  | Mentoring Resources Description (examples) |
| --- | --- |
| Personal contacts | Former boss, family friend, president of the local IIE chapter |
| Employer Program or Resources | Formal Mentor Development Programs |
| Community-based Programs | Local Chamber of Commerce<br>Community Leadership Development Programs |
| Professional Organizations | Society of Women Engineers (SWE)<br>IEEE Local Chapter<br>Women in Technology International (WITI) |
| Electronic Mentoring | Mentornet |

**TABLE 3.7** Biblio-MEntor-Collage (BMEC) Overview

| Area of Growth | Resource |
| --- | --- |
| Communication, public speaking | Books:<br>Websites/Blogs/E-Groups:<br>Other: |
| Better career planning | Books:<br>Websites/Blogs/E-Groups:<br>Other: |
| Managing Career and Family | Books:<br>Websites/Blogs/E-Groups:<br>Other: |

### Biblio-ME Summary Worksheet

**AREA** of focus for personal or career development:


**WHY** do I need to develop in this area?


**RESOURCE** (Book, Blog, Organization):


**HOW** does author of this resource suggest addressing this issue or developmental activity?


**WHEN** will I initiate this activity?


**SUMMARY** of actions to take to address this area:

**FIGURE 3.3**   Biblio-ME collage (BMEC) summary worksheet


Your BMEC should be developed by first identifying the top three areas where you can use guidance. After identifying the three areas, search for resources/books that provide self-help, professional development, or case studies in success for this area. The BMEC Summary Worksheet can be useful at helping you document the additional details you need to support your growth in each area (Figure 3.3).

## Networking

One of the most valuable tools used in modern day business is networking. All of us network among our college colleagues, with other people working in similar jobs, among managers of other companies, among our friends, and with family members. As social as we are, studies have shown that we do not use networking to the degree that we can in our careers. Women do not make optimum use of this tool. This does not need to remain the case nor does it have to impede your professional development because we can definitely learn to network. As relationship-oriented as studies have shown women to be, we should be able to master the art of networking.

As important as working hard at your profession is, hard work alone will not lead to success as a leader. According to psychologist Lois Frankel [23], if you're not spending 5% of your day building relationships, you're doing something wrong. This relationship development should be with your colleagues, superiors, and subordinates. The objective of this relationship development is two-fold: one is to share who you are and allow people to get to know your character, strengths, and value. The second objective is for you to learn about others and demonstrate your concern and value for them as a team member. This is vitally important because in healthy work environments people are not promoted simply because they work hard, but because the decision makers know the person's character and have a confidence in his/her ability do the job and promote collegial working relationships.

Electronic networking through social networking, blogs, and other community interaction sites has given a new level of possibility to networking. The activities available online to promote networking and professional development include being part of an online community, continuing your education or obtaining a certification, attending a conference remotely, taking part in a tutorial, starting a blog, and countless other opportunities.

One of the most powerful networking experiences I've ever had was when I attended the Women's International Research in Engineering Summit (WIRES), a National Science Foundation funded international workshop in Barcelona, Spain, in 2009. WIRES is the bi-annual, international summit for women who are interested in pursuing international collaborative researching opportunities. The main objective of this summit is to enable meaningful and sustainable research exchanges between female engineers from around the world while identifying issues faced by females pursuing careers in engineering that could benefit from a global strategy. My participation in this meeting was very focused as I had the specific goal of establishing international collaborations. Prior to going to the meeting I did my homework on the participants and was very clear about the type of strategic partners I would be seeking. Immediately upon arriving at this well-planned and efficiently organized event, I went to work on my plan to establish the needed research collaborations. As a result of the four days spent at this meeting I established two research collaborations that resulted in substantive outcomes including appointment to an international research committee, a funded National Science Foundation grant, a Guest Editor invitation for an international journal, and, within a period of four years, acceptance as a Fulbright Specialist/Scholar. The relationships I established at this meeting are still active and continue to add value to my research career.

Although you may not have access to an event such as WIRES, you do have an option to develop your own networking resources, skills, and relationships to support your leadership and career ambitions. Many of us shy away from networking because we feel that it is wrong or dishonest to get to know people so that the relationship can be used later. Nothing could be farther from the truth. Networking is not about using people. It is about creating a chain of people who can help each other in achieving common goals that benefit us all.

## Taking Things Personally

Leaders are "vision" focused on the associated mission and individual goals. Although leaders must be passionate about the vision, it is necessary for them to separate the vision from themselves. This is valuable in communicating objectively about the vision. In my experience I have identified two powerful tools that minimize the urge to take negative responses or situations personally. For this to be effective it requires me to focus on the "mission" or objective of my leadership activities rather than me personally. The two points that have guided me are as follows:

1. "It's not about me – it's the mission"
   Explanation: What I'm leading is for a cause that is bigger than me and is about the mission. People's acceptance, support, and engagement directly benefit the mission, and conversely their failure to support it negatively impacts the mission.
2. "Don't own other people's issues"
   Explanation: People's responses to me do not necessarily reflect on me, my vision, purpose, or relationship with them. Their responses are often a manifestation of their experiences, perceptions, and state in life. Determine whether I've effectively communicated and interacted regarding the issue, and, if not, make an effort to engage them again. Make sure to ask them to stay focused on the "issue" in their response and to clearly articulate all responses relevant to the issue. No matter how they respond, don't own or make it about you.

Along these same lines of personal issues we have to be very careful about bringing up the gender issue as a primary reason for pointing out bias in our organization. While our intent is not to let others forget that we are women, at the same time, we cannot focus on this as a major aspect of leadership. Remember, you are not a woman fighting for a cause; you are a leader who happens to be a woman.

Former head of the US Environmental Protection Agency in the Clinton Administration, Governor Christine Todd Whitman, provides a stellar example to illustrate this point. In 1990, when Governor Whitman was running for office against former basketball star Bill Bradley, she frequently tried to get him to engage in a formal debate with her. His office would ignore her calls, and after many attempts she decided to use the "gender card" very effectively. She went to the media and played up the fact Bill Bradley would not return the calls from her office regarding a request for a debate and she believed that he did not want to debate her because she was a woman. This brought an immediate response from him and he agreed to face the debate. The reason why he was not responding earlier may not have been the same as the one she propagated, but when she played this card his response was prompt. This is an example where the gender card was used appropriately and strategically, and it provided the desired results.

## CONCLUSION

There are many things we can say to summarize this chapter; the essence of this chapter is to recognize your talents, utilize your resources, and capitalize on the power you have to see your goals realized. As female leaders of the 21ˢᵗ century we have tremendous opportunities before us and a global society yearning to benefit from our leadership and creativity. In the process, however, we may deal with many challenges, but it is the management of these challenges that can bring rewards and a very satisfying career. If you are willing to deal with all of these things, then you are capable of being a leader. I have always agreed with this inspirational quote from Marianne Williamson's *A Return to Love*:

*We ask ourselves, who am I to be brilliant, gorgeous, talented, and fabulous? Actually, who are you not to be? You are a child of God. Your playing small does not serve the world. When we let our own light shine, we unconsciously give other people permission to do the same. [24]*

Although this quote flies in the face of everything I was taught over the course of my "good Baptist" upbringing, I say this with all due respect: the former attitude that was encouraged in me does not serve me or the world. There is no need to play it small in painting your goals and visions. Your dreams can impact the future and the lives of so many. It is time for us to accept the greatness within us and move forward into the exciting and challenging careers that we are so very capable of having today. You are a leader. You are an innovator. Let us go forth and conquer; go forth and prosper as the leaders and innovators we are destined to become in our personal and professional lives.

## ACTIONS FOR THE READER

1. Assess my current or future organization for the level of community to leadership development and innovation.
2. Take a cultural and personal inventory of my perspectives and perceptions of myself as a leader and innovator.
3. Take a cultural and personal inventory of my perspectives and perceptions of women as leaders and innovators.
4. Determine a list of my mentor needs and commit to identifying at least one mentor or mentoring resource in the next 30 days.
5. Create a Biblio-MEntor Collage (BMEC).
6. Identify three networking-related actions to implement in the next 90 days.

## CHAPTER RESOURCES

1. Recognizing when you're being stereotyped
2. Factors to guide in the assessment of your organization
3. Mentor Development Resource
4. Biblio-MEntor-Collage (BMEC)
5. Cross Cultural Model for Family and Career Leadership Success

# REFERENCES

[1] Catalyst. The Double-Blind Dilemma for Women in Leadership: Damned if You Do, Doomed if You Don't. Research Report. New York, NY: Catalyst; 2007.

[2] Bureau of Labor Statistics, Current Population Survey, "Employed and Experienced Unemployed Person by Detailed Occupation, Sex, Race and Hispanic or Latino Ethnicity, Annual Average 2005."

[3] Catalyst. Women "Take Care, " Men "Take Charge:" Stereotyping of U.S. Business Leaders Exposed. Research Report. New York, NY: Catalyst; 2005.

[4] Catalyst. Different Cultures, Similar Perceptions: Stereotyping of Western European Business Leaders. Research Report. New York, NY: Catalyst; 2006.

[5] Van Velsor E, McCauley CD, Ruderman MN. The Center for Creative Leadership Handbook of Leadership Development. 3rd ed. Hoboken, NJ: Jossey-Bass; 2010.

[6] Catalyst is a leading research and advisory organization working with business and the professions to build inclusive environments and expand opportunities for women at work. As an independent, nonprofit membership organization, Catalyst conducts research on all aspects of women's career advancement and provides strategic and web-based consulting services globally. From The Double-Bind Dilemma for Women in Leadership: Damned if You Do, Doomed if You Don't Research Report 2007; Catalyst.

[7] National Science Foundation, ADVANCE Program Brochure, www.nsf.gov (accessed May 24, 2012).

[8] Schaef AW. Women's Reality. In: Weaver VJ, Hill JC, editors. Smart Women, Smart Moves. New York, NY: AMACOM, A Division of American Management Association; 1994.

[9] Allen TD, Herst D, Bruck C, Sutton M. Consequences associated with work to family conflict: A review and agenda for future research. Journal of Occupational Health Psychology 2000;5: 278–308.

[9a] Byron K. A meta-analytic review of work–family conflict and its antecedents. Journal of Vocational Behavior 2000;67(2):169–98.

[10] Hochschild A. The Second Shift: Working Parents and the Revolution at Home. London: Piatkus Ltd; 1989.

[11] A Guide to Producing Statistics on Time Use: Measuring Paid and Unpaid Work. Department of Economic and Social Affairs, Statistics Division. United Nations; 2004, ST/ESA/STAT/SER.F/93.

[12] Galinsky E et al. Overwork in America: When the Way We Work Becomes Too Much. New York, NY: Families and Work Institute; 2005.

[13] Simard C, Henderson AD, Gilmartin S, Shiebinger L, Whitney T. Climbing the Technical Ladder: Obstacles and Solutions for Mid-level Women in Technology. Palo Alto, CA: Anita Borg Institute and Clayman Institute for Gender Research; 2008, p. 5.

[14] Cheung FM, Halpern DF. Women at the top: Powerful leaders define success as work + family in a culture of gender. American Psychologist; April 2010;65(3):182–93.

[15] Buckingham M, Clifton DO. Now, Discover Your Strengths. New York, NY: Simon & Schuster; 2001.

[16] Andros B. Book Summary of *Now, Discover your Strengths* (Buckingham and Clifton, 2001, Simon & Schuster, New York) and *Strengths Finder 2.0* (Rath, 2007, Gallup Press, New York). http://paulsmith.s5.com/ASTD-Feb2011/StrengthsFinder.pdf (accessed July 6, 2012).

[17] Bennis W, Nanus B. Leaders: The Strategies for Taking Charge. New York, NY: Harper and Row, Publishers; 2003.

[18] Wharton Executive Education, Knowledge@Wharton, http://knowledge.wharton.upenn.edu

[19] National Leadership Workshop on Mentoring Women in Biomedical Careers, Meeting Proceedings, Office of Research on Women's Health. National Institute of Health. Bethesda, MD; 2007.

[20] Macfarlane A, Luzzadder-Beach S. Achieving equity between women and men in the geosciences. Geological Society of America Bulletin, 1998;110:1590–1614.

[20a] Rosser SV. Using POWRE to ADVANCE: Institutional barriers identified by women scientists and engineers [Electronic version], 2004.

[21] Di Meglio F. What Women MBAs Want: Role Models. Bloomberg Business Week 2005 www.businessweek.com/bschools/content/oct2005/bs20051030_2564.htm (accessed March 30, 2012).

[22] Bush PM. Winners Don't Quit: Today They Call Me Doctor. Orlando, FL: IP Publishing; 2003.

[23] Frankel LP. Nice Girls Don't Get the Corner Office: 101 Unconscious Mistakes Women Make That Sabotage Their Careers. New York, NY: Time Warner Book Group; 2004.

[24] Williamson M. A Return to Love: Reflections on the Principles of 'A Course in Miracles.' New York, NY: Harper Collins; 1996.

## Chapter 4

# Leadership and Innovation Characteristics

*Career Innovation*

*Creating a customer oriented, career focus area that capitalizes on one's capabilities, interests, resources, and knowledge to meet current or emerging needs in a given area of* ***opportunity***.

As I was watching a recent commercial from a major oil and gas industry company, I recognized how artfully the marketing effort captured the concept of innovation. In this commercial a woman is driving down the street and observes a group of children playing on a hot summer day. The children are filling a balloon with water while playing. She observes and "associates" this seemingly unrelated experience to her technical need – initiating the possible innovative application. The scenes artfully move through the development steps to the

Transforming your STEM Career through Leadership and Innovation.
http://dx.doi.org/10.1016/B978-0-12-396993-4.00004-7

**63**

conception and development of a product. Most importantly the commercial demonstrated how the product adds value and has an impact in another country thousands of miles away. This is a great example of the culmination of various innovation activities to produce an innovation. The characteristics of leaders and innovators overlap in many respects as innovators can be described as "idea or thought leaders." To take a leadership role in moving an idea from conception to product is clearly a leadership activity. The discussion of characteristics for leaders and innovators should be considered as relevant to the development as an individual leader and the development of ideas that contribute to innovation.

## CHARACTERISTICS OF INNOVATORS

*Innovators' Core Skills*

- *Associating*
- *Questioning*
- *Observing*
- *Experimenting*
- *Networking*

**Source: Dyer, Gregersen, and Christensen (2011)**

The "Nature vs Nurture" argument can be invoked as we seek to understand the essence of innovation and what it takes to become an innovator. An understanding of the basis of innovation is also important as we desire to inspire the characteristics that lead to innovative behavior in individuals, the workforce, and organizations. When considering what the individual innovator looks like and what the innate characteristics that produce a mind that engages in innovation are, a number of common characteristics surface. According to research conducted by Jeffrey Dyer, Hal Gregersen and C. Christensen [1] which included a six-year study surveying 3,000 creative executives and conducting an additional 500 individual interviews, they found five "discovery skills" that distinguish these individuals as successful innovators. These "discovery skills" of innovators are outlined in their book, *The Innovator's DNA* [1], and all innovators evaluated possess these skills. Only one skill, associating, which is the making of connections across seemingly unrelated fields, problems, or ideas – is a cognitive skill. The other four – questioning, observing, networking, and experimenting – are behavioral skills. Thus, with a basic level of cognitive functioning and effort, essentially anyone can become an innovator.

**Associating** Most successful innovators tend to be very good at seeing connections between seemingly disparate ideas. For example, you might be at a soccer game and notice that one of the moms has come up with a way to make sure her kids have cold water – some kind of chiller. To take that idea and apply it in another environment – perhaps soldiers serving in hot climates like Afghanistan – is an association technique.

**Questioning** The ability to ask "what if," "why," and "why not" questions that challenge the status quo, see the bigger picture, and discover available resources. Asking how things are and how they might be changed.

**Observation** Carefully observing and watching the world around you to gain insights and ideas about emerging and current needs and different or new ways to meet these needs. Attention to details, most notably in other people's behavior. The success of a product is impacted by consumers' responses to it. Take notice!

**Experiment** Exploring by doing! Evaluating a concept, idea, or theory experientially by trying something new, taking things apart, building computer or physical simulations or prototypes. Experimenting can be seen in the consistent exploration of new worlds. While many of us are most comfortable in our own environment (we eat at the same restaurants, even order the same meals!), being able to experiment helps us develop the new and the different perspectives or ideas.

**Networking** Actively engaging in conversations and searching for new ideas by talking to people who offer diverse perspectives and viewpoints. The ability to talk and learn from people that you have nothing in common with is a valuable ability as an innovator. Having a certain comfort level talking to and learning from people that are very different from us is becoming more and more important for professionals in every walk of life. Networking is the foundation on which a lot of this is built.

So why do some people question, observe, network, and experiment more frequently than others? The authors say it has to do with courage. The more people practice these skills, the more confident they become. So a healthy combination of courage, confidence, and a willingness to do what hasn't been done is essential in stepping up your innovation potential.

As we look ahead to the next generation, it's important to understand how to encourage more innovation in our young people. Professor Tony Wagner, a member of Harvard's Technology Entrepreneurship Center, explores the characteristics and qualities that should be developed in young people to make them future innovators. In the book *Creating Innovators: The Making of Young People Who Will Change the World* [2], the author proposes four main qualities, similar to those previously discussed, as key characteristics of innovators. These qualities include:

- Curiosity: Consistently asking good questions and a desire to understand concepts or ideas at a deeper level
- Collaboration: An eagerness to listen to and learn from others who have distinct perspectives and expertise
- Associative or integrative thinking: The ability to relate ideas to different and diverse environments and bring together multiple perspectives about an idea
- A bias toward action and experimentation: Regularly conducting experiments, study, or some form of action to evaluate an idea

Again, these characteristics involve cognitive abilities but are more often a function of behavioral tendencies. Thus, with recognition of the cognitive and behavioral nature of innovators, we can all become innovators and develop considerably more innovators in the future.

Where are you today in terms of your level of innovativeness? You may be well on your way to being an innovator or not at all consider yourself a creative or innovative person. Take the Innovation Test in Table 4.1, adapted from the article "How to Tell If You Are an Innovator" [3].

This test may not be a scientifically validated approach to assess innovation, and, no matter the outcome of this test, as previously stated the premise of this book is that we can all be innovators. The approach outlined above is a thought-provoking tool to be used as a resource to gauge, initiate, and enhance your level of innovation. The objective of the outcome is to help you understand your thought process relative to innovation and offer guidance on areas where you can grow your innovation nature. In other words, we need to regularly score in the frequently high rating of each innovation skill to be consistent innovators. If we find that we are not frequently demonstrating these qualities there is an opportunity for us to grow in this area as an innovator. This is an iterative process and the more we innovate, the more confident we become and the better we become at it – let the process for bringing out the innovator in you move forward today!

Roles on the "Innovation Team" vary widely and there is a need for a variety of skill sets. Additionally, there are various roles that an individual can play in the innovation process (Figure 4.1) [4].

The opportunity to participate in the innovation process is broad with required input from a variety of technical experts, researchers, managers, and marketers. The leader of this team is tasked with ensuring continual interaction between the team to move the goal of innovating forward as efficiently as possible and with consideration for all relevant issues. In addition to the leader, the Capability Maturity Model Integration (CMMI) approach to innovation defines the following roles:

- Networker: Responsible for creating and maintaining relationships between relevant internal and external individuals or organizations
- Coordinator: May serve as the project manager and integrates all activities into a plan, schedule, and milestones to reach the desired outcome
- Builder: This individual(s) will likely have an in-depth understanding of the innovation technical area and is tasked with taking the concept into an initial design, production plan, and strategy for delivery
- Anthropologist: Provides the understanding to the team of how people are likely to interact with the project or service; may work closely with a marketing team member to understand and identify ways to make the product more targeted at meeting the end user needs

These roles may be held by one or more individuals and in some organizations a single person will hold multiple roles. After evaluating your innovation skills, this may assist you in determining the role that you are most apt to excel

**TABLE 4.1  Personal Innovation Test**

| Question | Description | Score<br>1 2 3<br>Not at all<br>Sometimes<br>Frequently |
|---|---|---|
| Do you think a lot about the future and the potential or possibility for new ideas? | Are you wondering not about the next calamity, but what the future will be like and how you can impact it?<br>Do you find yourself trying to understand what the emerging trends will be in an area?<br>Are you wondering what consumers will want next year, next decade and beyond? | |
| Do you find yourself questioning things as they are and are you not satisfied with the status quo? | Are you constantly trying to improve things – even things that don't seem to be broken?<br>Do you want to know how to improve things, eliminate obstacles, and offer new conveniences? | |
| Are you aware of the needs of others and are interested in identifying ways to meet these needs? | Do you think about the needs of others and how ideas, products, or innovations could change/improve their situations? | |
| Do you have a sense of openness to new ideas, willing to try new things (in a healthy sense)? | Are you open to new experiences and willing to "take action" in the evaluation or consideration of an idea?<br>Are you willing to test and prototype, and open to discovery? | |
| Are you stubborn and driven when you believe in something? | Are you determined and driven, even in the face of doubt and failure?<br>Are you committed to your ideas?<br>Are you committed enough to convince others of the value of your idea? | |
| Are you open to the exchange of insights and ideas? Do you value the expertise of others? | Do you understand that the best ideas are emergent and based on the insights and ideas from a broad range of settings?<br>Are you willing to listen, to absorb, and to incorporate inputs from a wide variety of sources? | |
| Do you want to solve real problems? | Are you interested in doing more than "talking" about ideas?<br>Do you regularly think of how to solve existing and emerging problems? | |

Source: Adapted from Phillips, How To Tell If You Are An Innovator.

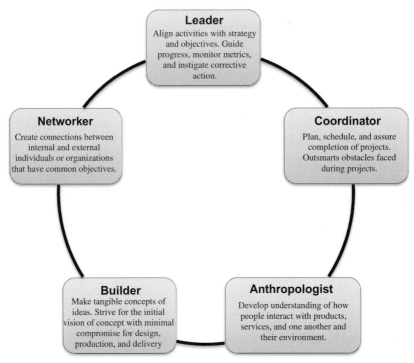

**FIGURE 4.1** Innovation roles. *Source: Essmann and Du Preez (2009).*

in during the innovation process. The objective is to make sure that all functions are covered to holistically address the innovation needs to take an idea from concept to a value-added product in the hands of a customer.

## *MYTHBUSTERS*® ON LEADERSHIP [5,6]

I love the show on the Discovery Channel known as *MythBusters*®. This award-winning show is intended to reveal the truth behind popular myths and legends by combining scientific methods with curiosity, ingenuity, and entertainment to create a television quality style of experimentation and explanation. Is it possible to beat a lie detector test, can plugging your finger into a gun barrel cause it to backfire (don't try this at home), and whether or not a dirty car is more fuel efficient than a clean car are but a few of the myths of focus. A scientific analysis is applied to the myth and a conclusion is reached, so by the end of the show the viewer is forced to confront what they may have believed to be true for a lifetime as a myth: simply put, the myths may be just that – myths that are far from truth.

The same perspectives confronted in *MythBusters*® can be present in our assessment of what it means to be a leader. In previous chapters we addressed

MythBusters® is a registered trademark owned by Discovery Communications, LLC, 2012.

stereotypes and cultural and corporate bias. The confronting of our perspectives on what leadership means requires us to take the same approach and seek the truth, based on research, experiential knowledge, and history. Consider the following "myths" of leadership.

1. Myth #1: Leadership is a rare skill

   Nothing can be further from the truth as this skill is present and demonstrated in almost everyone in one environment or another. While great leaders and recognition of tremendous leadership feats may be rare, everyone has leadership potential. More importantly, people may be leaders in one organization (i.e., professional societies, social organizations) and have quite ordinary roles in another (i.e., within one's work environment). The truth is that leadership skills are present at varying degrees in almost everyone. The degrees to which we develop those skills and apply them to the environments that matter to us determine the degree of leadership that will be realized.

2. Myth #2: Leaders are born, not made

   Don't believe this for a minute. The truth is that major capacities and competencies of leadership can be learned. We all have the capacity to learn, grow, and improve if the basic desire to develop is present.

3. Myth #3: Leaders are charismatic

   Some are, most aren't. Charisma is a useful tool but, in some cases, it is the result of effective leadership, not the other way around. When charisma is coupled with character, those who have it are granted a certain amount of respect and even awe by their followers, which increases the bond of attraction between them.

4. Myth #4: Leadership exists only at the top of the organization

   Leadership, leaders, and leadership opportunities, both formal and informal, exist at every level of the organization. The larger the organization, the more formal leadership roles it is likely to have in order to address the needs at varying levels and functions of the organization; however, in smaller organizations there may actually be more opportunity to experience various types of leadership requirements.

5. Myth #5: The leader controls, directs, prods, and manipulates

   This is perhaps the most damaging myth of all. Leadership is not about the exercise of power itself or a demonstration of individual power, rather it is the empowerment of others. Leaders are able to translate intentions and visions into reality by aligning the energies in the organization behind an attractive goal. Leaders lead by inspiring rather than insisting, and by encouraging the team to use their own initiative and experiences toward the mission.

6. Myth #6: How you behave outside of work and online does not affect your ability to lead

   Character is not circumstantial and integrity is not issue based. Whoever you are as a person will be reflected in your professional and personal life, thus your behavior outside of work absolutely affects your success as a leader.

7. **Myth #7: Leaders have all the answers**
   The best leaders I know surround themselves with bright people and seek input in areas where they need expertise, fully recognizing there are limits. Great leaders are eager to gain input and are not afraid to admit when they do not know something.

8. **Myth #8: Your team is there to serve you**
   As a leader, you and the team are to serve the "vision" as it relates to the good of the organization, constituents, shareholders, and all stakeholders. The best leaders set the example with selfless leadership demonstrated though a servant attitude, thinking about the vision first, the team second, stakeholders third, and finally themselves. This is servant leadership.

## CHARACTERISTICS OF LEADERSHIP

Now that we've addressed the myths associated with leadership it is important to get a clear understanding of what it means to be a leader and what leadership entails. Leadership is an activity that should take place throughout your career, whether you're leading yourself in a project, a small team, or an entire organization. The level of the position, however, is not the only indicator of the level of leadership. As organizations move toward an increased recognition of the value associated with human potential, many are seeking ways to further inspire employees through enlightened leadership.

The academic literature and self-help resources are replete with definitions of leadership and characteristics that leaders should possess. There is a good bit of consistency and Table 4.2 [7] provides a summary of some of these leadership behaviors from the literature.

Many of these characteristics will look familiar, as the lines between leading and innovating blend on multiple levels; recall – innovators are often considered "thought leaders." Clearly, leading an organization or initiating the development of a concept to a product both require an individual that is willing to stand out and demonstrate additional effort: in other words, this requires leadership. The difference is that the "Innovation Leader" focuses these characteristics on moving an idea or product forward whereas an "Organizational Leader" focuses on moving an organization or group of people forward. A more in-depth discussion is provided of select characteristics in the following section.

## VISION

"Where there is no vision, the people perish"; [8] this ancient wisdom has stood the test of time and is evident in business, education, and the community. While a vision may at some point have had its genesis in a dream, a vision is not a dream; it is an attainable reality that has yet to come into existence. Vision is palpable to leaders; their confidence in it and dedication to seeing it realized

**TABLE 4.2** Leadership Behaviors

| | |
|---|---|
| **Consulting** Checking with others before making plans or decisions that affect them | **Networking** Developing and maintaining relationships with others who may provide information or support resources |
| **Delegating** Authorizing others to have substantial responsibility and discretion | **Planning** Designing objectives, strategies, and procedures for accomplishing goals and coordinating with other parts of the organization in the most efficient manner |
| **Influencing Upward** Affecting others in positions of higher rank | **Problem-Solving** Identifying, analyzing, and acting decisively to remove impediments to work performance |
| **Inspiring Others** Motivating others towards greater enthusiasm for and commitment to work by appealing to emotion, values, logic, and personal example | **Rewarding** Providing praise, recognition, and financial remuneration when appropriate |
| **Intellectually Stimulating** Exciting the abilities of others to learn, perceive, understand, or reason | **Role Modeling/Setting the Example** Serving as a pattern standard of excellence to be imitated |
| **Mentoring** Facilitating the skill development and career advancement of subordinates | **Supporting** Encouraging, assisting, and providing resources for others |
| **Monitoring** Evaluating the performance of subordinates and the organizational unit for progress and quality | **Team-Building** Encouraging positive identification with the organization unit, encouraging cooperation and constructive conflict resolution |

Source: Catalyst, 2007.

is so strong they can devote long hours over many years to bring it into being. In this way, a vision acts as a force that compels a leader and team to action. It gives a leader purpose, and the power of the vision and the leader's devotion to it work to inspire, empower, and encourage others to work toward the vision with purpose.

In his book, *Developing the Leader in You*, John Maxwell states:

*All great leaders possess two things: one, they know where they are going and two, they are able to persuade others to follow. [9]*

*If you don't know where you're going, any road will get you there.*
                    **Lewis Caroll, adapted quote from** Alice in Wonderland *movie*

The leader knows where she's going because she is led by a vision; this vision, once shared, becomes the guiding force for a team, organization, or corporation. Additionally, a leader must inspire hope and faith – in the vision and oneself. These can only come from a clear and focused vision that we can articulate, accept, and share with others.

The attainment of your vision will be much more likely if you take the time to invest in creating and documenting a vision statement for you and the organization. Be realistic in what you plan and recognize that it can take several years to attain a vision. The following definitions apply to what will be needed, as a minimum, in the clarification and attainment of a vision.

Vision Statement (long-term perspective)
- A statement that represents the holistic view, intention, and purpose of your life and career. This statement is described with global or high level words and should be original and specific to the values, passion, and life views that you hold. It should be ambitious, inspiring, attractive, and, yet, attainable.

Mission Statement (goals to be attained in support of the mission; 1 to 3 years)
- The mission statement consists of actions that you will follow to achieve your vision. The statements connect specific action to vision.

Roadmap (action steps to achieve the mission in order to see vision realized)
- Schedule
- Milestones

Given the relationship between vision, mission, and roadmap it is essential that the vision development be followed by the creation of a mission statement and specific goals to be accomplished, or a roadmap. It is also important to keep in mind that a roadmap, accompanied with a schedule and milestones, can enable you to measure your progress and see if you are on track; in order to do this, the milestones need to contain specific metrics or measurable outcomes. Achieving these milestones will give you and your team the necessary feedback to promote a sense of achievement and continue to inspire movement toward the vision. To create a vision it is essential to know ones dreams, ambitions, values, and essentially know who you are today and who you want to be tomorrow. A few valuable points to remember when building a vision in addition to knowing yourself include:

- Ponder, imagine, and brainstorm for a large vision
- Focus on a vision that is consistent with your values, life purpose, and passion
- Don't limit your ambitions – dream big!

## Strength of Character

*Integrity can be neither lost nor concealed nor faked nor quenched nor artificially come by nor outlived, nor, I believe, in the long run, denied – **Eudora Welty***

The integrity quotient of a leader should be her strongest point. No one should be able to raise a finger against your ethics, integrity, and principles. Your skills and achievements may win you the admiration and approbation of those whom you lead but these are not the same as respect – respect for you, the person. While people may respect a position or office, the level of commitment that this perspective engenders does not begin to compare to the level of commitment attained when there is unquestionable respect for one that holds the position. Earning this type of respect is a function of consistent integrity, character, and mutual respect. Always ensure that your personal values and actions match the values you publicly endorse – it is difficult to be a trusted leader when you are considered double-minded or inconsistent.

As a leader you must be comfortable with public scrutiny, even expecting your public and private life to stand up to harsh criticism. Any contradictions in integrity, values, or honesty can be devastating to your career, movement, or organization. One of the synonyms for integrity has always been honesty. If the people around you question your honesty, your incorruptibility, they will question the very bedrock on which your leadership is based. They will doubt the motives behind all your actions and decisions. Your personal integrity should never be in doubt, and that will happen only when you project a clear image of an honest, principled, and scrupulous leader. It is not sufficient that you have the integrity; it is important that everyone else believes in your inherent integrity and trusts you.

When you have to make compromises, never let them be of your personal values. Make sure that all those involved know the reason for your actions and the resulting compromise. Never allow your motives to be questioned and speak in terms of the decision as it relates to the vision, mission, and overall benefit for the organization. People may not agree with what you say, but let there never be a question over your motives for saying what you have said or the decisions you have made for the team.

Clearly, leaders are multidimensional figures; however, there is no room for inconsistency in values and integrity within a leader. In the past, it was easy for leaders to minimize the importance of having consistency between one's personal and private lives. However, in the days of limited privacy, digital media, and instant dissemination (i.e., YouTube), if you didn't believe it before, you have new motivation to believe it today. Aside from the fact that virtually any statement or action we make can instantly become publication information, the public life, private life, and perceived person (image) that you are combines to form your individual persona; this persona, accurate or not, becomes the image of who you are to your followers, the public, and the world.

## Belief in the Idea, Organization, or Mission

Just as your supporters need to believe in you, you need to believe in your organization, as well as the associated vision and mission. Belief and conviction in the organization is what will give you the impetus to work for it in the most difficult, challenging, and uncertain times. You have to believe in its reasons for existence; in its modus operandi; in the work ethics; in the goals and its projects. If there are any differences of opinions in any of these areas take some time for organizational evaluation and personal introspection. In some cases, this will mean we need to compromise on some of our expectations (for those that do not violate our values), gain differing perspectives, and negotiate with the others to support the ultimate vision.

Being a leader without conviction and commitment to the organization is a sure road to disaster. If you're not passionate, totally committed and enthusiastic about the mission of your organization it will be much more difficult to convince others to follow you. In the absence of a high level of demonstrated commitment, your team is likely to sense hesitation on your part, and in many cases this can lead them to mediocrity, putting forth less than ultimate effort and half-hearted support of the organization.

Conviction is important, but blind conviction, without regard for others, is dangerous. Remember that there are many others working towards change and improvement, especially when these achievements can largely impact the world around you. For example, suppose you are working towards a more rigorous process for product evaluation and introduction while another group within the organization is trying to introduce procedures to get innovative products to market faster. These two objectives support the organizational vision but may conflict on some levels. In situations like this don't give up on your convictions, but re-evaluate your circumstances, the perspectives of others, and the environment as it relates to the mission. The willingness to give genuine consideration to changing situations and to adapt strategies and approaches in order to accommodate new realities should be in the game plan of all visionary leaders.

## Ability to Empower Others

So what does it mean to empower others? What is an empowering leader? This concept may vary across cultures, organizations, and genders, and, as such, a brief review of the literature will be beneficial here. A recent article by Srivastava et al. [10] provides an historical perspective on empowered leadership that is summarized in the following discussion.

According to several leadership scholars, [11,11a] empowerment was initially conceptualized as an aspect of the relational or power-sharing view. There are several academic roots of this perspective of empowering leadership, including the Ohio State leadership studies [12] on "consideration" (e.g., showing concern for subordinates' needs); work on supportive leadership; [13] participative leadership studies [14] and the coaching, participating, and delegating behaviors encompassed in situational leadership theory [15]. Many of these characteristics or behaviors are aligned with what are typically considered "feminine leadership traits" as defined by the Catalyst study [16]. As such, women should be more effective in empowering a team if these were the only considerations.

However, Conger and Kanungo [17] argued that a view of empowerment as "sharing power" is incomplete and that a complete conceptualization must also include the motivational effect of empowerment on subordinates [18]. This was work enhanced by Thomas and Velthouse [19] as they proposed a more complex model focused on intrinsic task motivation. Kirkman and Rosen [20] further extended the concept of empowerment to the team level. As we move toward innovative cultures, this concept of empowerment is most compatible with the needs of this environment.

*An empowered organization is one in which individuals have the knowledge, skill, desire, and opportunity to personally succeed in a way that leads to collective organizational success.*

**Stephen Covey**

The authors postulate that empowered teams perform at a higher level because they experience higher potency and autonomy in performing their tasks. The interpretation is that these team members find their tasks more meaningful and impactful engendering a stronger personal commitment and higher intrinsic motivation. Finally, the research [21] concludes that these perspectives complement one another and thus define empowering leadership as behaviors whereby power is shared with subordinates and their level of intrinsic motivation is raised. Behaviors of an empowering leader include: leading by example, participative decision making, coaching, informing, and showing concern. In summary, empowerment is the infusing of power in people or things. The best leaders are those who know how to infuse positive energy, enthusiasm, and a shared vision into others. This empowerment leads to powerful outcomes as it is the others – or the "team," not an individual leader – that bring about a change. Thus, it is important that leaders empower others not only in their technical focus areas, but to manage themselves, their projects, and to also lead. That means transferring knowledge and resources as well as providing mentorship and guidance as projects are executed. Empowering others develops trust; it teaches, it inspires, and, most importantly, it serves to train the next generation of leaders [22].

To empower others, they must believe we care – about them as individuals and the degree to which the vision impacts them. I love the quote, "People don't care how much you know, until they know how much you care." – Theodore Roosevelt. This is a powerful statement that rings true in almost every environment and is critical in the perception that a team has of its leader. Yes, the leader is at the helm of the organization, but the mindset should be that you as the leader are "**first among equals**." In other words, the skills that the leader brings must be considered as equal to those that each individual team member brings to the organization. To accomplish this, the leaders should regularly acknowledge the value and contribution of each team member throughout a project. This type of leadership is valuable in creating and maintaining a team environment.

Yes, your team needs a leader, but the leader needs a team just as much, or more than they need you. Your strength is the strength of your team, and, as an engaged leader, you can infuse this strength or power into your team. However, this can't be done from the outside. To do this, we have to learn to be in two places at the same time – in front and in the middle. In front, because that's where we stand as leaders; in the middle, because that is the heart of our team and the "team" is how we get things done!

Remember that, although they are a team working together for the same objective, the team is made up of individuals, all of whom have their different traits, abilities, and emotions. Get to know them personally. Let them relate to you on a one-to-one basis; do not be aloof on the hilltop, watching others while they work. Of course, if you have a large team, getting to know each person intimately will not be possible. This is additional motivation to develop others as leaders. Empower them to represent the vision and develop your team through them by focusing on the vision. The fact that you encourage others to take up leadership roles will boost the morale of your team and motivate them to do more for the cause, knowing that their efforts will be recognized.

## Communication Skills

Communication skills are sometimes less than exceptional for STEM professionals, as we have spent much of our education and career focused on the technical elements of our environment. However, as leaders it is imperative that our communication skills be strong. This is not to say you must be a great orator, but we must be able to decisively and convincingly share our thoughts, perspectives, and concerns.

*If you can dream it you can do it*

**Walt Disney**

The short yet powerful quote "If you can dream it, you can do it" [5] by visionary Walt Disney has been a constant source of inspiration for at least three generations. As a resident of central Florida, the home of the Walt Disney World Resorts, I am continually amazed, impressed, and inspired by the incredible leadership and vision of founder Walt Disney. The effect of this leadership has lasted and is being permeated on a global level with resorts in Paris, Tokyo, and other places throughout the world.

However, believing in one's dreams alone is not enough. Walt Disney was not just a dreamer – he was clearly a doer as well as a consistent communicator about the passion he had for his vision. Many people have held intoxicating visions and honorable intentions; however, in the absence of effective communication none of these visions will be realized. Leadership requires the communication of a compelling image for the goal state, and ideally the communication of this idea should induce enthusiasm, inspiration, and commitment in the team or followers.

Clearly, communication is one of the most powerful leadership tools at all levels. Communicating your vision and beliefs to engage others and inspire them to believe in them will lead to acceptance as a leader. Since most of us will not lead as dictators, but as consensual leaders, this requires a good bit of discussion and persuasion. This is why communication skills are so important. Whether it is making a speech to a large audience, talking informally to your supporters, or just sending an email, how you say it is as important as what you say.

It is important to realize that although your vision may be clear to you, and your plan of action has been well thought-out, if others do not understand what you plan to accomplish, then you have not achieved your first test – proper communication. Your communication skills are one of the most potent weapons you can use to fight for your cause.

I hope that even with all the issues I have raised throughout this chapter you are not afraid to learn what it takes to overcome those issues. Enroll in public speaking courses if you are afraid to address crowds. Make it a point to express your convictions during informal gatherings and meetings in a gentle, but firm way. While it's good to communicate with passion, people should remember what you have said rather than how you said it. Remember, if you can't communicate, how will people know who you are and what you're fighting for? If they do not know your cause or you, why would they support you?

Obviously, the way you communicate will be a function of the purpose of the message, size of the audience, and forum. Understanding how to be effective at communicating in various environments will go a long way in ensuring a broad understanding of you, your vision, and leadership capabilities. Finally, there will also be times when you need to communicate in difficult situations without letting your emotions get in the way. You'll be in situations where you feel like you weren't treated fairly, and being able to communicate in a way that allows you to share and receive information from individuals is crucial.

## Ability to Stand Up for Yourself

*Since 1977, when the women of the U.S. House of Representatives formed themselves into a women's caucus, these legislators have been the driving force behind major legislation benefiting women and their families. Many of these issues were complex and controversial, and progress could not have been achieved without a sustained effort, especially by the women members of the House, who have been willing to give the problems continuing priority. [23]*

It is just as important to become a leader as it is to remain one amidst all adversities and criticisms. While we are leaders for the cause and not ourselves, as the representative for the cause we must be willing to stand up for ourselves. All of us have at some time faced the barbs, the criticisms, and the attempts to "cut us down to size." As a leader it is doubly important that you learn to stand up straight, and fight for yourself and the cause or group you are leading. Standing up for yourself means addressing situations, individuals, or rules that limit your movement and the advancement of your cause. It may also mean competing to make sure your cause or issue is seen as a priority in the organization.

Charles A. O'Reilly III, Professor of Organizational Behavior at Stanford Graduate School of Business, has been especially interested in women's career attainment and the problem of why, despite definite gains in recent years in the areas of education and experience, women are still so largely underrepresented in the highest ranks of American corporations. In 1986, he initiated a study where he followed a group of MBA graduates from the University of California, Berkeley, to see if he could isolate those qualities that led to senior level corporate positions. His conclusion was surprisingly simple: success in a corporation is less a function of gender discrimination than of how hard a person chooses to compete. The issue is not hard work but rather competitiveness and demonstrating a willingness to do more than your counterparts to demonstrate commitment. And the folks that tend to compete most aggressively are the stereotypical "manly men."[1]

A sports analogy is offered by O'Reilly to explain this difference and suggests that we consider careers as a sort of competitive tournament. In the final rounds, you have the best athletes and thus players are usually matched pretty equally for ability. At that point, what differentiates winners from losers is effort – how many backhands a tennis player hits in practice, how many tackles a football player makes, or how many calls a sales representative is willing to make. "From an organization's perspective," he says, "those most likely to be promoted are those who both have the skills and are willing to put in the effort. Individuals who are more loyal, work longer hours, and are willing to sacrifice (including in personal and family lives) for the organization are the ones who will be rewarded."[2]

While we may not fully agree with all that is espoused in this study, it is important to realize the value of standing up for ourselves, as our health and well-being directly impacts the health of the vision. This includes being willing to engage in vigorous competitions to see our vision realized, and having the tenacity to see the issue through to the end.

## Ability to Make Tough Decisions

We all make hundreds of decisions in a day, and as a leader the results of your decisions can impact one to thousands. Many of our decisions may have unintended negative consequences for some, but in pursuit of the vision these decisions may be necessary. For example, if you realize that the direction a technical aspect of the project is taking will not accomplish the goals, you may have to

---

[1] Where are the Women? Article posted February 5, 2004. Isegoria website www.isegoria. net/2004/02/fast-company-where-are-women.html (accessed July 6, 2012).

[2] Where are the Women? Article posted February 5, 2004. Isegoria website www.isegoria. net/2004/02/fast-company-where-are-women.html (accessed July 6, 2012).

eliminate a department that contains valuable team members. Recall the discussion about separating the vision from yourself and allowing it to stand as its own entity. When considering the vision, the "value of the team members" remains unchanged; however, the "value to the vision of the project" has changed. As the leader, your commitment must be to the vision. Now, having said this, even with commitment to the vision, it is essential that these situations be handled with consideration, respect, and a demonstrated concern for those involved.

Other scenarios where tough decisions must be made could include realizing a short-term loss right now in order to achieve a long-term goal in the future. It could be strategic relationships that are not consistent with the organization, requiring the elimination of non-performers, and individuals or departments that don't support the corporate vision.

The tough decisions extend to impact our personal lives as we consider the work–family balance. A tough decision could mean being away from home on your child's birthday because your vision requires your presence on the road. These are but a few of the many instances where your mind will need to override your heart. Oftentimes, women are characterized as "leading from the heart." This should not be confused with thinking with your heart. Leading from the heart is what gives you the passion and strength to fight your battles. Alternatively, "thinking with our heart" can lead to decisions that are primarily based on emotion rather than the demonstrated facts and support for the vision we say we believe. A persistent focus on the vision with enlightened leadership, and knowledge of the long-term impact of our decisions, coupled with logic and reason are the tactics that enable us to make consistently good decisions.

Your ability to evaluate the pros and cons of a situation and make the correct decisions is what makes you a leader. To make the proper evaluation you need to be fully aware of the facts of the situation and the implications of your decision. There are three things that will help you make the right decision: knowledge of the facts, knowledge of the people involved, and experience. Are the unpleasant implications of your decision worth it? Is the short-term loss worth the potential future profits? You are the leader. You have to decide.

Once you have made your decision, stand by it. Never let your team see "you waver" or uncommitted to your decision – these will percolate down to them and demoralize them. The confidence you show in making your decisions will be reflected in the confidence with which your team will follow you.

Indecisiveness is an unhealthy quality in a leader. As a leader, you are required to make countless decisions and many of these involve difficult situations as well as uncertainty. Nonetheless, the decisions must be made. In these situations, reduce the uncertainty by making sure you have as much information as possible, reviewing relevant or common situations in other organizations, and, if time permits, seek input from your team, mentors, and advisors. After you've done this, make the decision and, most importantly, don't second guess yourself. Move forward with the decision and accept responsibility as the leader for whatever consequences (good or bad) result from your decision.

Leaders must be open-minded, particularly in the fast-paced innovation culture of today. It is imperative that we not let ourselves become a victim of tunnel vision. There is a lot going on in the world, particularly today, and ignoring this will lead to definite challenges. What happens outside your cause can affect what happens to you and your followers. Be aware of the world around you and how it is likely to affect your activities. Having said that, as often as possible try and be open in your decision-making process and share your motives with your team. To the best degree possible, include them as part of the process. A variety of decision-making styles will be used by a leader, depending on the circumstances, environment, and urgency of a response. Figure 4.2 provides examples

Five Levels of Decision Making

J.T. Taylor

Leaders make solid decisions and commit to seeing them through. Losers put off decisions and mess around with them once they are made. A key skill in becoming a successful leader is the skill of decision making. It is surprising how many people don't like to make decisions. They do all kinds of things to keep the moment of decision at arm's length including: gathering more data, talking to more people, not thinking about the decision, fretting over who the decision might offend, worrying about the resources needed to pull the decision off, hoping the problem will go away on its own, etc. Good leaders develop the skill of making the best decision possible with the best information possible in the timeliest manner. They are quick to decide and quick to take responsibility for their decisions – positive or negative.

Successful leaders have learned that action is vital. They know procrastination kills. They live with the reality of consequences and know there will always be uncertainty in decisions. No one can see all possible ramifications; no one can predict every contingency; no one can absolutely prevent failure. Leaders know that failure is not final, it is a learning opportunity. The real danger surrounding decision making is not "will I make the wrong decision" but "did I make the best decision possible given the facts and circumstances." Strong leaders will always recover from poor decisions – they learn and become wiser. But losers will mess around and miss opportunities. And once they finally make a decision, chances are their decision will have no momentum, no passion, and no urgency.

In addition to a bias for action, good decision makers approach decision making with some foundational strategies. These strategies can best be summed up with three questions:

1. What is the downside?

    If the liability involved is significant, and is even marginally possible, then the decision is "no, go find other options." One of the leader's most important jobs is to protect the organization. Exposing the organization to undue risk is never wise.

2. What is the cost/benefit ratio?

    Every decision is a trade-off between costs (usually company resources) and benefits (usually claims aimed at increasing company resources). Smart leaders use the cost/benefit ratio to leverage growth and profitability. Good decisions are highly leveraged with low cost/high benefit. Poor decisions are high cost/low benefit. When leaders find low cost/high benefit opportunities (with minor liability of course) the decision is, "Yes, let's do it."

3. Who needs to be involved with this decision?

Good leaders understand that making decisions goes far beyond being in charge and calling the shots. Decision making is also one of the best developmental tools at their disposal. In order to create momentum around decisions the leader must cultivate commitment. Asking for input, especially from key stakeholders, is critical for momentum and effective implementation.

## The Five Levels of Decision Making

The following are five levels of involvement leaders use when deciding who should be part of the decision making process:

Level One: Leader makes the decision alone.

This is used especially in emergency situations where immediate action is critical. Input is not helpful, quick action and immediate compliance is what counts.

Level Two: Leader makes the decision with input from key stakeholders.

The leader seeks input, usually to cover blind spots and enhance their depth of understanding around the issue to be decided. Stakeholders hold important information and not consulting them would be foolish.

Level Three: Consensus building – leader gets final say.

Leader solicits input from a variety of sources, builds consensus around a specific direction, allows the group to make a recommendation of which the leader must finally approve. This level takes considerable skill and is where developing leaders often make mistakes. Solid decision makers are well versed in the skill sets of this level.

Level Four: Delegate the decision to someone else.

The authority and responsibility are clearly shifted away from the leader (usually to a direct report). Both the leader and the direct report live with the consequences – good or bad. The leader reviews the decision but does not change it and uses it as an opportunity for development.

Level Five: True consensus.

Leader fully delegates the decision to a group (usually a committee). If the leader is part of the committee then he/she is just one vote among many. The group processes all the decisions involved, compromises positions until everyone is in agreement.

Strong leaders understand the process decisions must go through to be effective. As leaders move higher in organizations the demand upon their time and influence also increases. The temptation to use the power of position to make things happen is high. Rookie leaders will often get caught in this trap and learn expensive lessons when decisions go bad. Hopefully you can avoid these mistakes and make effective decisions by using the three questions.

**FIGURE 4.2**   Five levels of decision making. J.T. Taylor. *Source: www.teambuildingusa.com/ articles/making-effective-decisions/ (accessed July 2, 2012).*

of decision-making styles that leaders engage in; it is valuable to understand when and where you should use a particular style.

Although we know we are not perfect, oftentimes we hesitate in decision making because of fear: we fear we will make mistakes or we are worried about the impact of potential negative outcomes. Be sure as a leader; you will have times when things don't work as well as you'd planned and circumstances may necessitate a change in your path. When this happens, use the same tools that you began with as a leader: knowledge of the issues, knowledge of the people involved, and your experience and input from your team to make additional decisions that address the situation. Be open and honest in this process as your team will value your honesty, openness, and willingness to accept responsibility when the decisions you made weren't as successful as planned.

## Willingness to Think Outside the Box

As STEM professionals we often base our decisions, methodologies, and ideas on historic research, literature, and existing theories – thinking creatively and outside of the box can be a challenge for us. Additionally, the business community – prior to the innovation era – is comfortable with "what's been done." So being a leader requires a concerted effort to resist this mindset in pursuit of "better, faster, and more creative ways to accomplish our goals."

Leaders must be willing to do things in ways they have never been done before as well as encouraging the team to do the same. This is why innovation and leadership are so related. Innovation and new technologies have made it easier to accomplish our goals in untraditional ways. Leadership consultant Kevin Eikenberry [24] suggests the six steps below for leaders to encourage creative or "out of the box" thinking in your organization:

- Reward creativity when it's evident and encourage it with tangible or intangible rewards or recognition
- Have a clear and positive expectancy for new ideas from employees
- Allow time for people to be creative as it takes time to do things differently and ponder how to apply new ideas to solve a problem
- Provide a safety net by talking about the risk involved in new ideas and encouraging the team to innovate now and think about the risk later
- Provide stimuli that encourage creativity such as new experiences, articles, or questioning
- Model the behavior as the leader; if we want others to think outside the box we must be willing to model the behavior as this will signal sincerity from the leadership in seeking creativity

The application of out of the box thinking also applies to personal and career development outside of the office. A personal example of how technology has changed the way we do things is in distance education. Years ago when people wanted to go back to college, distance learning programs were rare. Thus, an aspiring student with a family had to make sure their kids were old enough to be left at home or they had to find babysitters. It was also necessary to find a college near them that was convenient. Today, classes can be taken from the comfort of your home – you don't even have to get in your car – you can get a certification that can propel you to the next level. This kind of innovative thinking could not have happened without the widespread use of technology, personal computers, and other innovative resources that make learning from your home possible.

## Patience and Resilience

If you read the biographies of the great innovators of our time you will see many people told them they could not do it and many times they had to get up when knocked down. So many people today want instant success and to be cheered on all along the way – while this may be the "stuff dreams are made of," it's a far cry from the real world or organizational leadership. Demonstrating an attitude of patience as a team works to develop innovative approaches to address challenges and unexpected situations benefits a leader as this can create an atmosphere of confidence, stability, and an air of faith in the team.

Many successful entrepreneurs/innovators were unable to realize a dream because they gave up too soon. As a leader with a passionate vision, a common perspective is to adapt, adjust, and evaluate, but never quit: it is always too soon to quit.

In his book *The 21 Irrefutable Laws of Leadership*, John Maxwell tells the story of the McDonald brothers who started a fast-food restaurant, made a success of it, but failed when they tried to expand the business. They were good restaurateurs and business managers, but they lacked the skills to progress to higher levels. They were able to franchise only 10 new restaurants. When they took in a man named Ray Kroc as a partner he soon became the leader who created the global entity that is McDonald's today. That is the difference between a manager and a leader [25]. Having the patience to see a challenge through or deal with failure as you move towards a goal can be the difference between a successful venture and one that was abandoned prematurely.

## Strong Team Building – Build Your Own Team

*Never doubt that a small group of thoughtful, committed people can change the world. Indeed. It is the only thing that ever has. – **Margaret Mead***

Building your own team does not always mean starting from scratch. You may have to take over a leadership position inherited from someone else. A lot of baggage will come with this – people you don't know and who don't know you; you will have to work with all of them to create your own team. Make it clear that you are now their leader, but do not be arrogant while doing so. Share your vision with them. Explain your way of working. Listen to what they have to say. Don't ignore complaints and queries. Understand them and try to deal with them sympathetically. If they are to be your team they have to work with you, not in spite of you. Let them understand that you need them as much as they need you. Once you have their loyalty, they are YOUR team. Never take their loyalty for granted. The team culture should demonstrate value for loyal behavior, otherwise it can diminish.

When given the opportunity, to the degree possible build your own team. Selection of team members should be a process that identifies individuals with skills, talent, relationships, and functions necessary to accomplish the vision and mission of the organization at the highest level. As you construct your team, include your innovation soundboard and core teammates. Having a personal accountability partner to support you along with a team to keep you accountable for your deadlines and goals, keep you on your feet, and help you where you lack the skill or expertise, will be essential for you. Most of us already have a team without realizing it. You probably have someone you talk to about taking care of your children, or a spouse you talk to about money. Maybe you keep in touch with an old college friend who likes to talk about career goals with you. Understand you need a team, build a team, identify people currently part of your world that are on your team, and go out to see/incorporate others – a mentor, for instance – who will be a positive addition to your team.

## Determination and Optimism

*A woman who is convinced that she deserves to accept only the best challenges herself to give the best. Then she is living phenomenally. –* ***Maya Angelou***

There has never been a leader who has not been plagued by some degree of doubts and uncertainty. Accept that nothing in life is guaranteed and that a small dose of uncertainty is a consistent part of life and necessary as we embark upon new challenges. The reason I bring this up is that so many of us begin undertakings with the attitude "I can do it if…" That "if" is one of the biggest pitfalls for a leader. If you're a leader, you have to be determined to succeed with no ifs, ands, or buts! There can be no conditional determination to succeed. There will be uncertainties, dangers, and the unexpected. Your success as a leader lies in how determined you are to carry on in the face of these. Remember they are all watching the leader. If your determination is in doubt, it will not be long before the determination of your team wanes.

Judy Miller in the book *Great Failures of the Extremely Successful* [26] talks about her battle for the custody of her children, and having to cope with a new and difficult job at the same time. If you find yourself having to manage significant personal and career challenges simultaneously, you may feel overwhelmed, but don't feel defeated. You can get through this situation. I promise. In the book, Miller's words hold true for all of us – "I found that we can be whatever we want to be whenever we want. You have to just go inside, get rid of all the voices that aren't yours, the 'should' and 'shouldn'ts' and hear yourself. That's when you hear the truth. That's what we have to listen to." [26] The point is you can get through it – the alternative is to fail and we simply cannot accept failure. At these times, we must force ourselves to see beyond the moment into our vision so that we can renew our determination and reach out to the resources, relationships, and the hope so that we can make it through the difficulty.

Let me clarify that by determination I do not mean blind stubbornness or narrow-mindedness. These are negative qualities that will always work against you. Not knowing when to stop when we are engaging in unhealthy activities is an example of stubbornness; however, refusing to withdraw from a fight that you know you're meant to win is called determination. There are times when a tactical withdrawal is necessary; however, this should be done in a way that allows you to still reach your goal.

An adjunct of determination is optimism. How can you be determined to succeed if you are not hopeful, positive, and optimistic that you will? I suppose you can be but it makes the journey considerably more enjoyable when the path is laced with the consistent presence of optimism. Optimism does not mean you're unrealistic about the risks, rather it means you understand them and are focused, determined, and expecting a positive outcome. It is important that the focus actually be on the positive outcome of the leadership activity rather than the challenges in the process or the risks. An example of the importance of focusing on positive outcomes rather than the risk is described by Bennis and Nanus [5] in the book *Leaders: The Strategies for Taking Charge* as the story of internationally known great tightrope aerialist Karl Wallenda is shared. The impact of focusing on worrying about the risks (pessimism and fear) rather than on the expected positive outcomes (optimism) is so significant that it has been termed the "Wallenda Factor" in this book.

"Shortly after Karl Wallenda fell to his death in 1978 (traversing a 75-foot high wire in downtown San Juan, Puerto Rico), his wife, also an aerialist, discussed that fateful San Juan walk, 'perhaps his most dangerous.' She recalled: 'All Karl thought about for three straight months prior to it was falling. It was the first time he'd ever thought about that, and it seemed to me that he put all his energies into **not falling** rather than walking the tightrope.' Mrs Wallenda added that her husband even went so far as to personally supervise the installation of the tightrope, making certain that the guide wires were secure, 'something he had never even thought of doing before.'" [5]

The interpretation is that the continual focus on the potential negative outcomes distracted from the positive energies that were needed for focusing on the activities to achieve success. Simply put, the direction of our greatest thoughts is where we are moving or "what we think about we bring about." Thus, as a leader it is imperative that we condition ourselves to focus on optimism and faith in spite of all the obstacles as this will encourage and inspire us – and our team – toward the attainment of the vision. If you have shared your vision with your team and passed on your passion and positive energy to them it is a small but critical step to inculcating in them your determination and optimism.

## POWER TIPS FOR WOMEN LEADERS

As you develop the leader in you, there are a few tips from the "field" that will be useful. These tips were collected in a *Newsweek* article that captured 20 top women corporate leaders in their various fields.[1] While much of what is said is consistent with the social science literature, the items below are not based on a scientific data collection exercise but rather experiential knowledge from these experienced leaders. The 10 power tips are quoted exactly as listed and include the following:[2]

1. **Be competitive:** "To succeed in business you have to want to win," says Liz Lange, founder and president of Liz Lange Maternity. "Too often, women feel they have to be nice. Don't," says Lange.

2. **It's not about friendship:** "Women want everyone to like them but it doesn't really matter what people think of you," says Renee Edelman, senior VP of Edelman. "It's that you get the job done and deliver results."

3. **Stand up for yourself:** Restaurateur Donatella Arpaia is responsible for two restaurants and 140 people. "I protect my interests, their interests. If someone is going to mess with that, I cut them out like cancer."

4. **Trust your instincts:** Dozens of people tried to talk Lange out of growing her business, now a major force with nationwide distribution at Target. "There are a lot of naysayers out there," says Lange. "Shut out negative noise and go for it."

5. **Always project confidence:** Oscar-winning film producer Cathy Schulman says presentation is key. "When someone asks 'How are you?' don't go into a litany of what's wrong with your life," says Schulman. Instead, present yourself as in control and happy.

6. **Own your success:** Say goodbye to fear and insecurity, says Arpaia. Have confidence in your decisions, and make them.

7. **Reach out to other women:** When Lange started her business, she called every woman (and man) she admired and asked to meet. "Don't be shy," she says. Schulman begins each day by noting colleagues' accomplishments with a quick call or e-mail. "We don't have golf so create other communities of support."

8. **Insist on being well paid:** Don't view wanting money as inelegant or "not classy," says Schulman. "Men make decisions on the bottom line. Why shouldn't we?"

9. **It's all right to make mistakes:** When Arpaia realized a business partnership was doomed, she cut ties and moved on. "Don't obsess over things," she says.

10. **Be a problem-solver:** If something on Schulman's desk seems difficult to deal with, she tackles it first. "Big problems are an opportunity to grow."

Integrating these power tips into the additional leadership characteristics can be valuable in creating a comprehensive image of what it takes for you to succeed as a leader.

---

[3] Power Tips. Newsweek Magazine, September 24, 2006 www.thedailybeast.com/ newsweek/2006/09/24/10-power-tips.html (accessed July 6, 2012).

[4] Power Tips. Newsweek Magazine, September 24, 2006 www.thedailybeast.com/ newsweek/2006/09/24/10-power-tips.html (accessed July 6, 2012).

## THE TRANSFORMATIONAL INNOVATION LEADER

A recent study evaluated the relationship between extraordinary leaders, or transformational leaders, and innovation. A study by Gumusluoğlu and Ilsev [27] investigated the impact of transformational leadership on organizational innovation to determine whether internal and external support for innovation as contextual conditions influence the level of organizational innovation. In this study, transformational leadership was hypothesized to have a positive influence on organizational innovation. In order to test these hypotheses, data were collected from 163 Research and Development employees and managers of 43 micro- and small-sized Turkish entrepreneurial software development companies. Hierarchical regression analysis was used to test the hypothesized effects. The results of the analysis provided support for the positive influence of transformational leadership on organizational innovation. This finding is significant because this positive effect was identified in micro- and small-sized companies while previous research focused mainly on large companies. In addition, external support for innovation was found to significantly moderate this effect. Specifically, the relationship between transformational leadership and organizational innovation was stronger when external support was at high levels than when there was no external support.

The key points made by the research suggest the following with respect to the impact of individual transformational leadership on innovation within an organization:

- Transformational leaders enhance innovation within the organizational context; in other words, the tendency of organizations to innovate.
- Transformational leaders have been suggested to have an impact on innovation as the individuals enhance the culture of innovation within the organizational context.
- The tendency of organizations to innovate is enhanced with transformational leadership [28] that has innovation as a priority.
- Transformational leaders promote creative ideas within their organizations and their behaviors are suggested to act as "creativity-enhancing forces"; individualized consideration "serves as a reward" for the followers, intellectual stimulation "enhances exploratory thinking," and inspirational motivation "provides encouragement into the idea generation process." [29]
- Howell and Higgins [30] state that this behavior reflects the "championing role" of the transformational leaders.
- This leader develops his or her followers' self-confidence, self-efficacy, and self-esteem.
- This leader motivates his or her followers by his or her vision, increases their willingness to perform beyond expectations, and challenges them to adopt innovative approaches in their work.
- The heightened levels of motivation and self-esteem in the followers are likely to enhance organizational innovation [31].

This study highlights the importance of external support in the organizational innovation process. The results implied that internal support for innovation by itself may not be sufficient to promote organizational innovation, in particular, incremental innovations. Rather, it is the support received from outside the organization that serves as leverage to the effect of transformational leadership on organizational innovation. Therefore, to boost the level of company innovation, managers, especially of micro- and small-sized entrepreneurial companies, should play external roles such as boundary spanning and entrepreneuring/championing and should build relationships with external institutions which provide technical and financial support.

Other implications of the study suggest that for a leader to function at a transformational level a high level of commitment to the vision and the organization is required. As a result of this commitment to people, the vision, and respect, the leader is able to inspire people and empower them to achieve the vision. The response would lead to the followers viewing the leader between levels four and five on the leadership continuum described by John Maxwell [32] and would be expected to provide outstanding outcomes toward the organizations' mission and vision.

## BEYOND TRANSFORMATIONAL INNOVATION LEADERSHIP

The levels of leadership espoused by Maxwell take the image of leadership to another level – beyond the vision to a level of leadership that integrates the vision, care for others, and the attainment of goals for a much bigger purpose (Figure 4.3).

Gaining an understanding of these levels of leadership can be instrumental in the establishment of our vision as well as the paths we take to reach our missions and goals.

### Leadership Assessment Test

A variety of complex leadership assessment techniques exist and should be utilized as you frame your leadership goals and develop as a leader. In the assessment of your potential effectiveness as a leader, a survey developed by Gaebler.com [33] to assess the entrepreneurial leadership skills of an individual may be a good place to start (Figure 4.4). Again, this survey is not designed to provide scientific, personality, or theoretically proven conclusions about your abilities as a leader, but rather it is a tool to assist in understanding your current leadership potential.

### SUMMARY

By this point, you've learned the elements of an innovator and a leader. Additionally, you have probably begun to understand where you are in the innovation and leader continuum and allowed some time to consider where you are and where

| Level One Leadership from Position | Level Two Leadership from Respect | Level Three Leadership from Results | Level Four Leadership from People Development | Level Five Leadership from Mentorship |
|---|---|---|---|---|
| This is the basic level of leadership. At this level people follow you because they have to. Your ability to lead people is totally geared to your position and does not exceed beyond the lines of your job description or authority granted to you by the company and your boss. | At the respect level of leadership people follow you because they want to. The core of Leadership from Respect is that people want to know that you care, before they care about what you know. People see you as a professional partner, sharing the same goals and the same challenges along the way. | People follow you because of what you have done for the company. People admire you for your accomplishments and respect your tenacity. At this point leadership becomes fun. Going to work is fun, work related challenges are seen to be opportunities for a more stable work environment and all tasks have a purpose in the minds of employees. | People follow you because of what you have done for them. It is a leader's responsibility to develop their people to do the work that is expected to contribute future growth opportunities to the company and the people who serve it. People are loyal to you because they see first hand personal growth opportunities for them as well as the company. | People follow you because they respect you. As a leader you are bigger than life and your success is shown through a life of accomplishments. People seek you out after you have left the company because you have left an indelible mark on the organization and the employees. Less than five percent of all leaders will get to this level. |

**FIGURE 4.3**   The five levels of leadership. *Source: Maxwell (2011).*

you aspire to be as a leader and/or innovator. To summarize the key points of innovators and leaders, from a career and personal perspective, consider the following:

1. **Vision:** Develop your vision statement for your career and life. Without a clear vision in your own mind, you cannot lead your team. You should know where you are going, how you are going to get there, and when you are going to get there.

2. **Belief in your cause or your organization:** Often our belief in our cause is half-hearted and this doubt gets transmitted to the rank and file of our supporters. Believe in your organization fully, and then lead others to work for it.

3. **Unquestionable Integrity:** Your personal life and your honesty and integrity should never be in doubt. No one should ever be able to raise a finger against you where moral and integral issues are concerned.

4. **Communication Skills:** It is just as important to know what you are doing as it is to be able to tell the others what you are doing. Many a cause has been lost to humanity because those who believed in it were not able to get it across to the general public. Learn the skills and use them.

5. **Work well with others:** You have to work with your group or followers – not above them. Be a hands-on leader, not a hands-off one.

## Leadership Test

The following survey is designed to measure your objective leadership ability. It's important to answer each question honestly, according to the skills and abilities you actually possess rather than the abilities you hope to possess in the future.

Please provide a simple "Yes" or "No" answer to the following questions:

___ Are you confident in your ability to analyze problems and make solid decisions?

___ Do you have a reputation for meeting goals and following through on commitments?

___ Can you clearly and effectively communicate your ideas to others?

___ Are you a good listener?

___ Do you embrace risk and real-world challenges?

___ Do you think in terms of the big picture?

___ Can you consistently spot problems and improve processes?

___ Are you adept at knowing, growing, and coaching other people?

___ Do you accept responsibility for outcomes?

___ Are you easily hurt by criticism?

___ Do you demonstrate a high level of integrity in your personal and professional life?

___ Are you able to inspire others to excellence?

___ Do you learn from mistakes and constantly seek to improve your skills?

Leadership Assessment Test Scoring

Scoring is based on the number of questions to which you answered "Yes."

10+: You demonstrate a high level of leadership abilities. Although there may be room for improvement in a few areas, you are well on your way to achieving your goals in business and leadership. In the meantime, you should think about ways you can share your expertise with others.

7–9: You exhibit several strong leadership traits and are on track to become a great leader. Your ability to grow as a leader will depend on your willingness to actively seek out resources and development tools to strengthen your areas of weakness. You may even want to consider finding a mentor to help you reach the next level of leadership.

4–6: There are indications that you may have leadership potential. You may be a young leader who needs to gain experience in order to become a capable and confident leader. Take advantage of opportunities to develop your skills and whenever possible, exercise leadership – no matter how small the assignment.

**FIGURE 4.4**    Leadership test. *Source: Gaebler ventures, resources for entrepreneurs. Business leadership: Leadership ability assessment.*

6.  **Make tough decisions:** It is part of your job persona as a leader to make tough decisions. The "buck stops at you" and in the final reckoning it is your call. Learn how to make those decisions after analyzing the situation, weighing the pros and cons, and then making an informed judgment.

7. Determination and optimism: These go side by side. You have to be determined to achieve your goals and optimistic that you are going to achieve them.
8. Stand up for yourself: Face up to criticism. Be your own greatest defender. Do not let them "cut you down to size." They will try – it is part of human nature.
9. Build a good team: You are only as great a leader as the weakest link in your chain. You have to build your team, nurture them, and make them strong and efficient. They are the ones who will help you achieve your goals. Without them you are just a one-woman army.
10. Do not be afraid to experiment and try new things.

## CHAPTER RESOURCES

1. Personal Innovation Test
2. Leadership Ability Assessment

## REFERENCES

[1]   Dyer J, Gregersen H, Christensen C. The Innovator's DNA: Mastering the Five Skills of Disruptive Innovators. Boston, Massachusetts: Harvard Business Review Press; 2011.
[2]   Wagner T. Creating Innovators: The Making of Young People Who Will Change the World. New York, NY: Scribner Publishing, An Imprint of Simon and Schuster Books for Young Readers; 2012.
[3]   Phillips J. How To Tell If You Are An Innovator. www.innovationexcellence.com; (accessed May 24, 2012).
[4]   Essmann H, Du Preez N. An innovation capability maturity model – development and initial application. World Academy of Science, Engineering, and Technology 2009;53:435–46.
[5]   Bennis W, Nanus B. Leaders: The Strategies for Taking Charge. New York, NY: Harper and Row; 1985.
[6]   The Ryan Leadership myths podcasts. www.insurancejournal.com/news/national/2010/07/14/111563.htm (accessed July 2, 2012).
[7]   Catalyst. The Double-blind Dilemma for Women in Leadership: Damned If You Do, Doomed If You Don't. New York, NY: Catalyst; 2007.
[8]   Proverbs 29:18.
[9]   Maxwell J. Developing the Leader in You. Nashville, TN: Thomas Nelson Inc.; 1998.
[10]  Srivastava A, Bartol K, Locke E. Empowering leadership in management teams: effect of knowledge sharing, efficacy and performance. Academy of Management Journal 2006;49(6):1239–51.
[11]  Burke W. Leadership as empowering others. In: Srivastava S, editor. Executive Power. San Francisco: Jossey-Bass; 1986. pp. 51–77.
[11a] Burpitt WJ, Bigoness WJ. Leadership and innovation among teams: the impact of empowerment. Small Group Research 1997;28(3):414–23.
[12]  (Fleishman, 1953)
[13]  Bowers DG, Seashore SE. Predicting organizational effectiveness with a four-factor theory of leadership. Administrative Science Quarterly 1966;11(2):238–63. Taylor J. An empirical examination of a four-factor theory of leadership using smallest space analysis. Organizational Behavior and Human Performance 1971;6(3):249–66.

[14] Locke EA, Schweiger DM. Participation in decision making: One more look. In: Staw BM, editor. Research in Organizational Behavior. Greenwich, CT: JAI Press; 1979. pp. 265–339; Labianca G, Gray B, Brass DJ. A grounded model of organizational schema change during empowerment. Organization Science, INFORMS 2000;11(2); March–April, 235–257; Vroom VH, Yetton PW. Leadership and decision-making. Pittsburg, PA: University of Pittsburg Press; 1973.

[15] Hersey P, Blanchard KH. Management of Organizational Behavior: Utilizing Human Resources. New Jersey: Prentice-Hall; 1993.

[16] Catalyst. The Double-Blind Dilemma for Women in Leadership: Damned If You Do, Doomed If You Don't. New York, NY: Catalyst; 2007.

[17] Conger J, Kanungo R. The empowerment process: integrating theory and practice. Academy of Management Review 1988;13(3):471–82.

[18] Jain N, Mukherji S. Communicating a holistic perspective to the world: Kautilya on leadership. Leadership & Organization Development Journal 2009;30(5):435–54.

[19] Thomas K, Velthouse B. Cognitive elements of empowerment: an 'interpretive' model of intrinsic motivation. Academy of Management Review 1990;15(4):666–81.

[20] Kirkman B, Rosen B. Beyond self-management: antecedents and consequences of team empowerment. Academy of Management Journal 1999;42(1):58–74.

[21] Srivastava A, Bartol K, Locke E. Empowering leadership in management teams: effect of knowledge sharing, efficacy and performance. Academy of Management Journal 2006;49(6):1239–51.

[22] Kachaturoff T. Leadership Qualities – Great leaders Empower Others. http://EzineArticles.com/3150889 (accessed May 29, 2012).

[23] Young D, editor. The Difference "Difference" Makes. Palo Alto, CA: Stanford University Press; 2003.

[24] Eikenberry K. Six Ways to Think Outside the Box. Innovation, Leadership, Learning. August 2, 2010 http://blog.kevineikenberry.com/leadership/six-ways-to-think-outside-the-box/ (accessed on March 21, 2012).

[25] Maxwell J. The 21 Irrefutable Laws of Leadership. Nashville, Tennessee: Thomas Nelson Publishers; 1998.

[26] Young S. Great Failures of the Extremely Successful. Beverly Hills, CA: Tallfellow Press; 2002.

[27] Gumusluoğlu L, Ilsev A. Transformational leadership and organizational innovation: the roles of internal and external support for innovation. Journal of Product Innovation Management 2009;26(3); May, 264–77.

[28] Elkins TK, Keller RT. Leadership in research and development organizations: a literature review and conceptual framework. Leadership Quarterly Aug–Oct 2003;14(4/5):587–606.

[29] Sosik JJ, Kahai SS, Avolio BJ. Inspiring group creativity. Small Group Research 1998;29(1):3–31.

[30] Howell JM, Higgins CA. Champions of technological innovation. Administrative Science Quarterly 1990;35(2):317–41.

[31] Mumford MD, Scott GM, Gaddis B, Strange JM. Leading creative people: Orchestrating expertise and relationships. Leadership Quarterly 2002;Q.13:705–50.

[32] Maxwell JC. The Five Levels of Leadership: Proven Steps to Maximize Your Potential. New York, NY: Center Street; 2011.

[33] Gaebler Ventures, Resources for Entrepreneurs. Business Leadership: Leadership Ability Assessment. www.gaebler.com/Leadership-Ability-Assessment.htm; (accessed July 2, 2012).

## Chapter 5

# Developing the Leader in You

*Raise your hands. Raise your voice. Be ambitious. Don't take no for an answer. The world would be a better place if more women were running it, and so long as that is true then ambition in women should be celebrated as a gift to us all.*

**Susan Estrich**

## Chapter Outline

The basis of the leadership development premise associated with this book is that we can all develop as leaders. The theoretical foundation for this perspective is found in the research conducted by the Center for Creative Leadership Development where leader development is defined as the expansion of a person's capacity to be effective in leadership roles and processes [1]. The question then becomes, how do people acquire or improve their capacity to be leaders and how should organizations approach this ever pressing issue? The use of

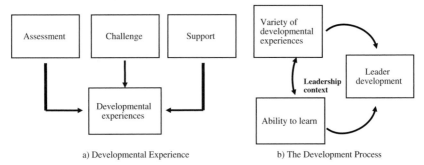

**FIGURE 5.1**   Leader Development Model. *Source: Van Velsor E, McCauley, C. D., Ruderman M. N. Feb 02, 2010, The Center of Creative Leadership Handbook. Jossey-Bass, Hooken, ISBN: 9780470570258. Chapter 2*

a developmental process and select developmental experiences can create the knowledge, experiential learning, and resources that have been shown to promote the development of leadership qualities (Figure 5.1). The developmental experiences should provide an opportunity (or challenge) accompanied with support, and finally an assessment of performance. Additionally, there should be a variety of developmental experiences.

The use of this process on an iterative basis to address developmental areas will result in knowledge, experiences, and evaluation, thereby producing in the individual the various characteristics required for effective leadership. These developmental experiences can take many forms including formal, informal, and experiential learning formats. However, before we discuss the types of developmental methods/opportunities, it is worthwhile to study the primary leadership development theories on which many of the developmental approaches or leadership models are based and designed to teach an array of leadership qualities.

## LEADERSHIP DEVELOPMENT THEORIES

A number of leadership development theories exist as the foundation for leadership styles. Additionally, within these leadership theories there are further classifications that are a function of the foundations of each theory (i.e., behavioral, biological). The categories of leadership theories can be classified as one of eight primary types: [2]

### "Great Man" Theories

The "Great Man" leadership theory became popular during the 19th century. This theory assumes that the capacity for leadership is inherent – that great leaders are born, not made. These theories often portray great leaders as heroic, mythic, and destined to rise to leadership when needed. Some of the world's most prominent leaders have contributed to the notion that great leaders are born rather than made. Figures such as Martin Luther King, Jr, Abraham Lincoln, Julius Caesar, Mahatma Gandhi, and many others to whom monuments have been erected, influence the perpetuation of this theory. Although this theory can apply to women (i.e., Mother Theresa, Catherine the Great) the term "Great Man" was used because, at the time, leadership was thought of primarily as a male quality, especially in terms of military leadership.

## Trait Theories

Trait theory, similar to Great Man Theory, is based on the assumption that people inherit or acquire certain qualities, characteristics, and traits that enable them to be better suited to lead. Trait theories often identify particular personality or behavioral characteristics shared by leaders. One of the challenges to this theory is the presumption that for an individual to have the characteristics associated with leadership is not enough, in itself, to create a leader. In other words, simply because a person has these qualities, that alone will not be a predictor of leadership ability. For example, there will be individuals with leadership characteristics as defined by this theory; however, for many reasons, they may never excel in leadership roles.

## Contingency Theories

Contingency theories of leadership are dynamic and focus on variables related to the environment that might determine which particular style of leadership is best suited for the situation. According to this theory, no leadership style is best in all situations. Success in leading depends upon the aggregate impact of a number of variables, including the environment, leadership style, qualities of the followers, and aspects of the situation.

## Situational Theories

Situational theories propose that there is no optimal style of leadership; rather, leaders choose the best course of action based upon situational variables. Additionally, the premise of this perspective is that leadership is task-relevant and the best approaches for each situation will depend on the individual job requirements, the leader, and those being influenced.

## Behavioral Theories

Behavioral theories of leadership are based upon the belief that great leaders are made, not born. According to this theory, people can *learn* to become leaders through experience, teaching, and observation. Leaders are made through a series of experiences, knowledge, and opportunities that lead to "conditioned responses" that are consistent with leadership behavior. The responses in this theory are outward manifestations or actions in response to the leadership need. This theory focuses on the actions of leaders not on mental qualities or internal states, and the evidence of leadership is the demonstrated activities.

## Participative Theories

Participative leadership theories assume that the input of many minds results in better leadership than a single decision maker. This theory espouses that the ideal leadership style is one that takes the input of others into account. These leaders encourage participation and contributions from group members and help group members feel more relevant and committed to the decision-making process.

## Transactional Theories

This theory states that people work for reward as well as working to minimize the likelihood of punishment. In this theory, successful completion of the work is rewarded whereas unsuccessful completion is punished. The focus in transactional theory is on the role of supervision, organization, and group performance toward the attainment of the goals.

## Relationship Theories

Relationship theories (i.e., transformational theories) focus upon the connections formed between leaders and followers. This theory assumes that through vision and passion a leader can achieve by inspiring and injecting enthusiasm and energy into a group. Transformational leaders motivate and inspire people by helping the group members see the importance and greater good of the vision and each associated task. These leaders are focused on the performance of the team but also want each person to fulfill his or her potential. In these situations, the result is a transformation of the group or organization that moves them toward attainment of the shared vision.

These theories are ultimately translated into implementable methods to infuse the desired leadership traits into an individual.

Several "positive" leadership theories have surfaced and include empowerment, transformation, charismatic, servant, spiritual, authoritative, and authentic leadership theories, to name a few. An article by Avolio and Gardner [3] compared authentic leadership to five other positive leadership theories: transformation leadership theory, behavioral theory, self-concept based theory, servant leadership theory, and spiritual leadership theory. In this article, the primary components of the leadership theory for authentic leadership were compared to determine the degree to which the other theories focused these same elements (Table 5.1).

**TABLE 5.1** Comparison of authentic leadership development theory with transformational, charismatic, servant, and spiritual leadership theories

| Components of authentic leadership development theory | | TL |
|---|---|---|
| Positive psychological capital | | D |
| Positive moral perspective | | FC |
| Leader self-awareness | | |
| | Values | FC |
| | Cognitions | FC |
| | Emotions | FC |
| Leader self-regulation | | |
| | Internalized | FC |
| | Balanced processing | FC |
| | Relational transparency | FC |
| | Authentic behavior | D |
| Leadership processes/behaviors | | |
| | Positive modeling | FC |
| | Personal and social identification | FC |
| | Emotional contagion | |
| | Supporting self-determination | FC |
| | Positive social exchanges | FC |
| Follower self-awareness | | |
| | Values | FC |
| | Cognitions | FC |
| | Emotions | FC |
| Follower self-regulation | | |
| | Internalized | FC |
| | Balanced processing | FC |
| | Relational transparency | D |
| | Authentic behavior | D |
| Follower development | | |

*Continued*

**TABLE 5.1** Comparison of authentic leadership development theory with transformational, charismatic, servant, and spiritual leadership theories — *Cont'd*

| Organizational context | | |
| --- | --- | --- |
| | Uncertainty | FC |
| | Inclusion | FC |
| | Ethical | FC |
| | Positive, strengths-based | |
| Performance | | |
| | Veritable | |
| | Sustained | FC |
| | Beyond expectations | FC |

Note:
(FC) – Focal Component
(D) – Discussed
Key:
TL – Transformational Leadership Theory
CL(B) – Behavioral Theory of Charismatic Leadership
CL(SC) – Self-Concept Based Theory of Charismatic Leadership
SVT – Servant Leadership Theory
SP – Spiritual Leadership Theory
Source: Avolio and Gardner (2005)

As we decide what theory of leadership we choose to subscribe to as a basis for our developmental activities, it is important to recognize that we can utilize an approach that considers elements of various types of leadership theories. The analysis in the study indicates that authentic and transformational theories are among the most comprehensive of these leadership styles. The theory or basis for the proposed leadership development strategies offered in this text is a hybrid of the authentic, transformational (Figure 5.2) [4], and servant leadership (Figure 5.3) theories. The premise for this hybrid approach (Figure 5.4) is that the integration of these theories can meet the developmental needs of various types of individual while supporting an integrated innovative culture. This will ultimately offer greater benefit to the organization over the use of the individual theories.

As you attempt to apply the guidance offered in the transformation of your STEM career, consider the specifics of your personal vision and organizational constraints and tailor the approach as necessary. The knowledge of how to tailor the approach for you will be gained through an understanding of your organization, clarification of your vision, and experiences. Finally, the plan that you

| Elements | Description |
|---|---|
| Charismatic Role Modeling | Using charisma (naturally occurring or cultivated), the leader inspires admiration, respect, and loyalty, while emphasizing the importance of having a common mission. |
| Inspirational Motivation | Takes place when the leader articulates an exciting vision of the future around the mission while showing the follower how to achieve the goals, and expresses a shared insight that is a vision not because the leaders tell them but because each individual identifies with the vision of the leader and is thus ''moved'' or inspired and believes that what they do supports the vision and at times, something greater than themselves or the leader. |
| Individualized Consideration | The leader builds one-on-one relationships with his or her team members, as well as gaining an understanding of their differing needs, skills, and aspirations. |
| Intellectual Stimulation | Integrated into this leadership style when the leader broadens and elevates the interest or thinking of his or her employees and stimulates followers to think about old problems in new ways. |

**FIGURE 5.2**   Transformational leadership. *Source: Bass (1998)*

create to meet your leadership development needs should be dynamic and adapt to your changing developmental requirements throughout your career.

## WHAT DOES IT MEAN TO DEVELOP YOUR LEADERSHIP SKILLS?

Now that we've discussed the various theories of leadership, perhaps you've identified with the type of leader you want to become or the elements of each theory that you'd like to see manifested in your leadership style. It is important to ask ourselves what characteristics we currently possess as well as those we need to acquire in order to become effective leaders. This process involves introspection, personal evaluation, and an analysis of one's self. Trusted friends, colleagues, or mentors can assist in supporting.

The introspection in this process is a two-fold activity: first, we must know who we are today and, second, we must know what type of leader we want to become. For the first step we will outline the process for the development of a Personal Vision Statement and for the latter a personal assessment of your leadership characteristics will be suggested.

### Establishing Your Vision and Mission Statement

I can clearly remember being a young, single mother with aspirations of a successful career and good life for my small daughter. Although I was using public assistance (welfare), struggling academically, and was unsure of what my future held, I managed to hold on to a vision of a better life. I spent time each week thinking about how my life would be when I didn't need welfare and how I was going to take trips, be a successful engineer, and create a great home for

| Elements | Description |
|---|---|
| **Listening** | Listens and pays attention to the spoken and unspoken messages. Motivated to listen to subordinates and support them in decision identification. |
| **Empathy** | Subordinates are not only considered employees, but also individuals worthy of respect and appreciation for their personal development, and this type of relationship ultimately generates a competitive advantage. |
| **Healing** | Seeks to help employees solve problems and conflicts in relationships, to encourage and support the personal development of each individual. This leads to the formation of an organizational culture that is dynamic, fun, and free from fear of failure. |
| **Awareness** | Gains general awareness and self-awareness. She has the ability to view situations from a more integrated and holistic perspective and as a result gains a better understanding about ethics and values. |
| **Persuasion** | Seeks to convince and persuade employees by sharing the value or benefit of the endeavor or vision. Does not take advantage of their power and status by coercing compliance. |
| **Conceptualization** | Sees beyond the day-to-day activities and limits of the operating business; also focuses on long-term operating goals. |
| **Foresight** | The ability to anticipate what the likely outcomes of various situations will be in the future. |
| **Stewardship** | An obligation and duty to help and serve others; the vision, mission, or organization function for the greater good of society. |
| **Commitment to the growth of people** | Nurtures the personal development of people as the belief is that people have intrinsic value beyond their contributions as workers. |
| **Building Community** | Identifies ways to build a strong community within her organization and seeks ways to develop a community among businesses, organizations, and institutions. |

**FIGURE 5.3** Servant leadership theory: Central characteristics in the development of servant leaders. *Source: Spears L. C. (2010) Character and Servant Leadership: Ten Characteristics of Effective, Caring Leaders. The Journal of Virtues & Leadership, 1(1), 25–30*

**FIGURE 5.4**   Hybrid leadership development theory

my daughter. These visions were a source of inspiration and encouragement in the lowest periods of my life and they were the foundation that moved me forward to the realization of my ambitions. Today, I still do the same thing in considering the next phase of my career. My leadership model has been refined, and, although motivation has changed, the process for getting there remains the same: create a vision, a mission, and execute the plan!

A simple approach to begin your journey into leadership whether you decide to subscribe to authentic or transformational leadership theories, or any other theory is to prepare a vision and mission statement for your personal career aspiration. This analysis helps to give you a better understanding of where your strengths lie, where your interests are, the opportunities you are faced with, and the threats which you must overcome to attain a particular goal. Try to be as objective as possible about yourself. Within this analysis not only will you understand your strengths and weaknesses, but you should also list your assets (not just your financials!) and your liabilities. If you have some really good friends whose opinion you value and trust, show them your list and ask for their comments. Remember, it's not always the big things that tell you about yourself. You may have raised a lot of money for a cause, which could infer that you're a good motivator, but if your workspace at home is always a mess then you may not be a good organizer. Unless you're a saint, your list of weaknesses will be on par with your strengths.

The development of a vision statement takes time; however, the investment of time will be well worth the effort in the long term. Upon development of your vision you will likely see your attitude enhanced and the frequency of your frustration with small matters in life may begin to be minimized. That is because, as I like to say, your mind will be on "higher" things, specifically your life vision. A vision is about a higher calling and vision-driven living is an exciting and impactful way to live.

Your vision statement should also cover the important areas of your life. It is a written description of your future desired life as you see it in your mind. There are no hard and fast rules about the "correct" format or length, although the more detailed and specific your vision is, the more connected to you it will

**TABLE 5.2** Personal Vision Statement Tool #1

| Things I Really Enjoy Doing | Issues or Causes I Care Deeply About | The Two Best Moments of My Past Week | Three Things I'd Do If Money or Time was Not an Issue |
|---|---|---|---|
| What I'd Like to Stop Doing or Do as Little as Possible | My Most Important Values (Circle) | Things I Can Do at the Good-to-Excellent Level | Things I Can Do to Serve the People that Matter the Most to Me |

**TABLE 5.3** Personal Vision Statement Tool #2

1. Based on my personal research, these are the main things that motivate me/bring me joy and satisfaction:

2. My greatest strengths/abilities/traits/things I do best:

3. At least two things I can start doing/do more often that use my strengths and bring me joy:

4. This is my Personal Vision Statement for myself (in 50 words or less):

be and the more likely you are to visualize it. A few useful questions to ask yourself as you develop your personal vision statement include:

- What do I believe my purpose is as a leader?
- What are my most important values?
- What are the things that I really enjoy?
- What brings me happiness/joy?
- What are the issues and causes that I care deeply about?
- What are my primary strengths?
- What are the things that I'd like to stop doing or do as little as possible?
- How can my purpose best serve the people that matter most to me?

Table 5.2 can be used to categorize your answers to these questions.

After you've completed these questions, consider the holistic perspective that results from the things that bring you happiness, your values, strengths, and desire to serve. Capture this perspective by summarizing your thoughts in Table 5.3.

## Your Personal Mission Statement

*Mission Statement*

*A mission statement is a brief description of what to focus on in the short term, and should direct your energy, actions, behaviors, and decisions towards the activities necessary to accomplish the vision.*

After the completion of your vision statement, it's time to put it in action with the development of a mission statement. In essence, the mission statement "operationalizes" your vision and provides a concise platform to align your thoughts and actions from your personal vision statement. Thus, creating the mission requires the evaluation of the vision as it relates to actions, resources, and the impact on the external groups. In other words, your Mission Statement is how you will manifest your Personal Vision in your daily life. It may be a few words or several pages, but it is not just a "to do" list. It reflects your uniqueness and must speak to you powerfully about the person you are, the person you are becoming, and the necessary actions to move you forward.

Based on the assessment of your strengths in previous chapters and the development of your personal vision you can now begin the development of your mission statement. When preparing the mission statement, it is helpful for the decision makers to consider: (1) what is to be accomplished to translate vision into action, (2) how the activities will be carried out and necessary resources, and finally (3) the beneficiaries of the mission being attained. Once your mission statement is complete, it is now time to create an actionable plan to begin moving toward the attainment of the vision. This series of actionable items will become your personal roadmap.

It will likely take multiple iterations to finalize your vision and mission statements, and it is advisable to take a few days to develop and ponder the vision as it relates to your overall life plan. Having a personal vision does not mean your life changes overnight. But with a personal vision statement, mission statement, and commitment your life will change. Your personal mission statement provides the plan and activities to get you there.

## PERSONAL ASSESSMENT OF LEADERSHIP CHARACTERISTICS

As we continue in the development of a leadership strategy we should first stop for a moment to reflect on the leadership characteristics we currently possess. As discussed in Chapter 4, too often we minimize our strengths and focus on our weaknesses. To move forward with confidence we should acknowledge and celebrate the leadership skills, strengths, and experiences we have today. This requires us to reflect on past activities, projects, and experiences in our personal and professional lives. Many of these experiences will have surfaced during the personal vision and mission statement exercise.

Scientific research, historic examples, and many of our personal experiences are solid proof that we can all grow as leaders. To do this requires effort and a desire to build leadership capacity. Once you know the direction you want to take, as a result of your vision statement the next phase is to create a personal leadership development plan. To assess your leadership skills consider the Leadership Development Assessment Survey by Peter Barron Stark Companies (Figure 5.5).

This survey should help you gain a perspective on your leadership skills and primary developmental areas as you create your leadership development plan.

**Assess your leadership skills on the following 10 statements using a 5-point scale.**

**1 = Not like you................................5 = Very much like you**

1. I have a clear overall vision, or concept of my organization/department's purpose, function, and responsibility (its contribution, mission, values, focus).

2. I spot the critical issues and upcoming problems my organization/department will need to deal with before they happen.

3. I have the facilitation skills necessary to effectively lead a group to consensus.

4. I teach, mentor, and coach people skillfully to help them handle specific challenges and problems.

5. I keep up-to-date on what's going on with my technical area, organization/department.

6. I keep an open mind when hearing others' opinions.

7. I show genuine concern for employees as individuals

8. I maintain good systems that help people work productively whether they are my subordinates or team members.

9. I set a good example with my work habits.

10. I foster a sense of teamwork and build enthusiasm for group projects and assignments.

**Scoring – Add your scores up and then find your total below.**

| | |
|---|---|
| 45–50 | You lead with confidence and your followers know where you are going. |
| 40–44 | You're well on your way to effective leadership; keep focused and stay on the road. |
| 35–39 | Sometimes you get off track and your followers are left wondering what to do next. |
| 30–34 | With no clear path in mind your followers are left to their own devices. |
| Less than 30 | Your followers are finding it difficult to follow your lead and may be looking for a new leader. |

**FIGURE 5.5** Leadership development assessment (LDA) survey. *Source:* www.pbsconsulting.com/samplelda.htm

The creation of your personal leader development plan should be an activity that empowers and encourages you. Just as crystallizing your vision provides focus and clarity, creating a leadership development plan can give you the direction and interim satisfaction of attaining milestones in the journey toward your vision, as this activity will increase the likelihood that your ultimate vision is attained.

## Creating Your Leadership Development Plan

The development of a series of developmental activities to enhance your capabilities should be based on your personal vision, career goals, personal life, and access to resources. Your leadership development plan should include a variety of methods including activities within your place of employment or professional society, or community-based activities and personal actions. As you create your developmental activities, evaluate each using the SMART model where each activity needs to meet the following criteria:

- *Specific*: know exactly what you are trying to achieve.
- *Measurable*: know how to determine when you've achieved it.
- *Action oriented*: define the activities you must perform to attain it.
- *Realistic*: make sure it is achievable in your current environment; use resources, technology, and relationships to exercise the utmost resourcefulness in assessing realism.
- *Time bound*: make sure you have a deadline and milestones if it will take more than a year to achieve.

*Development activities should be created with the SMART model in mind. Evaluate each opportunity to ensure that it is:*
*S - Specific*
*M - Measurable*
*A - Action Oriented*
*R - Realistic*
*T - Time bound*

**Source: Haughey, D. SMART Goals, www.projectsmart.co.uk/smart-goals.html**
**(accessed July 6, 2012)**

To begin the development of your plan, consider Figures 5.6a to 5.6c [5]. This series of templates can be used as a concise reference to contain your vision, goals, actions, and plan to track outcomes. The templates should be used as follows:

- Figure 5.6a Vision, Mission, and Goals: Insert your vision statement, mission statement, and goals that you have identified in the previous sections.
- Figure 5.6b Strength Enhancement: In this table, you will list the areas that you want to develop within your strengths. If you are doing this as an activity aside from your job, consider asking a mentor or trusted friend to serve in the manager's role. Alternatively, it would be a demonstration of leadership on your part to present such a plan to your manager, even if the organization doesn't currently have an employee development program. Be cautioned in these situations, as your manager may or may not be receptive to your forward thinking with respect to your career.
- Figure 5.6c Developmental Needs: In this table, you will list the top two areas that you want to focus on developing in the next six months. Your individual development plan should be updated at least every six months and the status of development be documented within each area.

**(a)**                 **Individual Development Plan**

Name: _____        Manager: _____
Position: _____        Date: _____
Date in Current Position: _____

| Section A: Career Plan |
| --- |
| Personal Mission Statement |
| |

| Short-Term Career Goals(1– 2 years) | |
| --- | --- |
| Area of Interest/ Position Title | Competencies/Skills/Knowledge Needed:(areas I need to develop) |
| | |
| | |
| | |

| Long-Term Career Goals(3–5 years) | |
| --- | --- |
| Area of Interest/ Position Title | Competencies/Skills/Knowledge Needed:(areas I need to develop) |
| | |
| | |
| | |

**FIGURE 5.6**    Individual development plan. *Source: Institute of Industrial Engineers, 2008.*

## LEADERSHIP IS IN ALL OF US

Given a cause, need, or situation which we are passionate about, we all have the potential to be leaders. This acknowledgment and realization is essential in visualizing yourself as the leader that you can become. Of course there are areas you will need to develop as a leader but commit today to yourself that you will recognize, appreciate, and develop the leader in you. Additionally, as you develop the leader in you, agree to lead as yourself! Understanding your vision, values, passion, and personality will be key in helping you define the leader you want to be and ultimately see the manifestation of this leadership. There may be times when our environment is not necessarily conducive to our commitment to authentic leadership. In those instances, we must as ourselves ask a few

**(b)**        **Individual Development Plan**

| Strength to Leverage: select at least <u>one</u> strength to continue to build upon | | | **AREA OF FOCUS:** | |
|---|---|---|---|---|
| Critical Behavior/Goals What specific behaviors do I need to model or exhibit in this competency or skill? | Developmental Activities/Action Steps (assignment, coaching, formal training) Remember SMART | Manager's Role (or involvement of others if applicable) | Target Dates/ Milestones | Results/Outcomes How have I succeeded in adapting my behavior or learning new skills? (Provide examples) |
| | | | | |

**(c)**        **Individual Development Plan**

| Area to Develop: focus on areas to develop that are critical to your performance; select 1 or 2 areas to work on at one time | | | **AREA OF FOCUS:** | |
|---|---|---|---|---|
| Critical Behaviors/Goals What specific behaviors do I need to model or exhibit in this competency or skill? | Developmental Activities/Action Steps (assignments, coaching, formal training) Remember SMART | Manager's Role (or involvement of others if applicable) | Target Dates/ Milestones | Results/Outcomes How have I succeeded in adapting my behavior or learning new skills? (Provide examples) |
| | | | | |

**FIGURE 5.6** *Continued*

questions such as, what changes are required by me and the organization for me to lead authentically here? If the answer results in a manageable response, it can be worthwhile to develop a plan to address these issues. In cases where there is not a workable solution that allows you to lead authentically you will need to weigh the value of staying in this environment vs identifying an environment where you can lead authentically and fulfill your vision.

## Set Your Sights on Leadership Roles

Once you've made the decision to commit yourself to leadership and you clarify your vision, let's proceed. Decide on a specific leadership role to try your new-found knowledge. You could be a leader who is the public face of her cause, or a leader who excels in gathering financial support, or the one who is the systems and organization leader. There are many facets and personas of a leader. It is essential that you find the role that suits you best. A tool I've developed experientially over the years to evaluate leadership opportunities is the Assess-Learn-Prepare-Proceed model. This model takes an approach that allows you to evaluate opportunities as they relate to your visions, learn what is entailed in the vision, leadership, and ultimate goals of the effort, prepare yourself to engage in the leadership of these opportunities, and, finally, understand what it takes to move forward or proceed into the leadership opportunity. The use of this approach has increased my confidence when I'm evaluating an opportunity and also steered me away from situations that "sounded good" but upon detailed assessment they were not aligned with my vision.

### Assess

In the initial stages of an assessment begin with determining whether or not the opportunity is compatible with your personal vision. Once this hurdle is cleared, assess the opportunity and the requirements of a leader that you believe would be effective based on historical data, current circumstances, and intended outcomes. To begin this process set aside time to do independent research via the Internet or other written resources, talk to involved individuals (previous or current participants), and evaluate related leadership activities. Study the cause in as many facets as reasonable; however, do not allow yourself to become paralyzed from moving forward through this analysis. Assess as much as possible about the cause, history, successes and failures, strengths and weaknesses of this leadership opportunity. Likewise, gain an understanding of where the vision for this effort has support and what the forces against the opportunity are as this will provide a new level of insight.

To assess the opportunity and the desired leader, consider using Table 5.4.

### Learn

Now that you have done your preliminary assessment of an opportunity it is time to take your understanding to a deeper level by learning about the area, leadership intentions (to the degree you can), and ultimate benefits of a successful outcome.

**TABLE 5.4** Opportunity Assessment Table

| Opportunity | Compatibility with measuring a leader |
|---|---|
| Time Commitment | Not at all<br>Somewhat<br>Moderate |
| Knowledge<br>Requirement | Do I have the knowledge?<br>If not, can I acquire it? |
| Relationship<br>Requirement | Do I have the relationships to gain the<br>opportunity and succeed at it? |
| - Competitive<br>- Expected<br>- Voluntary | * Is it a competitive opportunity, and, if so, can I compete?<br>* Is it expected, and how can I excel?<br>* Is it voluntary? |
| Vision or Overall<br>Purpose of Opportunity | How compatible is this with my visions<br>and goals? |

To do this, you may have to show your interest in this leadership opportunity through your engagement in conversation with current or former stakeholders, so weigh the implications of these actions in your environment.

- Gather knowledge about the opportunity's history, vision, and mission. Learn what it takes to gain that type of leadership position.
- Collect the resources: Besides the knowledge, you need the resources. Among the resources that will be needed are supporters – inside and outside the organization. You will need time, money, and effort. Garner these resources for the task ahead of you. Never be shy of seeking resources, or asking or fighting for them. They are not for you; they are for your cause. Remember, it's not about you but about the vision.
- Speak to the current and past leaders: Learn from what they have done and the way they have done it. Understand their vision for the future and work towards identifying the areas where new leadership is required.
- Study the other leaders: Study what other leaders have needed and used. Learn from the experience of others and use this knowledge to develop your own strategies. Make a list of "Lessons Learned" from previous leaders. Specifically, ask them their most significant lessons.

## Prepare

Once you have the necessary data and resources available to you, take some time to examine whether you are prepared to make the best use of them. Consider your strengths and development areas, and create a comprehensive list of leader development resources. Upon evaluation of these areas you must make a decision about whether or not you will prepare – or demonstrate – your current level of preparation in pursuit of this opportunity. If you've decided to proceed, create a timeline that allows you to do additional preparation prior to and during the leadership activity. Some activities include the following:

- Start with informal training: In the privacy of your home or with close friends, start the correction process. For example, if your dress sense is bad, take the guidance of someone who is considered to be well dressed. Or, if your body language is not positive enough, work on this with your friends. There is a lot you can do on your own to improve yourself.
- The next step is acquiring informal training/education: Do you need to acquire skills in public speaking or professional etiquette? Do you need to be educated on general or specific issues relevant to your cause? Start working on these gaps immediately. Join public speaking classes. Meet people more often and make a genuine effort to socially interact with all types of people.
- Become an expert in networking: You can never be a leader if no one knows who you are. The only way to establish your presence and your loyalty to the cause is to network. Attend meetings. Get to know people and more importantly allow them to know you. Don't be a silent bystander. Express your points of view and offer to help where you can. A word of caution here – never be pushy or give the appearance of being arrogant, but always be confident. Make your presence felt, so that the next time you are not there, they miss you!!
- Position yourself: Once you've established yourself, the next step is to position yourself. Where do you need to be for others to see you as a potential leader or offer you the position? The key here is to be in the right place at the right time. Another word of caution – never let your desire to lead overtake your contribution to the cause. Doing the right thing, while at the right place and for the right reason, is what opens doors.

## Proceed

At this point, you have committed to pursuing the leadership opportunity, and if you fully engaged in the three prior steps you are likely the most committed, knowledgeable, prepared, and qualified candidate to hold the position. The following steps should be used and tailored to your situation as you proceed toward your leadership opportunity:

- Take small steps first: Remember that you have to prove yourself every step of the way. Proceed in small steps. Work closely with the leader. Try to take some of the load off her. Perhaps you could, with her approval, fill in for her when she's not available. Look for things you can do that will show quick results and allow you to prove yourself. Once you take the first step, how and where to take the next ones becomes easier.
- Expect and deal with resistance firmly and with understanding: If you're going to be a leader who makes a difference to your cause you will face

resistance and challenges almost from the beginning. This does not mean that you are on the wrong track. Every challenge has a reason, good or bad, behind it. The way to overcome them is to understand why they have arisen and use this knowledge to overcome them. A leader is different from her followers. It is by being different that you make a difference.

- Don't expect to change the world in a day: It won't happen and you will not be ready for it. Remember that even the smallest changes can have a far-reaching impact that you may not be able to perceive. As Anita Roddick, founder of The Body Shop said, "If you think you're too small to have an impact, try going to bed with a mosquito." [6]

## Creativity

The difference you make and show is demonstrated by the creativity you display. This does not mean that you have to be different in everything you do. Understand how things were done in the past. Those who do not remember history are condemned to repeat it.

- Adapt, Adjust, and Change: Once you understand how things were done before, evaluate what changes need to be made for action in today's context to be successful. Circumstances, both internal and external, are always changing and the strength of a leader lies in her ability to adapt to them. Do not take shortcuts, but do not be a slave to the traditional methods of dealing with any situation. Be creative, adapt, adjust, and change. Your creativity, coupled with knowledge of what was, will equip you to deal with what is.
- Implement your plans: Finding creative solutions is not enough. As the leader, you have to lead in taking action to implement your plans. The implementation is even more important than the planning. Never let your creativity be colored by daydreaming or wishful thinking. Dreams are the foundations on which we build our goals, but unless you initiate action they will remain just that – dreams.
- Retain your personal touch: Always remember why people accept you as a leader. It is because of some aspects of your personality that encourages them to think that you are suitable for the job. It is your personal touch that makes you stand out among the multitude.
- Do not become arrogant: At the risk of repeating myself, let me once again caution you against the biggest pitfall and danger of leadership – arrogance. Creating your own style of leadership does not mean riding roughshod over the opinions and feelings of those whom you lead. An individual leadership style is one that others follow because they like it and want to be a part of it, not because they have no choice.
- Do not overlook your personal well-being: Having said that, it is also essential to remember how important you are. You are needed. Your cause needs you. Your family and friends need you. Even YOU need you. Leadership can

be a strain and over time it can drain you of your strength. Taking care of yourself does not denote selfishness. Devotion to a cause is a great thing. But if it becomes an obsession that deprives you of other things that provide balance and quality in your life, you cannot be a good leader. Your unique style comes from your multifaceted personality and your mental and physical attitudes. Do not neglect your mental and physical state; you are your own best friend.

## Be Creative in Our Approaches

The basic condition for a creative act is to combine known elements into new combinations or perspectives that have never before been considered [7]. Therefore, as we endeavor to be creative in our approach we need to consider all of our resources, options, and perspective but combine them in different and unique ways to address the challenge.

In examining common practices that get in the way of creativity and innovation, Klemm lists six common factors or "blinders" that inhibit creativeness and innovation in leaders. Some of these factors will look familiar as antonyms of favorable leadership characteristics. These factors include the following: [7]

1. Resistance to change
2. Reliance on rules and conformance
3. Fear and self-doubt
4. Overreliance on logic and precision
5. Black and white thinking
6. Overreliance on practicality or the status quo.

*My grandfather once told me that there were two kinds of people: those who do the work and those who take the credit. He told me to try to be in the first group. There is much less competition.*

**Indira Gandhi**

The challenge for STEM professionals is that we have been "taught" to base our decisions on at least four (2, 4, 5, and 6) of these six barriers to creativity in our education, research, and applications. Thus, we must "unlearn" these and other historically acceptable behaviors to truly engage our creative energies. To create an organization mindset that manages well through change, Hickman and Silva suggest actions for individual leaders and subordinates [8]. These actions, when taken by the individual, reduce the likelihood of the manifestation of uncreative behaviors in an organization. These suggestions have been adapted and are listed below:

1. Set a personal quota of at least one new idea a day.
2. Pick an organizational rule that gets in the way and break it (in a benign way that won't harm you or the organization).

3. Read literature on creativity and join a blog or electronic site to receive information regularly on creativity.
4. Allow yourself to indulge in fantasy and totally out of the box thinking for solutions, particularly when you are swamped with technical detail.
5. For any problem, force yourself to consider many solutions.
6. Defer immediate dismissal or evaluation of an idea (toy with it, explore its ramifications).

The "unlearning" of unhealthy behaviors to enhance leadership effectiveness and creativity is a task that must be aggressively confronted. Coupling these efforts with the engagement in actions that enhance strengths and promote results-oriented leadership which is consistent with our personal and organizational goals will provide a powerful combination in moving us forward toward our optimal innovation and leadership abilities.

## Learn to Deal With Adversity

While we all aspire to lead, we oftentimes do not consider the "cost" of leadership. This cost can be varying levels of adversity, isolation, loneliness, guilt, and, in some cases, loss of relationships we have held closely for years. The leader must be prepared for these situations by acquiring coping skills, resilience strategies, and a mindset that prepares you, to the degree possible, for the unexpected. More powerfully, if we can find ways to "harness adversity" we can actually use these unpleasant situations to propel us further ahead than had we not experienced them. Yes, it is possible to use these negative circumstances to our benefit as individuals and organizations.

A theory that encompasses the management of adversity and resilience has been the basis for the development of the Adversity Quotient (AQ) [9] and suggests that we can all "learn" to be more resilient. This is a powerful theory and, if true, we should all seek to learn how we can increase our ability to deal with adversity as it is a certainty in life. To begin the process we must understand where we currently reside with respect to our relationship with adversity. Stoltz [10] created the Adversity Continuum that provides five categories of the relationship we have with adversity. The categories and associated definitions are shown in Table 5.5. Take a moment to rate yourself on how you handle adversity using Table 5.5. In this exercise you will rate the approximate percentage of the time your approach to addressing adversity is compatible with the category described. If you do not feel the category fully describes your approach, find the most compatible category so you will begin to gain an understanding of how you view adversity.

If you found that most of the time you're not in the "harnessing adversity" category with your responses, don't despair – for two reasons. The first reason is that you can change! The second reason is much of response to adversity is conditioning and, unfortunately or fortunately, you're in good company. A survey by Stoltz included more than 1,000 companies in

**TABLE 5.5** My General Response to Adversity

| How You Respond to Adversity | Description of this behavior | Percent of time you use this approach (%) |
|---|---|---|
| Avoid | Procrastinating, postponing, delegating, ignoring, or sidestepping a difficulty that you could or should take care of? | |
| Survive | You just want to get through it alive! Not sure what to do after the challenge has passed. | |
| Cope | You spend a lot of energy just getting through the day as a result of the difficulty. | |
| Manage | In addition to coping with the situation, you find at least one positive thing to do or respond with as a result of the adversity. | |
| Harness | You use adversity to achieve gains and attain accomplishments that you could not have reached without the adversity. You allow the adversity to become fuel to move you forward with new motivation and intent. | |
| **Total** | | 100% |

53 countries regarding their rating on the adversity continuum. The results reveal that most (70–90%) of the time, people do some combination of avoiding, surviving, and coping as a response, and thus the adversity is consuming them. About 10–30% of the time people actually *manage* the adversity and very rarely (5%) do people and their enterprises truly harness adversity and use it to their benefit [10]. The measure of your ability to be resilient, or your AQ [11], is a function of four core dimensions which describe your CORE response to adversity (Table 5.6).

To improve your ability to deal with adversity focus on your CORE response to challenge and make a concerted effort to deliberately improve your CORE response in each of the four areas.

Of course, this sounds good and who wouldn't want to be more resilient? But how do we do it? How do we become leaders that manage adversity such that we minimize the impact on ourselves, our organization, and our followers? I believe the first step to doing this is realizing that everyone, and particularly every leader, faces adversity – and in some cases a lot of adversity. This adversity can be challenges directly related to the job or organization, failures on the part of your subordinates or yourself, or personal crises that inhibit your ability to lead. The best approach to deal with the inevitable challenges involves

**TABLE 5.6 Response to Adversity**

| Dimension | What it is... | What it determines... |
|---|---|---|
| Control | The extent to which someone perceives they can influence whatever happens next | Resilience, health, and tenacity |
| Ownership | The likelihood that someone will actually do *anything* to improve the situation, regardless of their formal responsibilities | Accountability, responsibility, action, and engagement |
| Reach | The extent to which someone perceives an adversity will "reach into" and affect other aspects of the situation or beyond | Burden, stress, energy, and effort; it tends to have cumulative effect |
| Endurance | The length of time the individual perceives the situation / adversity will last, or endure | Hope, optimism, and willingness to persevere |

Source: Stoltz and Weihenmayer (2008)

preparing for adversity, developing healthy coping skills, and creating a plan for bouncing back.

*Be careful of your thoughts, For your thoughts become your words; Be careful of your words, For your words become your deeds; Be careful of your deeds, For your deeds become your habits; Be careful of your habits, For your habits become your character; Be careful of your character, For your character becomes your destiny.*

*Author Anonymous*
*Source: Markkula Center for Applied Ethics, Santa Clara University www.scu.edu/ethics/publications/iie/v13n1/*

Knowing the demands of everyday life, a summary of research has been integrated into a list of resilience strategies by motivational coach Paula Davis. The 7 Simple Resilience Strategies for Busy, Complicated Lives (Figure 5.7) [12], are written to quickly get to the point as they are designed for the busy person. The foundation of these strategies is a combination of research in the areas of human behavior, leadership, and good old-fashioned optimism.

## Take Good Care of Yourself [13]

If the experts are correct that it is our reaction to external events that creates stress, it supports a basic premise that we need to take care of ourselves to effectively respond to the stress factors inherent in our jobs. Taking care of yourself often falls to the bottom of the to-do list for busy executives, ambitious young leaders, and middle managers. This can be even more of an issue if you are balancing the demands of career and family life. However, it is absolutely imperative that we gain a genuine understanding of the criticality, long-term

---

### Find satisfaction with your work

Amy Wrzesniewski's research summarizes that:

- those who consider their work to be a job are generally interested only in the material benefits from their work and don't seek or receive any other type of reward from it

- those who consider their work to be a career have a deeper personal investment in their work and generally seek to advance not only monetarily but also within the occupational structure

- those who consider their work to be a calling usually find that their work is inseparable from their life

"Those with a calling will work not for financial gain or for career advancement, but for the fulfillment that the work brings."

---

### Analyze what pushes your buttons

The following four-step process is a technique based on the work of Drs. Albert Ellis and Aaron Beck, and can help you better understand why you react the way you do to certain situations:

1. Describe factually what pushed your buttons (who, what, where, when)
2. Write down your reaction – both what you did and how you felt (I felt angry and yelled)
3. Write down exactly what you were thinking in-the-moment during the challenge
4. Ask yourself whether your reaction helped or hurt your ability to find a solution.

People tend to focus only on the reaction part of the equation, but those reactions are driven by how you think; so, if you want to change your reaction to a situation, you need to change the way you think about it.

---

### Find fun

- Kids have zest in abundance, but as we age, societal and organizational pressures quietly tell us that having fun and being serious don't go together. Not surprisingly, zest is one of the best predictors of work and life satisfaction.

- Fun helps you socialize, provides an outlet for learning and creativity, and has great health benefits.

- The Association for Applied and Therapeutic Humor (www.aath.org) posts numerous resources, including research, about the benefits of fun.

### Increase self-awareness by identifying your strengths

- Research by Christopher Peterson and his team shows that using your strengths in new ways every day for a week increases happiness and decreases depression.

- Harter et al. found that those who get to do what they do best at work on a daily basis have increased loyalty, retention, and productivity.

### Create "THE LIST"

- Creating "THE LIST" may be useful in helping you figure out your next step. It can help you reconnect with activities and general pursuits that you've always loved to do, but which may have disappeared in the hustle and bustle of life.

- To develop THE LIST, set aside some time to reflect on all of the things you've loved to do throughout your life. You will start to see patterns throughout your life when you felt great joy performing an activity or impacted someone's life because of the unique talents you bring to the table.

- Do more of the activities on THE LIST!

### Build self-efficacy

- In the children's book *The Little Engine that Could*, the phrase the engine kept saying was, "I think I can, I think I can." That is self-efficacy – your ability to believe you can accomplish what you want to accomplish.

- The tendency to remember and only dwell on the times when you've failed or done less than your best often thwarts your ability to remember what you've accomplished in life.

- To build your self-efficacy, keep a journal of "wins."
  - Write down all of the times in your life when you have exceeded expectations, accomplished tough goals, and were in control of your life.
  - Review this list often and keep adding to it.
- Encourage your kids to start building their list now.

- Don't be afraid to start small. Small victories create momentum which is a great foundation from which to succeed at more complicated tasks.

| Help others savor good news |
| --- |
| • Research by Shelly Gable shows that how you respond to a person's good news actually does more for building a relationship than how you respond to bad news. This applies across the board from personal relationships to business interactions.<br><br>    • Responding in an active and constructive way; that is, helping the bearer of good news savor it, is the only response that builds good relationships.<br><br>    • Killing the conversation by offering a terse response or hijacking the conversation by making it about you are quick ways to weaken a relationship. |

**FIGURE 5.7**    Simple resilience strategies for busy, complicated lives. *Source: Davis P. 7 Simple Resilience Strategies for Busy, Complicated Lives* www.inpowerwomen.com/7-simple-resilience-strategies-for-busy-complicated-lives/ *(accessed July 6, 2012)*

impact, and overall benefit we will reap if we make taking care of ourselves a regular aspect of our lives.

Ideally, to be the best leader you can be requires you to be "at your best" when you lead. Understanding what being at your best means for you is a personal exercise and as a minimum would include knowing what it means for you to be healthy physically, emotionally, spiritually, and relationally. The need to take care of yourself so that you can be highly effective is characterized in the *Seven Habits of Highly Effective People* by author Steven Covey [14] as the principle of balanced self-renewal. This principle includes four dimensions of renewal: physical, mental, social/emotional, and spiritual. Covey further points out how this habit of balanced self-renewal surrounds all the other habits and is the one that makes all the others habits that lead to being highly effective possible. Complete Table 5.7 to describe how you currently, or plan to, promote your well-being and personal renewal.

In the interest of providing a summary resource, the detailed list of tips for busy executives has been identified by Motivational Speaker and Personal Power Expert DeLores Pressley (Figure 5.8) [15].

## Prepare Young Women to Lead

While this aspect of leadership is most closely identified with the Servant Leadership Theory, it has clearly been documented that developing the next generation of leaders is a competitive strategy from an organizational perspective. While we are currently developing ourselves and setting our sights on our leadership objectives, it is our responsibility to prepare young women by first of all setting a positive example of leadership, and then mentoring, coaching, opportunity creation, and advocating. To see the gains necessary in leadership every woman leading or aspiring to leadership should commit to

**TABLE 5.7** Taking Good Care of Myself Status and Plan

| Physical | | Daily | Weekly | Monthly | Annually | Start date for New Activities |
|---|---|---|---|---|---|---|
| | What am I currently doing to support my physical well-being? | | | | | |
| | What are the things I need to do to improve my physical well-being? | | | | | |
| **Mental** | | Daily | Weekly | Monthly | Annually | Start date for New Activities |
| | What am I currently doing to support my mental or psychological well-being? | | | | | |
| | What are the things I need to do to improve my mental or psychological well-being? | | | | | |
| **Emotional** | | Daily | Weekly | Monthly | Annually | Start date for New Activities |
| | What am I currently doing to support my emotional well-being? | | | | | |
| | What are the things I need to do to improve my emotional well-being? | | | | | |
| **Spiritual** | | Daily | Weekly | Monthly | Annually | Start date for New Activities |
| | What am I currently doing to support my spiritual well-being? | | | | | |
| | What are the things I need to do to improve my spiritual well-being? | | | | | |

| 1. | Remember to smell the flowers | Take time out to enjoy the little things in life. Being just as impressed by small events as large ones helps to cultivate wisdom and clarity. |
|----|---|---|
| 2. | Stop living a "hit-and-miss life" | Living aimlessly is like shooting multiple arrows that miss their targets. This is a waste of time and not a trait of an effective leader. |
| 3. | Anxiety is anticipation run riot | Anticipating the worst keeps us from enjoying the present. Realize that anxiety does not facilitate self-control. |
| 4. | Remember to take breaks | Taking breaks during work helps you accomplish more during the time that you are working. |
| 5. | Avoid procrastination | Remove temptations around you such as an instant messenger program or magazines, which might tempt you from being efficient at work. |
| 6. | Keep things simple | Eliminate the things that cause clutter in your life, such as unnecessary magazine subscriptions, paper, and too many unused gadgets. |
| 7. | Take care of yourself | Executives who look haggard or tired tend to have more responsibilities heaped on them, because your physical condition and dress sends the message that you permit that. |
| 8. | Commit yourself to exercise at least three times a week | Keeping yourself in shape will help you perform efficiently in all areas of your life. |
| 9. | Always eat breakfast | Low blood sugar as a result of not eating properly can cause unproductive afternoons. |
| 10. | Take your vitamins | If you eat constantly on the run to save time, take vitamins to avoid potential slumps in energy. |
| 11. | Bag your lunch | Not only is this cheaper, but it is more nutritious because you have control over what you eat. This can spare you from eating empty calories that exhaust you. |
| 12. | Sit down with your family for dinner | This is the one thing that you can do each day to bond with family members. It also saves money and allows you to control your diet. |
| 13. | Make dates with your mate | Planning romantic outings keeps your relationship erotic and alive. |
| 14. | Get professional help | If you can't cope due to bad time management skills or emotional problems, get the help that you need. |
| 15. | Ask for help if you need it | Pride prevents most executives from asking for assistance from higher ups or colleagues. Being trained wastes less time than trying to figure out something yourself. |
| 16. | Make sure you have quiet time | Set personal time aside for yourself each week doing something that you enjoy doing alone. This gives you clarity and is a form of meditation. |

**FIGURE 5.8**   Tips for staying healthy as an executive. *Source: Pressley D. (2012)*

impact the life of at least one young woman annually. The form of impact can be tailored to your condition, environment, or resources, but a commitment and resulting action is necessary. The impact can be the result of personal mentoring, donation of finances or resources to organizations supporting the development of women, creating opportunities within your organization, and support of professional societies. The point is that women and men must make this an expected aspect of leadership if we are to see the benefits of gender equality and a fully engaged female workforce realized. The activities and importance of this are discussed in more detail in Chapter 7: Women Leaders Must Support Each Other.

| | |
|---|---|
| **17. Get enough sleep** | People who are sleep deprived make more time consuming mistakes and are too irritable to lead a quality life style. |
| **18. Never get too hungry** | People who are hungry are irritable and make mistakes so that things need to be done over again. |
| **19. Avoid people who suck your time** | Needy or emotionally disturbed individuals can seriously throw your plans for the day astray. Avoid them the best you can. |
| **20. Deal with anger** | Angry individuals are hasty, reckless, and make careless errors that cause time-consuming mistakes. |
| **21. If your are tired, rest** | It is better to rest and do a task twice as fast afterwards, rather than do it slowly because you are exhausted. |
| **22. Take life one day at a time** | Live in the present, not in the future, and you will accomplish more. |
| **23. Give back to the community** | Engage in one meaningful activity where money is "not the goal." This empowers you spiritually and prevents you from getting too stuck in your own problems. |
| **24. Make yourself inaccessible at certain times** | Let others know when you are working and cannot be disturbed. |
| **25. Reward yourself for a job well done** | Whenever you complete a big task make sure to keep motivated by giving yourself a reward. |
| **26. Seek out the good in every situation** | Disappointments and delays are a part of life. Learn how to make it up to your family if you are late and can't be there for them. |
| **27. Realize that you always have choices** | Make choices about how you spend your time, and do not be at the mercy of obligations that you cannot fulfill. |

**FIGURE 5.8**  *Continued*

## CONCLUSIONS

Although an individual may possess leadership strengths, no one is born a leader. The passion you have for your cause creates the desire to lead and contribute more. Your innate abilities may have given you a start, but your leadership role will continue to grow. If you want to succeed, you will have to keep growing both as a person and a leader so that you fit that role. There are two main factors in which you will have to accomplish prior to reaching that desired leadership role.

- The first factor is how to learn to work with your strengths and weaknesses. You are what you are – use your inherent powers to their optimum capacity.
- The second factor of your growth that will give you the advantage over others is that of knowledge and learning. The more you know about your cause, your opposition, and the environment you work in, the stronger you are. And the stronger you are, the faster you grow.

Remember that we have to invest in becoming leaders. Like every other area of life, the returns we get on our investment depend on both how much and how wisely we invest. How much you give is directly proportional to how much you get back. In essence, there are four things to remember:

- You have to invest time: Time is a very scarce commodity and everyone has very little to spare. But if you are aspiring to become a leader it is important to find the time to do so. This may mean reprioritizing or making judgment about areas where you're spending time that's not conducive to your vision. In these situations, this is time you can recoup to invest toward the vision. Invest your time judiciously, efficiently, and you will become a beacon for the others to follow.
- Invest your time *wisely*: Let us carry forward the metaphor of short- and long-term investments. You may be saving up for a new car (short term) and also be saving for your retirement (long term). So you will have to look at the short- and long-term investments for your time. A short-term time investment is one where you will get immediate recognition for some specific work where you took on the leadership role. A long-term investment is one where you devote time to building up your leadership skills and working your way up the organization. Both are important. The first gets you recognition and the second allows you to build on it.
- The other factor you have to invest in is effort. Being a leader does not mean that you can just sit back and tell others what to do. You lead with effort, energy, and by example.
- Lastly, take good care of yourself. It is easy to get overwhelmed and try to do everything at once. Accomplish these tasks in manageable doses, prioritize, and focus on one or two things at a time. Leaders sometimes neglect themselves for the good of others and the organization. While sacrifice is required, continually neglecting yourself will not benefit you as a leader. Take care of your whole person: Mind, Body, and Spirit.

## CHAPTER RESOURCES

1. Vision Statement Development Plan
2. Mission Statement Development Plan
3. Career Development Template
4. Leadership Assessment Survey
5. Assessment of Adversity Approaches

## REFERENCES

[1] Van Velsor E, McCauley CD, Ruderman MN. The Center for Creative Leadership Handbook. Hoboken, NJ: Jossey-Bass; 2010.
[2] Cherry K. Leadership Theories - 8 Major Leadership Theories. About.com Guide: http://psychology.about.com/od/leadership/p/leadtheories.htm (accessed July 5, 2012).

[3] Avolio BJ, Gardner WL. Authentic leadership development: Getting to the root of positive forms of leadership. The Leadership Quarterly 2005;16:315–38.

[4] Bass BM. Transformational Leadership: Industrial, Military, and Educational Impact. Mahwah, NJ: Lawrence Erlbaum Associates; 1998.

[5] Takeda K, Hlutkowsky R, Sinclair S, Tompkin J, Kilmer K. IIE Annual Conference and Expo 2008 Conference Proceedings. Session: From IE to Management - How You Take Flight; Title: "Succession Planning Strategies, understanding developing IE's". Session participants: Takeda K, Hlutkowsky R, Sinclair S, Tompkin J, Kilmer K. Powerpoint presentations (2008), Institute of Industrial Engineers www.iienet2.org/ (accessed February 10, 2012).

[6] Quoted in: http://en.thinkexist.com/quotes/anita_roddick/ (accessed July 5, 2012).

[7] Klemm WR. Leadership: Creativity and Innovation. Prepared for Air University "Concepts for Air Force Leadership." 2003: www.au.af.mil/au/awc/awcgate/au-24/au24-401.htm (accessed July 8, 2012).

[8] Hickman CR, Silva MA. Creating Excellence: Managing Corporate Culture Strategy and Change in the New Age. New York, NY: New American Library; 1984.

[9] Reed J, Stoltz PG. Put Your Mindset to Work: The One Asset You Really Need to Win and Keep the Job You Love. New York, NY: Penguin Group; 2011.

[10] Stoltz P. When Adversity Strikes, What Do You Do? Harvard Business Review blog, 2010; http://blogs.hbr.org/cs/2010/07/when_adversity_strikes_what_do.html (accessed July 5, 2012).

[11] Stoltz PG, Weihenmayer E. The Adversity Advantage. New York, NY: Fireside, A Division of Simon and Schuster; 2008.

[12] Davis Paula. 7 Simple Resilience Strategies for Busy, Complicated Lives. www.inpowerwomen. com/7-simple-resilience-strategies-for-busy-complicated-lives/ (accessed July 6, 2012).

[13] Metzger C. Balancing Leadership and Personal Growth: The School Administrator's Guide. Thousand Oaks, CA: Corwin Press; 2006.

[14] Covey SR. The 7 Habits of Highly Effective People. New York: Simon and Schuster; 1989.

[15] Pressley D. (May 8, 2012) 27 Tips for Staying Healthy as an Executive. Smart Business www. sbnonline.com/2012/05/27-tips-for-staying-healthy-as-an-executive/ (accessed July 5, 2012).

## Chapter 6

# Innovate Today!

*Declaration: I take action toward achieving my goal knowing that whatever the result, it will be beneficial to me. There is no such thing as failure because I view all situations as opportunities to learn something new about myself.*

*Helene Lerner*

## Chapter Outline

Transforming your STEM Career through Leadership and Innovation.
http://dx.doi.org/10.1016/B978-0-12-396993-4.00006-0

The actual approaches we take to innovation within organizations and our careers has been changed by technology, globalization, and a type of social conditioning that expects new technology on a constant basis. This wave of change is also impacting how we manage our careers. To be credible we must meet and exceed the expectations from a technical or function perspective; however, to stand out as a leader and innovator we will need to introduce value-added products, processes, or activities. While many organizations provide career development resources, the primary responsibility for career management lies with the individual. Research [1–3] has demonstrated a shift in expectations for personal development and illustrates that the responsibility for managing careers has been gradually transferred from the organization to the individual. Given the criticality of innovation, demonstrating an ability to be an innovator in your organization can lead to recognition and opportunity for leadership. Thus, it is important to understand how to bring value to your career through the use of innovation.

What does innovation mean for you, your career, and environment? Is it required for advancement? Will it create new opportunities for you? Maybe innovation means coming up with new and creative ways to do things or new products and ideas to expand the life and growth of your organization. Another question you should ask yourself is whether or not your company has an innovative culture. The corporation's culture must be innovative if it's going to encourage innovation among its employees, but what does this mean to an individual? The following sections will address some of these questions.

## INNOVATION AND YOUR CAREER

Decide first of all if you want to be an Innovator – I assume you do or you are at least considering it. What are the factors within the decision-making process that you need to be aware of? Then identify a need, and come up with an idea to meet this need. This idea can be a very general concept. For example, if you realized that when you finish working out at the gym before work you don't have time to wash your hair so you have to put hot rollers in it – an innovative idea is a tool that you can put in while you are working out so when you finish, your hair is already done and ready to go. This concept offers no design, no materials, it may not even be feasible – it's just a general idea to meet the need for nice post-workout hair.

Next, determine your process. This is the step where you start to think seriously about how you would go about the process. Evaluate the idea and determine what you have to do. At this point you might seek external resources or private organizations that can help you design or produce your product.

### Decide To Become an Innovator

If you answered "no" to the question "Do you want to be an innovator?" I implore you to reconsider! Nurture the innovator in you and bring that person out. Ask yourself: what qualities do I have that are good for innovation? What qualities do I need to develop? Understand why these qualities matter. Don't necessarily focus on your weaknesses, but enhance your strength and mitigate your weaknesses (review Chapter 4).

## Habits of Innovators

Here are seven habits found in highly innovative and creative people that I've organized and summarized from Scott Berkun's *The Myths of Innovation* [4].

### Persistence

Innovation rarely happens overnight. It involves more than just great ideas. You need faith, hard work, and focus to keep your persistence going. Don't be deterred by difficulties; innovation by nature takes time and there are challenges at every stage. Take it from the man who gave us the light bulb:

*Invention is 1% inspiration, 99% perspiration*

**Thomas A. Edison**

### Remove Self-limiting Inhibitions

As discussed in previous chapters, often the number one person who gets in our way is ourself. Get out of your own way! How many times have you considered an idea and before you have even stood up from your thinking chair you have talked yourself out of it? A few years ago I was considering the development of a product for biomechanical analysis that could be used in the entertainment industry and the athletic industry. This idea was based on some research and expert witness testimonies I had conducted, and I got the idea because I had to do some research analysis that wasn't really possible at the time because the resources weren't there. All I had were 2-D figures, and I needed 3-D figures in order to do a full biomechanical analysis. I wrote down a little paragraph about it, and I bounced the idea off my husband and a few other people, and I received plenty of positive feedback from my inner circle. But when I sat down to think about it, I started thinking about why it wouldn't work. While it's important to understand those challenges, I effectively talked myself out of further pursuing it without doing any research. I analyzed and reasoned that I didn't have the resources, the technology was not quite ready for such an innovation and, if so, I probably wouldn't be able to find someone to provide the funding I needed to create a prototype. So I put that idea on the shelf for over a year. Today, much to my sadness, I'm seeing an innovation that is very close to that idea. With the pace of technology I could have clearly been in the running for creating this technology, but I talked myself out of it and never gave myself a chance.

Free yourself from these constraints you've created. Whether you are an over-analyzer and think your idea is impossible, or you don't think you are brilliant and wonderful, it just isn't true. Be open to new ideas and don't set limits;

as an innovator, understand that a criticism like "It's never been done before" is probably the most heartwarming thing you will hear – if it's never been done before, you are on the right track! "Remember, innovation is more about psychology than intellect." [4] In other words, we don't utilize our intellect because we are deterred by negative psychological feedback.

## Risk Taking and Comfort With Making Mistakes

No one likes to fail. We expect success, view ourselves as successful, and are often unprepared for mistakes. This attitude has to change if you want to be an innovator. Expect that things will fail over the process of learning. That's what prototypes are for. Even your brand new cell phone probably has something you would like to change about it. Don't sweat it! It's a learning experience, and you can bet someone who works for your phone company is working on fixing that problem. I always tell my students, you don't need to be a perfectionist to be a person of excellence. Don't turn in a project late because you spent so much time going over a particular concept when you should have the confidence that it will work out because of your intellect. Perfectionism is not a healthy trait. When things don't work out, in the research field, we don't call it a failure – we call it a research outcome. So we should apply this to innovation and call these innovation outcomes – rather than failures. It just means we need to try something else.

## Comfort in Your Environment

The more relaxed and calm we are internally, the more receptive we are to tap into our flowing creativity. Our feelings impact how we think, the way we think impacts our level of creativity, and our creativity impacts the ideas we generate which ultimately affects the level of innovation that will be realized. So find a way to achieve calm creativity.

Find a space that makes you susceptible to that creativity. Some work environments aren't conducive to creativity, so spend some time at lunch or before work focusing on these things. Although the innovator may have the "EUREKA" moment in the shower, that idea is a culmination of multiple interactions throughout the day, week, or even month. Each of us has different triggers for our creative energy: during tea time, before bed, while exercising, in the shower, wherever it is, find your creative zone! I get into my creative zone from sitting in a comfortable chair in a room with fragrant candles burning, holding a warm cup of French vanilla coffee, with jazz playing softly in the background. Many great thinkers go on long walks to help them solve problems. Experiment and find what works for you. Sometimes it is helpful to make a list of the ideas you have at the time, an hour later, and then a day later, because sometimes ideas take time to incubate.

## Writing Things Down

Writing an idea down makes it real, tangible, and more likely to be obtained. You can keep Post-it® notes or sketch paper around, or type it into your computer, smart phone or smart pad. Make a folder or envelope that you put your ideas in. Keep them going, and don't lose or forget about them! A thought is a fleeting and mysterious little thing – you need to capture it! And your thoughts and ideas are valuable to the world. If you don't believe me, go look up how much Bill Gates spent on Leonardo Da Vinci's notebook (answer: US$30.8 million in 1994!).

### Find Patterns and Create Combinations

Ideas come from other ideas. You can increase your exposure to new ideas by looking for patterns and finding ways to combine ideas or improve upon existing solutions. Did you know that Edison wasn't the first one who came up with the invention of the light bulb? He was the first to build a workable carbon filament inside a glass tube, which made the light bulbs last longer. His competitors, and those who came up with the first one, were no less brilliant or capable; they may have even had comparable resources. However, they were not the ones who ultimately saw the innovation realized.

### Curiosity

Many innovators are just curious, inquisitive people who like to solve problems. Practice seeing things differently. For example, when seeing the solution to a problem, ask yourself "What are some alternative ways to do this?" By asking questions you can challenge the norms or existing methods, and asking the right questions is the best way to gain a better understanding of the problem.

## Recognizing Opportunities for Innovation

Wherever you see a need, problem, or challenge, there is the potential for innovation. Opportunities for innovation are all around us! Know your area of expertise and the global challenges in your area. Just because an innovation doesn't have potential to affect your community, it doesn't mean it won't be useful elsewhere. If you find yourself with what you believe is a truly valuable idea but you're not getting the traction to move it forward in your environment, this may be a sign that it's time to expand your team or collaborators. Remember this simple equation:

$$(\text{Technology} + \text{Design}) \times \text{Creativity}^n \rightarrow \text{Innovation [5]}$$

In this case, Creativity can be interpreted as "collaborative ideation" (where n represents the number of minds involved in the process). This collaborative ideation should involve individuals with varying perspectives from different backgrounds, communities, or countries. Approaching creativity in this manner increases the likelihood that you will create an innovation that has broad, and hopefully global, appeal.

## How to Become an Innovator: Moving You Forward!

Various models of career development with respect to innovation exist, but they are usually focused on how an organization rather than an individual can innovate. Innovation is about thinking differently, having the confidence to do what others won't, and taking risks. The focus of this discussion on innovation is how to move you forward in your thinking, actions, and confidence to become an innovator. I have adapted a six-step program proposed by Helene Lerner in *Smart Women Take Risks* [6] and modified it such that it can be used as a tool for women to develop as innovators. These six steps for Smart Innovation Risk Taking include:

- Step 1: Commit to becoming an innovator and select an idea
- Step 2: Calculate the risk
- Step 3: Build and consult with your team (and make sure they're winners!)
- Step 4: Take the leap into the innovation
- Step 5: Claim victory: anticipate, expect, and celebrate your courage
- Step 6: Don't stop! Success breeds success so become a serial innovator!

### *Step 1: Commit to Becoming an Innovator and Select an Idea*

Sheryl Sandberg has achieved extraordinary success at 41 years of age, holding the position of Chief Operations Officer at Facebook, and prior to this appointment served as Vice President of Global Online Sales and Operations at Google. Sandberg points out the importance of women demonstrating self confidence and a willingness to take on new responsibilities [7]. Sandberg goes on to state:

*A lot of getting ahead in the workplace has to do with being willing to raise your hand*

In terms of becoming an innovator, this "hand raising" is an outward manifestation of our commitment, confidence, and recognition that we are capable of leading an opportunity. Raise your hand to yourself, your colleagues, and your boss to say that you are an innovator and you want the opportunity. This is a serious point and we must understand the overall impact it can have on our careers. A study by Catalyst [8] stated that 40% of women in corporate leadership positions stated that seeking difficult or highly visible assignments was a very important strategy for advancement. So in order to move forward we must be willing to do this throughout our careers. So let's start today. Some critical ingredients for making the commitment to raise your hand and lead an innovation include: [6]

- Know your value! You bring talents, strengths, and bottom line value to your organization.
- Being confident and recalling your strengths, as well as the success we've had, in taking on new challenges within or outside of your organization.

- Being honest with yourself and confronting mindsets, behaviors, or habits that are getting in the way of our moving forward.
- Be passionate about your ideas and your career! It's your responsibility and no one should be more passionate about seeing your ideas move forward.

If you feel fearful at the mere thought of raising your hand, demanding an opportunity, or striking out with a commitment toward an idea – don't worry – it just means you're moving in the right direction. Turning fear into excitement and enthusiasm can generate the additional fuel you need to blaze the path into your new level of commitment. Fear and excitement are closely related emotions and, if we reflect on times of excitement, even in positive situations we can identify some of the common feelings we have when we're fearful. So whatever you do, don't ever let fear be a reason to hesitate in committing to your goals.

## Step 2: Calculate the Risk

Any new endeavor will involve risks and the level of risks must be determined to recognize that to succeed in innovation requires a willingness to accept a higher level of risk than non-innovators. Lerner states that "accomplished people take Smart Risks by analyzing the possible outcomes of their actions, looking at the timing of a goal, consideration of the compatibility with their passions, weighing it with their priorities, and trusting their intuition about the 'rightness of taking the risk.'" [6] When these factors are all evaluated and align more positively than negatively, this should signal a need to accept the risks. To assess the risk, Lerner provides a Risk Quotient that is comprised of three components: [6]

1. Analyzing the pros and cons of taking a risk using a Risk Quotient Balance Sheet.
   - Create a table that shows the Pros vs Cons for each major decision factor in assessing the risk
   - Attach a priority level from 1 (not important) to 5 (extremely important) and assign a priority level to each Pro and Con in your table
   - Sum the values for each column and compare them; the highest rating gives you the guidance to make your decision about whether or not the risk should be taken.

I have provided an example of how to use the Risk Quotient Balance Sheet through my evaluation of whether or not to take a visiting professorship in the Department of Aeronautics and Astronautics at the Massachusetts Institute of Technology (MIT) in 1998 (Figure 6.1).

At the time of my decision, I did not have the benefit of this tool; however, my decision was to accept the challenge and take the visiting professorship at MIT.

| Risk Being Evaluated: Accepting a Visiting Professorship in Department of Aeronautics and Astronautics at the Massachusetts Institute of Technology (MIT) | |
|---|---|
| Pros | Cons |
| Establishment of new relationships with key researchers in my field (4) | Will require me to be separated from my husband (5) |
| Opportunity to focus only on research for 18 months without teaching and service responsibilities (5) | Currently going through the tenure process and don't want this to be perceived as lack of commitment to home institution (4) |
| High visibility as a Visiting Scholar at MIT (3) | Don't know anyone within three states of Massachusetts (1) |
| Prestige of National Science Foundation Funding in Professorship (3) | May produce moderate financial strain due to requirement to maintain two households (3) |
| Access to quality equipment, lab, and resources (4) | Daughter is in first year of college and I won't be near her campus (3) |
| Might improve changes of being selected to be an astronaut (2) | Different culture that I'm not at all familiar with given it's a private institution and in the N.E. (2) |
| Add credibility to my reputation (3) | Low levels of diversity in gender and African Americans (2) |
| **Total: 24** | **Total: 20** |

**FIGURE 6.1**    Risk quotient balance sheet example

2. Considering timing and our other priorities

   Timing is a major factor in decision making, and it seems even more important for women when considering family issues such as child bearing, parenting, and consideration of a partner's career. Consider your career management plan, long-term vision, and family plans in the evaluation of the appropriateness of the timing for a decision. For example, in my evaluation of whether or not to go to MIT, if the opportunity had come a year earlier during my daughter's senior year in high school, the timing would have prevented me from accepting the opportunity.

3. Listening to our gut sense (this is the most important aspect of the quotient) or inner voice.

   This evaluation criterion requires us to take time to get in touch with our thoughts, feelings, and emotions about an idea. For this it is best to set aside time to spend alone and in a quiet, comfortable place to focus on the idea and what it means to you. In this time, you should get a sense of what the pursuit of it really means to you on a totally personal level.

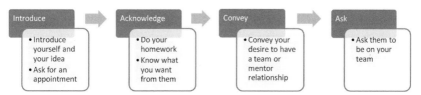

**FIGURE 6.2**    How to approach team members. *Source: Lerner (2006)*

## Step 3: Build and Consult With Your Team (And Make Sure They're Winners!)

Author Laurie Beth Jones profiles Jesus Christ as a visionary leader in the book *Jesus, CEO* [9] and points out that when he began his work in earnest he wasted no time in building his own team. The previous chapters have provided guidance in establishing relationships with individuals who can serve on your personal innovation team. The team will provide the needed guidance, shore up areas where you are weak, and add the array of skills necessary to holistically see your innovations and career developed. This team of risk takers or "innovation encouragers" should be diverse, skilled in their areas of expertise, available to support you, and comfortable enough with you to provide direct honest input. The team may include your mentors, boss, or respected individuals in the area. Often candidates for these roles can be identified in professional societies, at business or technical meetings, and via electronic or social media. Lerner offered an example with a four-step approach to approaching potential team members by introducing yourself, acknowledging what you want from them, conveying your desire to have them on your team or in a mentor relationship, and asking them to join your team (Figure 6.2) [6].

## Step 4: Take the Leap into the Innovation

After you have made the commitment, performed a risk assessment, and consulted with your team, in the words of the famous Nike slogan – it's time to "Just Do It!" At this point it's time to launch and follow through. This following through may be a long-term commitment to see your innovation or personal development needs to support your innovation fully realized. Personality traits that can get in the way of the attainment of your goals include perfectionism, second guessing, procrastinating, and over analyzing. Give yourself a specific timeframe to begin and follow your schedule or career management plan to make sure you're tracking the rate and success of your developmental and innovation activities.

## Step 5: Claim Victory: Anticipate, Expect, and Celebrate Your Courage

If you've made it to step 5 in your process, take a minute to reach over your shoulder and pat yourself on the back! You have done what many people would never do and you're still standing – you may not have fully achieved your goal but you've acted on what you thought was best, given the concept due diligence in evaluation, and taken a step to do something that really matters to you. Lerner suggests two exercises to further claim the victory. The first is to look into a mirror and state your name and the smart risk you've taken followed by what you have achieved or learned. This should be said many times in a loud and affirming voice. The second exercise is to identify a family member, colleague, or professional associate with whom you can "casually" share the fact that you've taken a smart risk, what you've learned, and how it's benefited you. Finally, at the point of celebration, find women's networks to provide continued support and reinforcement as you continue in the path of a risk taker and innovator. Joining organizations such as these will also give you an opportunity to share your risk-taking experiences and encourage other women to do the same.

### Step 6: Don't Stop! Success Breeds Success So Become a Serial Innovator!

As you grow in your use of the risk-taking process, your comfort level and confidence will increase. Continue to maintain innovation goals. This may be a time to broaden your risk taking to consider the evaluation of relationships or whether or not to take on a new community service endeavor. To make sure you keep a fresh history of your innovation successes, consider putting mementos or reminders around each of the six steps in your risk-taking projects. These can be emails you sent to prospective team members, your first (or tenth) rejection letter from a bank, and any number of other factors. The point is to remind yourself that you did it, survived it and are thriving but most importantly "you can do it again."

## An Innovation Process: Moving Your Idea Forward!

Now that we've established a process for *you* to become an innovator, we need to establish the process to see your idea move into an innovation. Once you recognize the need and come up with an idea to solve it, the most time-consuming aspect of innovating will be the process. I've broken down the process into a few steps adapted from Langdon Morris' "How to Innovate: The Innovation Process": [10]

### Step 1: Strategic Thinking

The innovation process begins with the goal to create a strategic advantage in the marketplace. In this stage we think specifically about how innovation is going to add value to our strategic intents and target the areas where innovation has the greatest potential to provide strategic advantage. Some important things to keep in mind during this stage are to think big, and think collaboratively – who would be good to work with to accomplish these ideas? The result is "Idea Creation."

The strategic thinking stage is not just about your current job, but your entire career. Where do you want to make the greatest impact? As a researcher? A teacher? Or more categorically speaking, do you want to make a social impact? Economic impact? What are the things that really matter to you and where can you have the greatest impact?

If there are many categories you find important, start with one and fold the others into it. Establish one to three "ideas" or innovations that you would like to see realized in each category. This becomes your personal "Idea Portfolio" (IP), an organized and descriptive listing of the primary career ideas you plan to pursue. Creating an Idea Portfolio Log (Table 6.1) will assist you in quickly noting ideas that you believe to have potential to be innovations.

The items in your Idea Portfolio Log should be further evaluated and prioritized. Prioritize the items by dividing them into categories based on innovations you feel you *must* do, *should* do for your career, and those that are just good ideas you want to see realized. When prioritizing, take into account your interest level, the resources available, and timing. Exercise some wisdom in understanding from a career, organizational, and marketing standpoint.

## Step 2: Career Management and Metrics

One of the important underlying facts of innovation management is the necessity of failure. We are by definition trying to do something new, and as we proceed on the innovation journey we do not in fact know if we are going to succeed. There will be speed bumps, bruises, and wrong turns. We must have confidence that we'll succeed eventually, and, although many attempts will never come to fruition, the ultimate idea will.

**TABLE 6.1** Idea Portfolio Log

| Date | Name of idea | Description | What need does it meet? | How is the need being met today? | Who would buy it? |
|------|------|------|------|------|------|
|  |  |  |  |  |  |
|  |  |  |  |  |  |
|  |  |  |  |  |  |
|  |  |  |  |  |  |
|  |  |  |  |  |  |

## Establish a Plan for Innovation Career Management

To achieve your visions of leadership, creating a career management plan (Figure 6.3) can be very useful. The elements of this plan should include your goals, vision, resources required, and a tentative schedule.

Using the career management plan from Chapter 4, you can track and plan the execution of topics from your innovation portfolio. Using the career

**My Career Management Plan**

Name: _____  Accountability Partner: _____

Date: _____

| Goal |
|---|
| **Personal Vision Statement** |
|  |

| Short-Term Leadership Goals (1-2 years) | | |
|---|---|---|
| **Area of Focus/Leadership Position** | **Competencies/Skills/Knowledge Needed:** (areas I need to develop) | **Completion Date** |
|  |  |  |
|  |  |  |
|  |  |  |

| Long-Term Leadership Goals (3-5 years) | | |
|---|---|---|
| **Area of Focus/Leadership Position** | **Competencies/Skills/Knowledge Needed:** (areas I need to develop) | **Completion Date** |
|  |  |  |
|  |  |  |
|  |  |  |

| Resources Required | |
|---|---|
| **Short Term** |  |
| **Long Term** |  |

**FIGURE 6.3** My career management plan. *Source:* www.iienet2.org; *Institute for Industrial Engineers.*[11]

management table, create a schedule for you to pursue each item in your idea portfolio. Identify the ideas that are most important for the current stage of your life, so you can get the most of that 5 years, 10 years, or however long you decide to plan for in your Career Management Plan.

As you are constructing your innovation goals, keep in mind the personal development goals created with your comprehensive Career Management Plan. Set a regularly scheduled time-out to focus on your Career Management Plan and IP. Remember, your Career is *your* responsibility. While many of us have been fortunate to have mentors, supportive bosses, and a supportive family, even with all of this, our career is our responsibility and we need to treat it as such. This means having a current vision, understanding what is needed to achieve that vision, and, if I want to be an innovator, giving myself the opportunity to learn how to accomplish these things. Innovation has become such a critical component to STEM careers that I felt I needed to grow within the field by educating myself on this component.

Some of the best advice I ever received from my mentor, Dr Howard G. Adams, was "take four hours per week to work on yourself," and he told me this as I was entering my career as an engineering professor. While I never thought I had more than two weeks out of the year where I actually had a full four hours to devote to this task, I am very mindful of that advice and it has been a source of motivation and encouragement for me over the years. Take the time to put yourself in that environment where you can be creative and envision your plans realized.

## Step 3: Risk Assessment and Research

Perform a Risk Assessment on each of your ideas, taking note of its potential value, potential challenges you may face, who will be impacted, to what degree they will be impacted, the financial implications of a failure, and the short- vs long-term implications of a failure. If the short-term failure is a loss of $5,000 and the realization of the goal means $5 million, it may be worth about a thousand failures!

### What if I fail?

I had a professor who used to say, "Just because you make a great grade on the test, it doesn't mean you're going to get an A in the class; and just because you get an F on a test, it doesn't mean you're going to fail." Failure is not always final, and there's no way your knowledge *won't* be advanced if you are invested in something. Given the likelihood of failure in trying totally new ideas, it is important to weigh the impact of a failure on your ultimate career goal.

So, what if you fail? You will survive! You'll learn! You'll get through it! The more important questions are not "what if's" but something more along the following:

- How will this impact my current position if the plan fails?
- How can I learn or benefit even if the innovative activity fails? (i.e., new relationships, advanced knowledge, etc.)

- Is this innovative activity a 1, 2, or 3 on my list where the rankings mean:
  1. Must do for career and/or personal success
  2. Should do, there are definite benefits to career or personal goals
  3. Would be nice to do, but not clear on the benefits to career or personal goals

After answering those questions, an interesting new question is: What are some potential positive outcomes of failure? For instance, experience from the innovation process and enhanced knowledge? Establishment of new relationships? These are all value added in the career development and innovation culture equation.

If your organization has a culture of innovation it will be understood that failures are part of the process of innovation. If you're risking failure, you're doing your job.

Risk assessment requires research: look deeply at the idea to understand the factors involved, and integrate that into what you have come up with as a proposed solution. However, do not let your assessment become a dissertation – and stall your progress. Research not only why your innovation will add value, but why it is innovative – what gaps will it fill? At this point you can only hypothesize about the impact your idea – turned innovation – will have because it doesn't exist yet! Through research you will be able to master a wide range of unknowns, including emerging areas of research, technologies, societal change, and customer values; and in the process will likely expose significant opportunities for innovation.

## Step 4: Insight

In the course of our explorations, the light bulb occasionally illuminates, and we grasp the very best way to address a future possibility. The innovation and the target are clarified. We begin to understand what the right value proposition is for the target audience. Note that the innovation process described here is not the same as random idea generation; *insight* is the result of a dedicated process of examination and development. It doesn't occur just because someone had a good idea in the shower, but because individuals and teams of people were working collaboratively, constructively, and persistently toward a goal.

## Step 5: Innovation Development

Innovation development is the process of designing, engineering, prototyping, and testing, that results in a finished product, service, and business design. This can also include designing a plan for advancing your career, which may mean obtaining an advanced degree, learning a foreign language, or volunteering for a foreign assignment. Understanding the process of innovation development is essential at this stage. We've looked at the process for innovation development, so being willing to write down the process as part of your strategic plan for your career is important as well.

## Step 6: Market Development

This aspect of the business planning process begins with brand identification and development, and continues through the preparation of customers to understand and choose this innovation. If you are in academia, your market may be funding agencies that you need to impress. Your market will likely include colleagues nationwide and globally who will evaluate your work from a publication standpoint as a peer reviewer, or possibly from a proposal standpoint as a proposal evaluator. This aspect of the business process is essential because it determines how people react to your innovation and how receptive they will be of your brand. Market development continues all the way down to the preparation of customers to help them choose the innovation.

## Step 7: Selling

This is the step where the real payoff is achieved. Now you earn the financial or personal return by successfully selling or implementing the new products, services, or resources. A personal return might be a promotion or the realization of an innovation. Perhaps you've always had a desire to see a women's shelter erected in your neighborhood because you've witnessed homelessness. While you won't be seeing a financial return on your investment, the social impact is substantial and meaningful for you. This is where *passion* becomes really important because you need to use that enthusiasm to sell your product or service and acquire advocates.

## How to Get Advocates for Your Research, Idea, Product, or Service

For an idea to become an innovation, it must "sell" to others. Whether there's an idea I'm trying to convey, or I'm seeking financial support for one of my funding agencies, or trying to communicate on a personal level, the following six steps have done well by me:

1. **Clearly articulated vision for the product, research proposal, or project**
   If you can't clearly state your vision to someone it is unlikely that people will be able to follow.
2. **Enthusiasm and passion**
   We've talked about passion many times throughout this book. You've got to maintain the enthusiasm and passion for your vision, particularly when you get to this point, because you're probably getting tired by now. You may have been working on an idea for 2 years 7 months and 12 days and you've finally decided that it's not going to be successful. While I would encourage you to decide based on your background analysis and understanding, I would also caution you not to give up too quickly because success may come in 2 years 7 months and 14 days.

3. **Knowledge of value of the innovation**
   Clearly explain why your idea is beneficial and how it varies from comparable or competitive ideas.
4. **Knowledge of the subject area**
   Knowing the subject area reduces your innovation process time. If we know our subject area we can quickly assess the state of the market from that perspective. If you have a collaborator who is an expert in the area you are analyzing, that can help short-circuit the innovation cycle and move things along more rapidly.
5. **Acknowledgment of limitations**
   Nobody believes someone who comes to them with an innovation that can do everything, including cut your grass, fix your breakfast, and scratch your back – that's just unlikely. So understanding your limitations becomes a credibility factor.
6. **Understanding and articulation of the impact**
   If you fully understand the impact of your innovation and can communicate that to potential advocates, then you will be better off than someone who hasn't done all the research or can't fully express an understanding for the impact their work will have on the community.

## Protecting Your Innovation

While you may love and trust everybody, you still need to protect your ideas! Write down your idea and make sure it's clear that this is your/your team's innovation. Do preliminary, low-cost documentation initially, and as the idea materializes consider legal guidance in patent or trademark licensing. If you don't have the means to get them to market there's a good chance you'll be sharing your ideas with a larger company or individuals with resources that can afford to help you. If your idea is so unusual that it's patentable, before you show it off you'll want to have that company sign a nondisclosure agreement promising it won't steal your idea. Ideally, you should have an experienced attorney draft the nondisclosure and have it signed prior to your meeting to share your ideas. If you don't have the means to have an attorney draft the document consider identifying nondisclosure templates from trusted legal sources and adapt them for your idea as this will provide documentation should you find yourself in a legal battle over your ideas in the future.

The extension of your idea portfolio log into an "Innovation Notebook" can also provide additional protection for your ideas. This Innovation Notebook should provide additional details about your idea including:

- Detailed description of the idea
- How you came up with the idea
- What does the idea look like in practice?

- How does it work?
- What problem does it solve?
- Potential product names
- Drawing of the idea (even a rudimentary drawing will do)

The further defining of your idea with the steps above provides confidence and additional evidence of the originality of your idea. This activity leads to more protection and reduces the likelihood that your idea will be stolen.

## Make Innovation a Part of Your Everyday Life!

Make innovation a part of your everyday life – it's an exciting way to live! As Steve Jobs once said, "Being the richest man in the cemetery doesn't matter to me… Going to bed at night saying we've done something wonderful…that's what matters to me." [12] According to Maslow's theory of the "hierarchy of basic needs," [13] this sense of fulfillment is extremely important – probably even more important than your salary.

Remember – it's never too late to innovate.

## SUMMARY

As we look forward to understanding the impact of innovation, we should be empowered now that we are equipped with knowledge of how to become innovators on an individual level and how to move our ideas forward. This guidance should be tailored to meet your innovation needs and be useful in clarifying your innovation goals.

An innovation process to move an idea forward is offered that takes the idea from strategic planning to selling the resulting product or service. Likewise, to develop personally as an innovator this chapter proposes Smart Innovation Risk Taking that is accomplished with the six steps below:

- Step 1: Commit to becoming an innovator and select an idea
- Step 2: Calculate the risk
- Step 3: Build and consult with your team (and make sure they're winners!)
- Step 4: Take the leap into the innovation
- Step 5: Claim victory: anticipate, expect, and celebrate your courage
- Step 6: Don't stop! Success breeds success so become a serial innovator!

## CHAPTER RESOURCES

1. Six-Step Process to Become A Risk-Taking Innovator
2. Risk Quotient Balance Sheet
3. Idea Portfolio Log

## REFERENCES

[1] Appelbaum SH, Ayre H, Shapiro BT. Career management in information technology: a case study. Career Development International 2002;7(3):142–58.

[2] Murphy SE, Ensher EA. The role of mentoring support and self-management strategies on reported career outcomes. Journal of Career Development 2001;27(4):229–46.

[3] Orpen C. The effects of organizational and individual career management on career success. International Journal of Manpower 1994;15(1):27–37.

[4] Berkun S. The Myths of Innovation. CA: O'Reilly Media, Sebastopol, CA; 2007.

[5] The Innovation Equation, by Anusha Sthanunathan, Three Minds Digital Marketing. http://threeminds.organic.com/about-threeminds (accessed June 28, 2012).

[6] Lerner H. Smart Women Take Risks: 6 Steps for Conquering your Fears and making the Leap to Success. New York: McGraw-Hill; 2006.

[7] Brzezinski M. Knowing Your Value: Women, Money and Getting What You're Worth; 2010.

[8] Catalyst. The Double-Bind Dilemma for Women in Leadership: Damned if You Do, Doomed if You Don't; 2007. Retrieved January 15, 2012. http://www.catalyst.org/publication/83/the-double-bind-dilemma-for-women-in-leadership-damned-if-you-do-doomed-if-you-dont

[9] Jones LB. Jesus, CEO: Using Ancient Wisdom for Visionary Leadership. New York, NY: Hyperion; 1992.

[10] Morris L. How to Innovate: The Innovation Process. Innovation Management. 2011. www.innovationmanagement.se/2011/09/16/how-to-innovate-the-innovation-process/ (accessed April 2, 2012).

[11] Takeda K, Hlutkowsky R, Sinclair S, Tompkin J, Kilmer K. IIE Annual Conference and Expo 2008 Conference Proceedings. Session: From IE to Management - How You Take Flight; Title: "Succession Planning Strategies, understanding developing IE's". Session participants: Takeda K, Hlutkowsky R, Sinclair S, Tompkin J, Kilmer K. Powerpoint presentations (2008); (accessed February 10, 2012).

[12] Steve Jobs's Best Quotes, Digits, WSJ. The Wall Street Journal. 1993. http://blogs.wsj.com/digits/2011/08/24/steve-jobss-best-quotes/ (accessed April 2, 2012).

[13] Classical Texts in Psychology – A. H. Maslow (1943) A Theory of Human Motivation. http://psychcentral.com/classics/Maslow/motivation.htm (accessed April 2, 2012).

## Chapter 7

# Women Leaders Must Support Each Other

*This is my wish for Women's History Month: That we not just celebrate how far we've come, but realize that we did it **together**, and that we need to **stick together** and continue to bust through that ridiculously cliché glass ceiling.*

**Katie Sluiter**

I remember having an exciting sense of "woman power" when Carleton S. (Carly) Fiorina was named president and chief executive officer of Hewlett-Packard Company in 1999. As an engineering graduate from the University of Oklahoma, I had seen many of my classmates seek and secure careers with this amazing company, and the fact that a woman was now in charge thrilled me and

Transforming your STEM Career through Leadership and Innovation.
http://dx.doi.org/10.1016/B978-0-12-396993-4.00007-2

the members of my professional "sister circle." This Sister Circle is comprised of like-minded women or as one sister calls us "Diverse women." We're diverse in that we focus on multiple factors including careers, family, being there for each other, and supporting other women professionally.

I followed the career of the new CEO and as her difficulties became public I happened to be at a technical conference in my home town, Orlando, Florida. As I entered the lunch event, I hurried to the first available seat that was nearest to the door to get back to my office and get some work done after participating in the meeting. I quickly introduced myself to my luncheon companions and learned one of them was from HP, and she was a woman! I was sure we'd have a great conversation about how exciting it was that she had a powerful, female CEO in this major technical company. I wondered how it had changed things, if the level of innovation was thriving even more, and how it was impacting the corporate culture. Well, the slice of "corporate culture" that I interacted with was woefully disappointing as this HP employee began to openly describe her dissatisfaction with her new CEO; she went on to say how bad "Carly" was as a CEO. I was feeling uncomfortable and almost taking it personally as this HP employee freely lamented about the failings of her new CEO. It is a major mistake to talk like this in public with people you really don't know – not only was it her company and the leadership, but she was talking about the first female CEO of HP! I was trying to respond to everything she said with a deflecting positive comment while making overt efforts to redirect the conversation; however, she continued. My discomfort, irritation, and surprise continued as she persisted in sharing her thoughts of the dismal job Carly was doing – not only was she saying this to me but there was a **table full of men**! I was thinking to myself, "Doesn't she know *we're* not supposed to do this?" "Does she realize what she's doing to herself? To other women? To Carly?" Didn't she read Gail Evans' books?!! I wanted to reach across the table and grab her by the shoulder and then shake her and yell "No matter how bad Carly is – *we* don't talk about her in front of these men!!" That was my "authentic self" of course, but my social self maintained my composure and fortunately we were able to strike up another topic among this lunch crowd and finally move on to another subject.

## WHY DOES IT MATTER?

Referring back to the story of my experience with my luncheon companion who "ran down" Carly Fiorina, my disappointment that this woman didn't seem to realize that what she was doing was "bad" for all women. Research has revealed a persistent stereotyping of women that negatively impacts perceptions of leadership and access to opportunities. These stereotypic beliefs spill over from the popular press, entertaining reality shows, and personal experiences to create perceptions of women as leaders in the workplace. The perceptions pose an invisible and powerful threat to women leaders. Gender stereotypes portray women as lacking the essential qualities that people commonly associate with effective leadership. As a result, they often create false perceptions that women leaders just don't measure up to men in important ways.

As I sat at the table, I realized that everyone had some form of stereotyping that formed their opinion about a woman's ability to lead, particularly in a large technical giant such as HP. The fact that another woman was sitting at the table tearing down the "first female CEO of HP" is powerful fuel that can reinforce any negative stereotypes about women's leadership abilities. That's why it was so "bad."

It was bad for all women because when this happened most of the people at the table were not just hearing that "Carly is a bad CEO" but "Carly, the woman, is a bad CEO." Although women today comprise an increasing proportion of science and engineering majors and middle managers within organizations, there is still a very low percentage of women in the senior level jobs or "C" level jobs (e.g., Chief Technology Officer, Chief Executive Officer). This is particularly true for CEO positions within Fortune 500 companies. In 2011, the percentage of female CEOs in Fortune 500 companies was a mere 2.4%. So we don't have the "luxury" of being classified just as a bad manager, leader, or CEO. We are most likely classified as "bad female manager leader, or CEO." As a result, this can and has inhibited opportunities for other women as they seek the positions.

Additionally, working women need to work together to see changes occur and gain the power to lead. While men have been helpful in some cases when it comes to supporting changes that benefit women, these efforts must be led by a collective group of women. Consider the meeting in 1848, where a group of abolitionist activists were invited by Elizabeth Cady Stanton and Lucretia Mott to Seneca Falls, New York, to discuss the problem of women's rights, or the lack of rights. This group of delegates consisted of a collection of determined women and a few men. Most of the delegates agreed: American women were autonomous individuals who deserved their own political identities and power. It was evident it would not be "given" to them and this movement was designed to create a force or collective group that would take this power. Examples that prove the value of women working together and standing up for each other and change range from the historic suffragette movement to the Lilly Ledbetter Fair Pay Restoration Act signed in 2009 by President Obama. When we support each other and work together it matters.

## No More Cheerleader Mentality

Becoming a cheerleader meant I had to smile broadly, be likeable, yell loudly, and make sure the judges knew I was "better" than at least 60 other girls vying for the 10 spots on the Hayfield High School Freshmen Cheerleading Squad. Since I had recently moved to the area, I had to quickly adapt to the "cool girls" mindset in this Virginia community. There was no such thing as a "team" concern; I wanted to be one of the few, the accepted, the recognized: the cheer-leaders. And, although we had a cheerleading squad, in the 1970s for me, it was about "me" not the team. It was my "Cheerleader Mentality."

Fortunately, I grew out of this mindset and today when I see it in the work-place, aside from being ashamed that I ever had this perspective (even as a teenager), it frustrates me and makes me want to yell "Ready OK"(that's how we started a cheer in the 1970s!) – but that's not all, I want to quickly and more loudly yell "Stop the Madness!"

This is what I wanted to say in 2010 when once again Carly Fiorina was the focus of a conversation regarding how women treat each other. Unfortu-nately, this time she was the perpetrator. The former Hewlett-Packard CEO had just become the Republican nominee for the U.S. Senate in the state of California, and began the primary race facing Democratic incumbent Sena-tor Barbara Boxer. Prior to an interview, although her microphone was off, Fiorina was recorded attacking Boxer like a teenage cheerleader instead of attacking her political record. Fiorina made it personal, unprofessional, and petty, going after the senator's hair. With a mean grin, reminiscent of the "popular girls," Fiorina was recorded smirking and saying "God, what is that hair? Soooo yesterday" [1], again, thinking her microphone was off. The media, women, advocates for women's leadership, and liberal men nationwide responded; emotions ranged from anger to disappointment as well as total shock to indifference. Is it possible that a woman can achieve so much in corporate America, win a party nomination for the U.S. Senate and still be so catty?! I noted the comments of one "liberal man" who said that women dress for women, so from that perspective…Carly's statement is natural. But does this mean it's acceptable? Is it right? And what in the world does it have to do with a U.S. Senate race?! Absolutely nothing. Stop the madness!!!!

Of course, we all have our moments where we find ourselves doing or say-ing things that really are "beneath" the vision and purpose that we should have for our lives. When we find ourselves in these situations, one of the best ways to make a course correction is to use the four simple steps below.

1. Recognize the "error of our thinking, actions, or words."
2. Recognize that destructive words, thinking, and actions can prevent me from attaining the vision; however, this is something that I can control.
3. Make a commitment to stop – immediately. Then stop and don't allow your-self to go back to it.
4. Replace the negative words or thinking with "new" words, thoughts, or actions that are positive, constructive, and consistent with the vision.

With women holding so few key political roles and leadership positions in corporate America, particularly in STEM fields, you would think they would build each other up rather than tear each other down. The Fiorina gaffe and countless others serve as reminders that we still have a long way to go. A 2010 study by the Workplace Bullying Institute found that 35% of the U.S. workforce reported being bullied at work. Among those who mistreat their co-workers, women were more likely to target other women (80%), compared to men who bully other men (46%) [2].

"It's a dirty little secret among women that we don't support one another," said Susan Shapiro Barash, who teaches gender studies at Marymount Manhattan College and is author of *Tripping the Prom Queen: The Truth About Women and Rivalry* [3] and *Toxic Friends: The Antidote for Women Stuck in Complicated Friendships* [4].

Barash believes that because we live in what is still a male-dominated society, women are apt to feel like there's not enough to go around for them, which feeds jealousy and resentment among women, fighting (they believe) for a smaller piece of the pie. "If you're the gender that yields the power, you don't have to feel that way," she said [3].

If we are to build the "team" in the workplace, we have to shed the *cheerleader mentality*. In many environments, being the only woman is a title insecure women don't want to shed. Being the only woman does mean that you get a lot of attention, you've made it, and perhaps you're different (i.e., better) than other women. And yes, you can use this extra attention to your benefit, but is that all you want, to stand out because of your gender? A woman who is content with being the "only woman" is not just limiting herself but is propagating the concept that women in positions of power are the exception rather than the rule.

## We're on the Same Team

When Gail Evans, one of the most senior executives of CNN, was asked if women need teams to enhance their power, she said "My solution to this is that we need to help each other. The idea is that I care about your success, that your success matters to me, that I understand the connection between your success and mine." [5] In her book, *She Wins, You Win*, Evans says that it is not enough that women understand and play by the rules that men "wrote," they must learn to create and follow their own rules. She writes, "…we are constantly being forced to second-guess ourselves, even when we decide to follow all the male rules. We are always expected to jump through hoops without understanding why. That's because our way isn't the expected way. The female psyche is not the role model for the business psyche; the male's is. …We need to know the male rules of business. But we must create and play by our own rules. **We should be talking to each other; we should be planning with each other;** we should be working to improve the situation for everyone of us, not for just one of us. We should launch a new strategy to advance our careers as a whole rather than advance our own careers at the expense of other women." [5]

## Do You "Want" to Join the Team?

Many women do not necessarily want to be identified as a member of the team as they relate such actions to reasons ranging from a belief that it will damage their careers to the mindset that it's not necessary and quite frankly a waste of time. If you're somewhere along this continuum I challenge you to reconsider your position and ask yourself if you are letting fear be the barrier to your willingness to be on the team. Evans outlines common fears and the associated realities that women impact women's interest in joining the team [5]. I have adapted these "fears" to be inclusive of additional issues (fears) among women from ethnically different backgrounds.

*Fear #1:* If you join that women's organization in your company, you'll be seen as an old-fashioned feminista.

*Reality #1:* Feminist isn't an ugly word or a bad word. Women have allowed men, religion, and society to define too many words for us and when we're not engaged in the establishment of a definition we lose. Consider the term aggressive – when used to describe a man it's a favorable connotation, and on the contrary when it's used to describe a woman it's almost exclusively a negative characterization. According to Webster's dictionary, feminism is the concept that women should have political, economic, and social rights equal to those of men. Feminism is a good word. It's about doing what's right and fair. Period.

*Fear #2:* By joining the women's team, you will have to sacrifice your individuality.

*Reality #2:* As women we like to see ourselves as unique, interesting, and unusual and these qualities make us attractive as individuals to our partners and society. They do not lead to a strong team spirit. Each member brings a unique talent to the team that should be appreciated, utilized, and engaged as necessary for the benefit of the team.

*Fear #3:* The idea of being on a team scares you.

*Reality #3*: Maybe you're a former "cheerleader," or the idea of a man's definition for team is what's concerning you. The male teams are generally characterized by a tough leader who commands through strict rules no individuality or shifting situations as this is believed to be what's necessary to win. I love the stories my husband Michael shares about his days of football at Alabama State University where he was captain of the team in his senior year. I have laughed for years at his recounting of various times on the football team, including Coach Scott's insistence on running the same play (of course, I always assume it was working) in a game. When he tells the story, he changes his voice to mock his revered Coach Scott. Coach would stand close to the team, have them gather around and state with total coolness and clarity "We're going to run the same damn play." And run the same damn play they did!

This mindset can be difficult for women as we're constantly adapting, adjusting, and revising to accommodate the dynamic nature of our professional and personal lives. The good news is our women's teams do the same things. While our objective (and focus) is clearly to win, we're also interested in understanding the importance of "our win."

The bottom line about teams is this – you're on the team anyway. Whether you believe it or not, there are people in the organization and society that have "put" you on the team. For "Women of Color," you're on a second team. It's the African American, Hispanic/Latino, Asian, or Native American Team! In some cases, we even get to choose a couple of these teams! Yes, it's true. You've been "teamed" up by society, your company, and the world. The smart thing for us to do is to recognize where we are, know the team can be good for us, and learn how to be a good team member. This means understanding what it means for the team to win and recognizing that when the team wins we all win.

*Fear #4:* If women spend our time working for and thinking about other women we will become ghettoized and marginalized.

*Reality #4:* Being on the team is not about limiting our opportunities, but about creating force in numbers to jointly increase access, opportunities, and recognition of our strengths. Evans tells a story of how she created a daytime show while at CNN that would allow women to discuss significant issues of the day from politics to education and of course women-specific issues. Much to her surprise, most of the men loved the show and gave it a green light but many of the women began to panic as they feared this type of show would remove women from the main discussions and "lock them into a half hour program." [5] Evans argued that the show would not do that and instead would increase the profile of the women and position them to appear in other venues once the industry saw them showcased as articulate, smart women in this format. Despite resistance, the show proceeded, was a success, and in no way marginalized or ghettoized the women. Many of these women went on to become media stars as a result of their participation in this program.

*Fear #5:* There isn't enough time to do our work and join the team.

*Reality #5:* Women often don't go out with co-workers to have a cocktail after work because there's so much work at the office and then even more work at home. But women must do this – not necessarily drink – but socialize with co-workers outside of the office. Maybe if it doesn't work for you to do it after work, you can try lunch, afternoon coffee, or walking together to the next meeting in a nearby facility. This time together builds the types of relationships that build trust, enhance confidence in your abilities, and become the pathway to new opportunities within your company. It also allows your colleagues to see you in a different light and gain insight into your strengths.

I recall my first few years as an assistant professor seeking tenure, at the University of Central Florida, while raising my high school daughter, focusing on being a wife and adjusting to a new community. If it had not been for the wisdom and guidance of an insightful and supportive boss, Dr William Swart, I too may have thought this type of socializing wasn't necessary or work. At least three times a week, he'd call his three new, nervous female assistant professors to his office for coffee to see "how we were doing." He also encouraged us to spend time together and collaborate, and as a result we became the best of friends and all felt we had someone there who understood us. While we all didn't go out with the guys for a drink, when one of us did, we shared it with the others and this kept us all in the loop. We quickly learned, as Evans points out, "this type of socializing is a completely legitimate form of work." [5]

*Fear #6:* If you build relationships with other women, hoping that you will profit from them some day, you are being manipulative.

*Reality #6:* As women we don't mind talking with other women about daycare, the best gynecologist or hair stylist, or the best place for a designer pair of shoes. So why do we stop using our outstanding relationship and networking skills when it comes to something so important as our careers? We get information about all types of things all the time from our networks, except at work, where we back down because we think we're supposed to make it on our own in this environment. That is just not the way we need to think – that's not the way it is ladies.

*Fear #7:* For women of color – if I join the women's team (translation – white women's team) they (my people) will feel like I'm "selling out" to the race.

*Reality:* You are already on both teams. Whether you accept it or not, you are viewed as a *woman* and a *woman of color*. Notice, I did not say a "person of color" but a "woman of color." There is no escaping this reality and it is in our best interest to support both teams. I recall having this very dilemma when I was a graduate student, and an African American businessman, whom I trusted greatly, advised me against "signing up to be with the white girls." He said the issues they have are not your issues. I trusted his opinion greatly but even as a young graduate student I thought – how does *he* know? He's an African American man – not a woman. I think the fear that some men of color have about this is that they believe our efforts to support the women's team will minimize the importance of our ethnic causes – despite the fact that in many of these organizations we are not given equal access to leadership opportunities. To this I say – relax guys. We are on both teams and we can support both of them.

## Being on the Team

Now that you're on the team, it's time to understand the rules and how we play the game to win. Although we will each tailor our teams and specific rules to meet the overall success of individuals in our organization, Evans suggests seven "tips" for each team member (Figure 7.1) in order to advance the team.

Evans adds additional insight into each tip as follows.

### Be a Mentor

*Mentoring isn't a discussion, it's an obligation.*

*Gail Evans*

**FIGURE 7.1**   Team tips for women working together. *Source: Evans (2003)*

A common obstacle for women leaders is the difficulty in obtaining mentors and access to informal networks of advice, contacts, and support. In surveys of upper-level management, between a third to a half of women cite the lack of influential mentors as a major barrier to advancement [6]. Of course, you're busy in your new position and may not think you have time, but this is something that you must focus on now or in the near future if you are going to build the team. Additionally, the importance of mentoring is clear for the mentee but also brings value to the mentor as studies have shown that the rewards run in both directions. "Quite apart from the satisfaction that comes from assisting those who need assistance, senior colleagues may receive more tangible benefits from the loyalty and influence that their efforts secure. Talented junior colleagues generally want to work for effective mentors and to support them in seeking and exercising leadership." [6]

### Be a Rainmaker

Rainmaking is about creating business opportunities for other women. We should actively (and first) consider women when we need to hire someone. This includes hiring women for small, medium, and large projects in our organizations, in our home, and in organizations that we belong to in the community. Rainmaking means taking time to consider who you currently have on your organizational and personal team. Have you considered hiring a woman as your attorney, accountant, chiropractor, home builder, and any other service? To be effective rainmakers, we must get beyond the typical areas, suggested the author in *The Difference "Difference" Makes*, edited by Deborah Rhode. We must move beyond traditional fields that we're accustomed to identifying women for, such as obstetrics, personal services, and child care, and open the door for women to gain access to other areas of opportunity in our world [7].

## Uncover and Share Information

It's not enough to be an expert in your area alone. As we progress to higher levels of leadership we must have a broader understanding of areas outside of our departments, technical areas, and organization. Leaders and innovators require a sphere of knowledge, although you don't have to be an expert in other areas. The level of confidence in you will increase when you're able to converse about other areas outside of your expertise. To do this in an organization means you will need to establish relationships with women outside of your department and agree to the need and willingness to share information. Talk about work when you're together, mix personal and business conversations, and most importantly ask questions. This also means that you should share information and recognize that it's being shared for a purpose, so don't share anything that should be kept confidential.

Get comfortable talking to women in other business settings, while traveling on public transportation to the office, and even on airplanes. Some of the nicest flights I've ever had were when I engaged in conversation with people on the flight. Although we're often so glad to sit down and turn on our music or DVD, flying can be a great way to establish new business relationships. I recall a long flight from Boston to Orlando when I was commuting from MIT to home. This flight led to a delightful conversation, continued communication, and a concept for a new book. Seated next to me was a pleasant woman who appeared to be close to my age and as I sat down we exchanged pleasantries – that seemed almost like greetings from real friends. In the course of the flight, I learned that she was a photographer and lived not far from me in Florida. When we talked about my writing goals we quickly moved to discussing how we might collaborate in a photograph and motivational project. We drafted out a concept on our notebooks and added areas for further evaluation once we were at our computers on the ground. After additional dialog our concept for a book of photos that captures the similarities, fears, ambitions, dreams, and hopes of women worldwide was born. We will travel to at least 10 countries and Katherine will capture candid photographs of women. We will talk to them and I will capture the "essence" and universal meaning and impact of the situation such that women worldwide can appreciate and to some degree "experience" the environment. The objective is to connect women globally and encourage us to value each other, our communities, and our passions as we move women forward worldwide. We agreed we would donate the proceeds to a woman's organization once we find a publisher smart enough to see the value of this concept. As of today, we've written the concept paper and plan to submit it to a publisher under the title "The Universal Language of Womanhood." We are hopeful that we will identify a publisher and sponsor for what we believe is a powerful concept to show women worldwide that we share so much in common and together we can make a difference.

## Keep Quiet – Don't Talk About Other Women!

We have discussed this issue in the opening of the chapter, but it bears repeating. When it comes to business information, share as much as possible, but we need to keep our mouths shout when it comes to talking to men about other women, especially within our organization. As the Catalyst studies have demonstrated, women are not only working to achieve the same goals as men, but are additionally fighting against negative stereotypes. Perhaps you think with female CEOs at giants such as Xerox (Ursula Burns) and IBM (Virginia "Ginni" Rommety) that this rally is no longer a factor in corporate America. You are absolutely wrong if this is what you believe. Even in 2012, when a woman in business speaks about another woman, she is giving validity and power to any negatives that have been spoken about that woman. As a result, the detrimental stereotypes are perpetuated and reinforced.

## Unite with All Women at All Times

Some of the most powerful, knowledgeable, and respected women in an organization are the assistants, secretaries, and associates. Everything you do affects other women; playing on the women's team doesn't mean playing just with the women at your level or levels that you aspire to reach. Almost every woman will experience some of the workplace issues we've discussed, from the cleaning staff to the senior executive offices.

Gloria Steinman's story of how female faculty were not being promoted at a university illustrates the power of team tips. The female faculty members at this university were frustrated at the lack of promotion for women to the rank of full professor. The female faculty came together to express their concern in committee meetings, a strike, and a task force, all to no avail. Nothing changed. Until, that is, one day a female professor described this situation to her secretary, who sympathized deeply with her. But she didn't stop at sympathy. The secretaries went on strike to support the female professors. Shortly after this, the male power structure gave in and a commitment was made for tenured and promotion opportunities for female faculty [5]. Understanding the impact we can have on others and how we can prevent injustices should be a powerful motivator for each of us. I recall in the early days when I was seeking tenure, I would often be in my office until the late hours of the night working on publications, proposals, and class preparation. I welcomed the gentle knock on my door from a pleasant and always cheerful Jamaican cleaning lady. Over the months and years, we began to chat and she always asked how I was doing on my "work." It was almost as if she had a sense of pride that a woman, and a woman who was also her color, had one of the offices in the professors' row. I would offer her a Diet Coke (which she never accepted) and we'd chat briefly. One evening when she came in, her cheerful disposition was absent as she shared with me that she was expecting to be terminated. Her story was that the new supervisor did not like her and wanted to hire his "friends" so he stated that she wasn't doing her job. She fought back the tears as she prepared to exit my office. I quickly stood up, dismayed at the thought that I wouldn't see her pleasant face again, and calming my "fighting" instinct that was already in solution mode. "Sit down," I said. "How can they say you're not doing your work?" "This just doesn't seem fair." She shared that the supervisor's boss really didn't care about people at her level and she was sure she would be fired. Again, in solution mode – I simply could not accept this – I told her I wanted to help. She looked totally shocked. I told her to "relax" as I was confident we could work through this together. Truth is, I had no idea how we were going to do this but I recognized injustice and knew I wasn't going to sit by and do nothing. I told her to stop by my office the next night to pick up a letter that I'd have ready for her. I crafted a letter of support on my university letterhead offering my knowledge of the long history of high quality of work I had witnessed in this woman. I was on travel for several weeks but upon my return I was working late and I heard an eager knock on my door. As I opened the door, she embraced me and the tears began to flow. "They didn't fire me!" she said through the sobs. She said her supervisor's boss got the letter and the only thing they asked is "How do you know this woman?" "How do you know a professor?" "Why would she write a letter for you?" She said she told them, she is my friend. She is my "sister." This small gesture on my part meant more than I could begin to imagine to this woman and her family. It was my pleasure to help her and we must be willing to support all women as injustice exists at all levels of the work environment. Needless to say, I had the cleanest office in the building throughout her time at the university and my success in being a professor clearly impacted this woman's life.

## Make Team-Related Choices

When we're on a team, we're not only looking out for ourselves. It's about the team, and if the team is good we should all benefit. This is not to suggest that we put aside our personal ambitions (or that I think others will) for each other. We should all be working toward our vision and purpose, with a strategic approach that promotes other women while building the power of the team. The point is there will be times when a decision has to be made about how the team or women will speak on behalf of other women. For example, when the Provost is looking for an interim Dean for the College of Engineering, I quickly poll the female faculty to see who "we" can nominate. Of course, if there is more than one woman that wants this opportunity, and if we want to come to the Provost as a united block of female faculty, it will be more powerful for all of us to present the female candidate to him. Every team member should at some point be "the woman" that the team is advocating to the leadership. If not, and you're finding that you or other women are not being supported at the level necessary, then it's time to reevaluate the team focus and strategy.

## Weave a Female Opportunity Web

Finally, it's important to weave a female web of women and men in your professional, personal, and social environments. This will be accomplished though networking, connecting with everyone you meet, being prepared to interact, and utilizing technology, social media, and Internet communication.

## Seek the Support of Other Women

*Fuse with incredible women to attain the impossible.*

*Vicki L. Malazzo*

As I sat in the beautiful meeting room as a member of the International Committee on Critical Infrastructure, I was admiring the Italian sculpture. I was enjoying the presence of the art, appreciating the details and the presence of beautiful art in this university in Milan, Italy. This was a far cry from any American University auditorium. My art appreciation or mental break from the speaker's comments was interrupted as I was approached by the committee chair, Dr Elias Kravis. Elias asked me to facilitate a session as the original facilitator had an emergency and was required to leave for his home country. He shared that it was a topic similar to my research and, as a new member of the committee, he thought I could use the visibility. Visibility – something men instantly recognize as important. Being one of only three women and the only person of African descent, it quickly crossed my mind that they could already see me! But within milliseconds, I realized what he was really saying. The committee needed to see me as a "peer" with knowledge, expertise, and the ability to communicate with them as a leader; standing in front of them facilitating a technical session. Yes, I got it, and quickly accepted the invitation. This may be much more than he was attempting to say, but I heard him. I heard him, and I was appreciative of the confidence from Elias and the opportunity to have a more active role in the meeting, engage in more detail with the other researchers, and increase my visibility.

After the session, I reflected on my path to serving as the U.S. representative on an international research-based committee. The interaction with, and support of, a single woman, Dr Michaela Album from Polytechnic University in Romania, had resulted in election to this committee providing interaction with engineers and scientists from Europe, Asia, and Africa. Seeking the support of women can be valuable and lead to faster results, particularly when we don't have to prove ourselves and prove that we're worthy of their support. As we grow in our career, we will need to have the support of senior and junior women within and outside of our organizations.

Author and entrepreneur Vicki L. Milazzo describes "female fusion" as the bond that occurs when women come together and share their passions, visions, experiences, fears, and promises. This bond leads to the emergence of a brilliance and insight that none of these women alone could have inspired [8]. This can lead to empowering supportive relationships in the professional and personal environments. According to a research study by UCLA [7], the type of bonding that comes from female fusion benefits is good for our professional, emotional, and physical well-being. This is not a social or networking activity but interaction specifically aimed at improving a woman's life. Thus, every woman in the group must have a goal to improve an aspect of her life. The format for this female fusion is not rigid but does have some structure. The guidance for a female fusion event includes the following:

- Keep it simple
- Three or more women (10 maximum)
- Two to four hours of uninterrupted time for the first Female Fusion
- A goal for the Fusion (i.e., establishment of a revised career vision)
- Creation of a safe environment by agreeing on the following:
  1. How to offer advice. Only when asked for? Or openly and freely?
  2. A confidentiality agreement. An informal agreement or simple document that every woman signs.

The truth of the matter is that many women would eagerly welcome an invitation for a Female Fusion event given the documented loneliness that many women experience as they acquire leadership positions and career distinction. The fusion exercises include your most audacious desire (Figure 7.2), your personal promises and the fusion circle, all designed to bring out the strengths, affirm, and move the women forward.

### Recognize That Your Leadership Role Can Impact Other Women

Women leaders should have an active role in demonstrating support for other women and showing that other women support us. Just as a woman leader has the right to expect support from her cause or organization, she has a duty to offer support to other women leaders, both established and aspiring. Mutual respect and understanding of the difficulties each one faces should form the basis of this support. In her book *The Difference "Difference" Makes*, Muzette Hill states very eloquently, "That's when difference makes a difference. When every 'first' makes it her business to guarantee that there will be a second. When we use our success, leadership and influence to support each other to affect change both inside and outside our organizations so that the definition of leadership is enlarged to embrace all of us – that's when difference makes a difference." [7]

Imagine someone you care about – your mother, daughter, niece, sister, or best friend – being in a leadership position. How would you like the world to view her and respond to her role? Would you like her to be viewed as an exception to the rule? Or for them to believe that women still are only entitled to a limited role to play in the leadership process? Or instead would you like for them to think of her as an individual who, through her leadership skills,

*Exercise 1: Your Most Audacious Desire*

*In this exercise, it's a good idea for the woman who brought all the others together to go first, because she will probably feel most comfortable.*

*Disclose secret wish, something very few people know. Start this disclosure with the word that most defines your wish, selected from the following list:*

| | | |
|---|---|---|
| • **Love** | • **Fun** | • **Respect** |
| • **Health** | • **Power** | • **Knowledge** |
| • **Peace** | • **Ecstasy** | • **Excitement** |
| • **Wealth** | • **Justice** | • **Fame** |

*The woman speaking describes her wish and a personal experience that simulated her wish.*

*She takes a **full five minutes,** using vivid detail. Speaking for five minutes is critical for the woman to go deep. While she's talking, everyone else jots down one of the 10 strengths that can help her attain her wish.*

*When she's finished, everyone in turn affirms her audacious desire.*

*After each woman has presented her positive comments with speaker, she takes an additional minute to respond to what she has heard.*

**FIGURE 7.2**   Fusion exercise #1. *Source: Milazzo, V.L. (2011) p. 303 [8]*

can make positive contributions? Don't you think that her success should be applauded because she is a good leader by herself and not because she is efficient despite being a woman?

## Create Opportunities for Other Women

Bring other women forward – they are your future network and support. You overcame the many barriers you faced to be where you are now. Don't forget those who helped you along the way. Now it's your turn to help others. Turn the obstacles you faced into opportunities for those following your footsteps. Set examples and create precedents to help other women on the road to leadership. If you stretch out a hand to help another woman cross the hurdle you are creating a chain, because then she can help others behind her. This is the chain of leadership! The strength of this chain depends on how you use your position to create opportunities for other women – not just in other spheres, but within your own organization. There is a tendency to look on other leaders of the same cause as competition. This is true to some extent.

However, in the case of women leaders, there is another far more important side to this picture. The greater the number of women leaders, the greater the number of women who will be their support systems. The greater the number of women leaders, the less the issue that you are a "woman" leader becomes, allowing you to focus more on your leadership.

Identify your areas of influence/control and see if you can create an opportunity for at least one woman within the next six months. This could be a leadership opportunity on a project, a nomination for an award, or participation on your project team. You might recommend someone for a promotion or project.

Dr Mary Juhas, Associate Professor and Associate Dean of Engineering at Ohio State University, is a person who wakes up thinking about how she can help other women. As a PhD in Engineering there haven't been many women in her field of study, but she supports junior faculty members, female faculty throughout the nation, and students in any way she can. She is so passionate about this that she accepted a prestigious rotation as a Program Director in the Engineering Directorate at the National Science Foundation. That leadership position allowed her to create a concept for the programs that will make a difference for women, such as the project she conceived known as the Women's International Research and Engineering Summit (WIRES). WIRES is about helping women in engineering academic positions go to "next levels" and become a part of the global community. WIRES has resulted in an international impact on women in STEM careers. The tangible outcomes include increased confidence in women to pursue these now necessary international collaborations for career success, multiple research projects funded by the U.S. and other countries, scores of scientific publications, and enduring research collaborations among engineering women worldwide. This is a simple but powerful example of one woman using her passion to create opportunities for other women. She did this with a plan, strategy, and team focus and in doing so positioned herself as a team member who not only benefited other women but built a powerful "international bridge" for other women to cross.

Although we can't all give hundreds of thousands of dollars to support women's research, we can find a project for a junior female to lead, or we can take a page from Dr Juhas' "philosophical book" and do something such as nominating a woman for an award, recommending a female colleague for a leadership position, or supporting each other for promotions or projects. In essence, we must establish a mindset where we are automatically thinking of ways to create opportunities for one another and thinking about how we can enhance one another's reputations and value each other. We can start doing this within our circle of supporters, collaborators, and friends and then let the "ripple effect" take place. It will spread.

*There is a special place in hell for women who do not help other women.*

*Madeline Albright*

I love the quote by former Secretary of State, Madeline Albright, "There is a special place in hell for women who do not help other women." Ideally, "helping each other" means creating opportunities, mentoring, and developing. It is also important to recognize when helping a woman means "helping her understand" that she may not be ready for an opportunity. It is important to handle these situations so that it becomes a developmental experience rather than a detrimental one. As you share your perspectives regarding her suitability to seek an opportunity, if you don't feel she's ready, be sure to propose developmental activities that can help her establish the needed skills, credibility, or relationships. To the degree possible, offer to be a part of her developmental plan as this will increase the likelihood that she understands you are in fact helping her, despite the fact that the perspective you have doesn't move her to where she desires today.

## Establish a Diverse Circle of Women Supporters

Diversity in gender, nationality, culture, and perspectives is not just a good idea, it really makes a difference in the creative activities of a team and an organization. It's important that all women, particularly women of color, understand the importance of this principle. Establish a diverse circle of female supporters, and enhance the quality of your leadership and innovation by broadening your inner circle and increasing the audience that recognizes your capabilities. Include women of different disciplines, careers, race, culture, ethnicity, religion, and leadership styles. Interacting with diverse individuals will require you to learn about different cultures and therefore add to your knowledge base regarding interaction with different cultures. This can raise your value as a leader, help you develop a style that allows a circle of support that is representative of the individuals you want to lead, and help you gain an appreciation of the uniqueness that all will bring to the team.

## Test your Commitment to the Team!

To give us an idea of how we are doing in the support of women, I have developed a quiz to assess ourselves (Figure 7.3). To rate your level of "commitment to the team" answer the following questions using a scale from 1 (not at all describes me) to 5 (describes my behavior extremely well).

If you scored an A or a B – congratulations!!! We need more women operating like this on the team. However, my education and experience leads me to believe that over half of the women who take this test will score in the failing category. That's largely the reason we are where we are today. The good news is

1. I have formally or informally mentored, coached, or advised at least one woman in the last year (this can be in your organization or professional community).

2. I am a paid member of at least one organization designed to support the advancement of women in my professional community.

3. I actively seek opportunities for women who are junior to me in the organization or community.

4. I believe women working together in the workplace can make a difference for all women.

5. I do not openly criticize my female colleagues at work or in social settings.

6. I would welcome a female CEO in my organization.

7. I have had favorable relationships with female leaders and mentors.

8. People would describe me as someone who makes a difference for women.

9. I have had younger women come to me for guidance in the workplace or community regarding gender issues they face in work, education, or the community.

10. I actively look for ways to advance the causes of women in my organization, professional society, and the community.

Sum your score for your 10 responses.
**Scoring interpretation (standard academic scale):**

| Score | Grade | |
|---|---|---|
| 46 – 50 | A | |
| 41 – 45 | B | |
| 36 – 40 | C | |
| 30 – 35 | D | |
| less than 30 | F – Sister, you are failing! | |

**FIGURE 7.3**   Commitment to the woman team quiz.

that we can learn. We can learn to be better team members, increase our score, and make a positive impact on the team. I encourage you to begin today.

## SUMMARY

It is imperative that we realize the importance of our unity. Together we all succeed. Make the decision to commit to the success of other women today. Often we are so focused on the equation, technology, innovation, academic proposal, or generating publications. While those are the universal metrics – the number of innovations created, the research funding, the material reward – it is equally important for us to understand the more abstract fruits of our daily labors. This is where our vision includes not just our personal vision but the collective success of our peers. We really need to commit to the success of other women. Find one woman in your world that you can support this year and really make a difference in her career. If you're in a position to recognize a woman or to promote her, make an effort to create opportunities and do that which is in your power to see another woman succeed.

The perspective on the importance of "women supporting each other" varies greatly even among women in technical fields reading Cate Sevilla's account of her experience in a panel discussion for Oxford University's Oxford Women in Politics group, titled "Are Women in Tech Their Our own Worst Enemies?" [9] While Sevilla was expecting the group to be "like-minded" in her perspective that women not supporting each other was one of the greatest professional challenges we face, she was abruptly shown that some of her fellow panel members shared different perspectives. Comments included:

*"Well, maybe it's a good thing if women don't always open doors for other women. You know, you have to work harder," one woman said.*

*"Maybe it's better if everyone doesn't share their contacts. It makes you find them out for yourself," another suggested with raised eyebrow.*

*We shouldn't be perpetuating the stereotype that women are catty to each other... If there is friction between women in business, surely it's just symptomatic of the system. The system is the problem.*

Based on the comments from the panel discussion, the perspectives on whether or not women "generally" support each other vary greatly. The responses to this topic brought to mind some of the conversations I've had with other women about this issue. Obviously, many women have had positive working relationships with female superiors and colleagues. Likewise, there is an equally loud group of women that can give multiple accounts of negative experiences with female bosses, colleagues, and even subordinates.

So the three issues that we have to pose this question to include:

1. Does it matter (to the corporation, society, women) if women support each other?
2. Do we need to support other women for them to be successful (should we let them tough it out and will this make them better)?
3. Are we currently supporting each other (what's the real deal of how we treat each other at work today)?

The literature, scientific research, society, and the current status of women globally provide objective evidence that our answers to these questions do matter. There is a direct relationship between women work-ing together and positive outcomes for the team. My response to questions 1, 2, and 3 are: Yes, Yes, and Yes. It matters and we need to do more to work with and support other women, particularly in male-dominated fields such as STEM. Support other women in their quest to become leaders, recognize the collective value we bring, and join the team, and together we all win.

## CHAPTER RESOURCES

1. Tips for the Team (by Gail Evans)
2. Commitment to the Women's Team Quiz

## REFERENCES

[1] ABC News.com. http://abcnews.go.com/Politics/video/carly-fiorina-mocks-barbara-boxers-hair-10874207. Accessed: August 13, 2012.

[2] Workplace Bullying Institute 2010 Survey. http://www.workplacebullying.org/wbiresearch/2010-wbi-national-survey/.

[3] Barash SS. Tripping the Prom Queen: The Truth about Women and Rivalry. New York, NY: St. Martin's Press; 2006.

[4] Barash SS. Toxic Friends: The Antidote for Women Stuck in Complicated Friendships. New York, NY: St. Martin's Press; 2009.

[5] Evans G. She Wins, You Win: The Most Important Rule Every Businesswoman Needs to Know. New York, NY: Gotham Books; 2003.

[6] Catalyst. Women in Corporate Leadership: Progress and Prospects. Catalyst; 1996.

[7] Rhode DL, editor. The Difference "Difference" Makes: Women and Leadership. Palo Alto, CA: Stanford University Press; 2003.

[8] Milazzo VL. Wicked Success is Inside Every Woman. Hoboken, NJ: John Wiley & Sons; 2011.

[9] Sevilla, C. Do Women Really Need to Help Out Other women, Computerweekly.com, November 2009. www.computerweekly.com/blogs/witsend/2009/11/do-women-really-need-to-help-out-other-women.html (accessed June 29, 2012).

## Chapter 8

# Winners Don't Quit: A Plan for Sustained Leadership and Innovation

*Never give up, for that is just the place and time that the tide will turn.*

*Harriet Beecher Stowe*

The essence of this chapter is to bring together all the lessons we've learned thus far throughout the book to create a workable plan for the management of your career and the attainment of your innovation goals. We know what leadership is, we know what innovation is, and hopefully you've taken some time to learn about your field and discover some opportunities for yourself. Now it's time to take what we've been theorizing about and apply some skills to our lives. Don't ask for permission, don't wait for someone to offer, don't even wait until the timing is perfect – make your move NOW! You may not be able to get everything done today, but you need to get started today.

I've never known a person who consistently applied these steps and principles and did not ultimately achieve her goal, or come very close to it. In most cases, the application of these simple guidelines on a consistent basis will lead to you actually exceeding your goal. My life is certainly an example of this occurring. My original goal was to get my BS in engineering, own a BMW, and raise my daughter. I always share with young people that I didn't even

Transforming your STEM Career through Leadership and Innovation.
http://dx.doi.org/10.1016/B978-0-12-396993-4.00008-4

know what the initials PhD meant – when Dr Howard Adams told me I should consider this as my ultimate academic goal. I applied these simple steps I'm sharing here and the result was exceeding the goals I'd set for myself. The reasons are many, including the new-found vision I had, each small success causing me encouragement, my increased knowledge and confidence, and, last, but certainly not least, the many people eager to support me in attaining those goals.

There will be times when things we can't control are preventing or delaying the attainment of our goal. But please, don't let this be a reason to let go of your dreams, vision, and goals. Maybe you are not in the right "season" for the attainment of these goals, but that doesn't mean that in six months or maybe six years you can't overcome that barrier, or that other resources won't be in place to help. Ask yourself if the plan you've come up with for yourself is right for the season of your life and if it is manageable. Have you considered all of your resources? Are you allowing other things to "crowd" out the time, commitment, and resources needed to attain your goals?

There comes a time when we must each ask ourselves: what are we doing that is unrelated to the attainment of our goals and how is that impacting our quest? Often it is a sense of obligation or something that impacts our sense of identity – maybe you see yourself as a wife and homemaker first. Maybe you felt obligated to join a book club your friend started because you wanted to support her, but your support is no longer needed. It's okay to say no. In fact, it's healthy. Be *honest* with yourself. Sit down and talk with someone if you are really having problems doing what you want and make sure you are not the one getting in the way of your own goals.

The previous chapters have shared the importance on a national and global level of our willingness to engage in leadership and innovation in the realization of our greatest dreams. The impact as well as personal satisfaction that comes from realizing your vision has also been discussed. Then we shared some of the challenges, obstacles, and resistance that we may face in pursuit of these goals from a cultural, personal, and organizational level.

The bottom line is this: we are fully capable of moving our dreams, visions, and most awesome ambitions into the passionate life we want to live. Yes, as sure as you are reading the pages of this book – you *can* live your dream (see Figure 8.1). The question then becomes, will we do what we need to do in order to see it realized? The obvious answer is yes, but this decision must be made and recommitted to throughout the process, in the toughest times and most difficult times, and sometimes on a daily basis. We must be committed enough to get back up when we're knocked down and when everyone in our world is saying that we can't do it. It's those times when the strength of our commitment to our visions is tested. Pass the test. The rewards are great when we pass the test. Remember you are a winner – winners may fall back for a time, fall down, adapt the plan, regroup, or even stop to rest for a moment. But we always get back up because winners will not take no for an answer. Winners Don't Quit.

**FIGURE 8.1**  Living your dream. Source: Pamela McCauley Bush

## MAKE THE DECISION

It is time to move beyond the beautiful dream and grand vision that rests in your mind. The dream must move to the decision stage in order for you to start doing rather than dreaming. The three primary focus areas you will need to consider in the decision include your career vision, your personal vision (family life), and the organization, company, or professional environment in which you expect to attain your goals. If we fail to consider any of these areas in our decision making, we will likely not have a comprehensive picture of the major factors impacting the outcome of our goals. In Chapter 3 we discussed the reasons more women do not lead or innovate, and these factors should be considered as you make your decisions as it will help you understand the cultural, individual, and organizational factors regarding your situation. In Chapter 5, we discussed a plan to develop the leader in you with a career management plan and strategies to manage adversity. At this point, the research (or process to do the research) has been provided for you to gain the insight you need to make a good decision. There is, however, one area that bears discussing with respect to the relationship between you and your organization. Oftentimes, we will have a "relationship" with our organization, as described by Weaver and Hill in the book *Smart Women, Smart Moves* [1], that is not conducive to the attainment of the goals. It is imperative that we be completely honest with ourselves about how our organization views and values us. Additionally, we must evaluate the commitment that we have to the organization. Failure to do this can lead to "acceptance" by default of situations that will prevent us from achieving our goals. Gail Evans refers to this as making your decisions from a "position of power." [2] This position of power means you're not letting yourself feel like a victim, even if things haven't worked out the way you had hoped in your organization. Instead, you examine your organization and determine the best decision for you to make to move toward your goals.

The feminine perspective on relationships with our employers tends to mirror the liaisons we pursue in our personal lives, specifically those with a significant other. This relationship that we develop can be based on the entire organization, our department, or management. The Feminine Relationship Model developed by Weaver and Hill characterizes five distinct relationship stages that are based on the outcome of four factors:

1. How a woman is identified or described within her organization
2. A woman's needs that she is trying to meet through her relationship with the organization
3. The level of investment and commitment she is willing to make
4. The organization's agenda for her

Upon review of each of these factors, a woman's relationship with her organization can be categorized by one of the following stages:

Stage 1: Dating – playing the field, searching, unattached, neophyte
Stage 2: Girlfriend – exclusive commitment, going steady
Stage 3A: Mistress – maverick, opportunistic or used, emotionally vulnerable
Stage 3B: Fiancée – engaged, limited partner, chosen one
Stage 4: Spouse – full partner, married, totally committed and loyal

A Work Relationship Indicator (WRI) [1] can help you determine where you are in your relationship with your organization by assessing three things: how you view yourself in your organization, your needs at this time from your employer, and your level of investment or commitment to your current organization (Table 8.1) [1].

After you've selected the categories that best describe you for the Descriptors, Needs Assessment, and Level of Investment determine where you are based on the relationship description in Table 8.2:

For each of the categories, write down (in Table 8.3) the relationship stage that you have assessed:

Interpretation.

- Same stage for all three categories: You are definitely in this phase of the relationship
- Two categories are the same: Your category with two common descriptors is your dominant relationship stage
- All three categories are different: You are in transition in this relationship

**TABLE 8.1** Work relationship indicator – personal assessment [1]

| Descriptors | Needs Assessment | Level of Investment |
|---|---|---|
| Circle the letter in the one box of descriptors that best describes how you view yourself in your current job. | Circle the letter in the one box that best reflects your needs at this time | Circle the letter by the one statement that accurately reflects your level of investment or commitment to your current organization |
| A<br>Neophyte, new to the organization. Experimenting with jobs and roles and trying to find the right one. | A<br>Security, social acceptance, approval, shared burden, shared risks, feeling of belonging in the club, full benefits, stock options, cars, upgraded travel, money, status, insider, sense of history and connectedness | A<br>My loyalty and commitment to the organization is based on comparable loyalty and commitment to me from the organization |
| B<br>"Going steady" with the organization. Testing or looking for a long-term relationship with the organization. Flirting with recruiters but will turn down offers. | B<br>Control, respect, inclusion, an alternative to long-term commitment, less emotional attachment and vulnerability, and getting what I've earned | B<br>I am loyal and committed. However, I reserve the right to determine the level of personal sacrifice I'm willing to make for the benefit of the organization |
| C<br>Limited partner. Formally engaged to the organization. Chosen for potential including into the inner circle. Willing to make some sacrifices. | C<br>Mutual commitment, trust, shared risks, part of the club, mentor/sponsor, skills utilized, strengths leveraged, deficits trained out, ability to affect company culture and policy | C<br>I am extremely loyal and very committed. I have sacrificed and/or am willing to sacrifice my personal and social needs for the benefit of my organization |
| D<br>Maverick. Opportunisitic. In control of relationship – or vulnerable and feel manipulated, used, or restricted. | D<br>Skills base, independence, a professional identity, status, beginning rites of passage in the workforce | D<br>I'm committed to learning and doing my job. I feel I'm too new to think of loyalty and commitment in any serious sense right now |

*Continued*

**TABLE 8.1** Work relationship indicator – personal assessment [1]—*Cont'd*

| Descriptors | Needs Assessment | Level of Investment |
|---|---|---|
| E | E | E |
| Full partner. Self-sacrificing. Married to the organization. Totally committed for better or worse. Considered an insider, publicly support the organization. | Financial security, belonging, status, professional validation, dependability, predictability, a solid foundation | I want to be committed and loyal; right now I'm trying to figure out what that means to the organization and to me |

**TABLE 8.2** Interpretation of personal assessment

| Descriptors | Needs Assessment | Level of Investment |
|---|---|---|
| A=Dating | A=Marriage | A=Mistress |
| B=Girlfriend | B=Mistress | B=Fiancée |
| C=Fiancée | C=Fiancée | C=Marriage |
| D=Mistress | D=Dating | D=Dating |
| E=Marriage | E= Girlfriend | E=Girlfriend |

**TABLE 8.3** Your relationship status with your organization (please put the appropriate term that you assessed in the boxes below)

| | Descriptors | Needs Assessment | Level of Investment |
|---|---|---|---|
| Stage: | | | |

This information should be used to support your decision making regarding whether or not you will stay in your current organization to pursue your goals. This is a personal choice and should be based on where and how you want to be viewed and your personal vision.

Good decision making is a combination of instinct, confidence, decision-making skills, and external influences. The degree to which we use each of these tools varies from one decision to another. Your decision-making style will dictate the process to making your decisions; however, a process outlined by Hereford can be useful to any decision-making process [3]. The process includes the following seven steps in making a quality decision:

1. Identify the decision to be made as well as the objectives or outcome you want to achieve.
2. Do your homework. Gather as many facts and as much information you can to assess your options. You must do the research in order to make a well thought-out decision, but don't let analysis lead to paralysis.
3. Brainstorm and come up with several possible choices. Determine whether the options are compatible with your values, interests, and abilities. When my daughter found herself at a crossroad in her life where she needed to make a career move we took the time to discuss and weigh the possibilities. While she had a good position that had the possibility for growth and economic stability that she wanted, it didn't give her the quality of life she wanted. She made a change, and she made her choice with confidence. It is important to be confident with your choice because you've now weighed your options and done the most you could to arrive at that decision.
4. Weigh the probabilities or possible outcomes. In other words, what is the worst that can happen? What will happen if I do A, B, or C, and can I live with the consequences?
5. Make a list of the pros and cons. Prioritize which considerations are very important to you and which are less so. Sometimes when you match the pros against the cons you may find them dramatically lopsided.
6. Solicit opinions and obtain feedback from those you trust or who have experienced a similar situation. If there are no similar situations go on blogs or social networks, or look for chat rooms; the Internet is a beautiful thing! There may be some aspects you haven't thought about in your evaluation.
7. Make the decision and monitor your results. Make sure you obtain the desired outcome and get the feedback that you need.

After a detailed process such as this, you should feel comfortable that you're making a well thought-out and informed decision.

## ESTABLISH YOUR GOALS

My mother is the most optimistic person I've ever known and always told us to speak positively about ourselves and our situation. She proves her unflappable optimism on a daily basis, at least annually as a resident of "tornado alley." One of the most active regions in the United States for tornadoes. Being a native Oklahoman, even in the worst tornado threats, her optimism remains with statements such as "well if that tornado comes our way at least we'll get a nice breeze [wind]!" Now that's optimism! I am consistently grateful that she has passed this trait on to me, as well as her insistence upon speaking only positive words about our goals. If you haven't been fortunate enough to be a natural optimist, don't despair – you can still see great things happening in your future.

Yes, you can still "learn" to see yourself attaining your goals. The first step has been completed: you've written them down. Step two involves taking five minutes right now to close your eyes and visualize yourself achieving this goal. Step three involves you speaking your goal out loud – to yourself. Don't mumble. Speak it clearly, loudly, and with confidence. The fourth step is to tell someone. Tell a trusted friend or mentor of the goal you've set for yourself – and ***really tell it!*** To "really tell it" differs from just "telling it" in that you speak with confidence, enthusiasm, and detail. Explain why it's your goal, how you arrived at it and what it means to you to attain it. Consider the example below of my vision:

Pamela *telling it*: "I have a goal of inspiring people and helping them achieve their dreams."

Pamela *really telling it*: "Ever since I was a little girl gazing up at the stars from my grandmother's back yard I have believed in dreaming big. I dreamed of being a doctor, an astronaut, and a television star! As hopeful as I was about my goals, when I was a young woman I was tested; I had several difficulties, made many bad choices, and put myself in situations that could have stopped me from achieving my goals. However, I learned that there's always a way out – if we will believe. Believe, work, and act. I also learned that there is something within each of us, when *sparked* by a passion and knowledge of the possible – that drives us forward no matter how dark a situation may be or how many times you've failed, or even if no one else believes in you. You can still make it happen. Success is not a mystery. My goal is to help millions of people realize this and attain their dreams. This is totally possible and can be done by helping them to understand how powerful they are and how bright their futures can be – this is real. With knowledge, commitment, work, and the right mix of resources we can do the impossible. My goal is to provide the inspiration, guidance, and tools to help anyone who's willing to believe move from dreams to a great reality!"

Stop for a moment and think about how you "felt" when you read each of those descriptions of my goal. Ask yourself, which of these descriptions of my goal gave you the most confidence that I would achieve it? Ask yourself, which of these descriptions sounded like the most confident person? By now, you should be getting the picture of how powerful it is for you and everyone who will support you to hear you "really telling it." It makes a difference. Now take some time to really tell it!!

Much of what was shared in the previous chapters will contribute to the development of, and the formalization of, your goals. Take time to plan, understand what you will need to do, prepare, and make a commitment to the execution of your plan. I recognize that planning comes easier for some than others, but most STEM professionals have experience with planning at some point in their life. Learn how to organize yourself and plan ahead, but keep up that "winners don't quit" mindset, and make sure to carry out the plan.

In a study conducted on 149 participants from around the world, researchers compared those who wrote down goals with those who did not and analyzed the rate at which they obtained those goals [4]. They concluded that simply writing it down increases your chances of fulfilling your goal. Individuals who wrote their goals down achieved an average of just over six goals whereas those who didn't write them down achieved an average of four of their goals within a given period of time. While this may not seem significant, imagine how different you life would be if for 10 years you obtained two additional goals per year over what you would without writing them down. This leads to an additional *twenty* goals attained. These twenty goals may mean completing a master's degree, buying your dream home, building a stronger relationship with a loved one, or establishing a scholarship in the name of your parents. Whatever it is, this matters. So write down your goal, the steps you will take to get there, the resources you will need, and your timeline, and then check your plan every month or week to make sure it's underway.

Now that you have moved from the dream stage and made a decision it is time to establish concrete goals. Determine your goals and relate them to where you want to be in the future – there is a lot of power in understanding our goals. Goal setting should be done with consideration for all areas of your life including career, family, financial, health, community, and all other areas relevant to you. A number of goal-setting templates are available online; however, much of the same can be accomplished with a legal pad or through the use of a spreadsheet. Whatever format you use, fill out a chart or table similar to Table 8.4 to organize and clarify your goals. Then you will need to list each individual goal on another page (spreadsheet) and determine the short-term and mid-term goals required to attain the ultimate goal. Finally, you will need to schedule the start (the date on which you will start working toward this goal) and completion dates for each goal. Utilize the Career Management Chart developed in previous chapters to populate this chart and add the additional details for attaining each series of goals or use the Goal Establishment Chart in Table 8.4.

## PLAN, PREPARE – AND *EXECUTE*!

If you are now thinking Big, it's time to plan and prepare in just as grand a fashion. I want to stress the importance of the plan and preparation; however, as women and especially women in STEM, I've witnessed us spending too much time on the planning – never thinking we're *quite* ready. Again, it's critical to plan and prepare because we may fail – for totally avoidable reasons. I experienced this with the development of a technical engineering firm, largely because I didn't properly prepare, but it also was not my true vision. I had been a consultant for about 10 years on a part-time basis while growing my academic reputation. When the consulting work grew so much that it was too much for me to handle, I assumed I could start an engineering services firm to accomplish the

**TABLE 8.4** Goal establishment chart

| | Long Term | Mid Term (3 to 5 years) | Short Term (1 to 5 years) |
|---|---|---|---|
| Career Goals | | | |
| Family Goals | | | |
| Financial Goals | | | |
| Spiritual Goals | | | |
| Health & Fitness Goals | | | |
| Community Service Goals | | | |

goals of this customer. Going from an individual consultant to running a business with employees, payroll, benefits, and hiring requirements is a totally different experience.

*If your ship doesn't come in, swim out to meet it.*

**Jonathan Winters**

Well, I made two major mistakes (among many that I made in this business) – first, I started it for the wrong reason: my customer needed more help than I alone could provide. Rather than starting a full business, a smarter thing to do would have been to contract with an additional consultant to support me in the effort. In any case, though I managed to run the business for over 10 years it never realized its full potential. As a result, I learned some very valuable and sometimes painful lessons. Among the most important lessons is the fact that preparation is essential in the planning process. I was not at all prepared to run a business – especially when my employees and most of the work was located at a military installation four states away! Take the time to prepare by using the following Key Steps to Planning in Figure 8.2.

In addition to the plan, you will need a plan's best friend: a timeline. Just as in school we got midterm reports and final evaluations, it is important to do a personal quarterly, midterm, and annual evaluation of your own progress in order to monitor yourself and hold yourself accountable for moving toward your goals.

## HARD WORK AND SMART WORK

Success requires hard work, but it also involves working smart. While there is no substitute for hard work, we live in an age where we have many resources available that can make working more efficient and integrated and can have a greater breadth of impact. In our technology-rich environment hard work is taking on a different persona. There was a time when you wanted to be the first

For each short-term goal answer the following:

1. How much time will it take to attain this goal?
2. What resources do I need to attain this goal?
3. What preparation is needed to attain this goal?
4. What are the financial implications or requirements?
5. What are the existing resources I have which can provide support for the attainment of this goal?
6. How much time commitment is required from me to attain this goal on a weekly, monthly, and annual basis?
7. What activities am I currently doing that pursuing this goal will impact?
8. What type of schedule should I implement to complete this goal?
9. When will I begin?
10. How will I know when I have achieved this goal?

**FIGURE 8.2**   Key steps to planning

and last one in the office to show your boss that you were his or her most valuable resource.

While "presence" is still important, it can be manifested in different ways given our technology resources. Thanks, or no thanks, to technology, you may be working for someone you have never laid eyes on. We are in our beds at 11 at night and responding to e-mails or meeting with colleagues halfway across the world. It is possible to work hard in 2012 in a way that is totally different than 15 years ago.

The key is to understand the following: How much of my plan requires me to be in certain physical locations to successfully execute?

1. What are these locations?
2. Do I have access to them?
3. How much time do I need to spend in them?
4. What are the times I need to spend in the given locations?
5. Who do I need to know?

While working hard will always matter, the higher you climb up the organizational and innovation ladder, the more important it is to work *smart*. It's about understanding how to accomplish what you need to in the most efficient way possible. Keep in mind this includes cultivating relationships that will help you in the environment you're working in today and where you hope to be working in the future. Understanding what resources you need to work is especially important. If you need a certain kind of computer, smart phone, network, or other technology that allows you to work remotely, you'd better be sure you have access to it if you want to work as efficiently as possible. Working smart also means recognizing when you need to pull back and take some time to recover. I've always believed the world looks best through rested eyes.

Knowing what resources we need, how to access them, and how to use them is very valuable. For example, if you want to go back to school to pursue a graduate degree because you recognize that everyone at the level you want to achieve in the workplace has a master's degree, you need to understand the resources you will require to accomplish this goal. Your assessment of resources should include financial, relationships, equipment, time away from work, etc., so you can choose a program that is flexible to fit into your schedule. Then you would see if necessary resources were available: maybe your organization will reimburse you. Perhaps they have an on-site program or relationship with an institution to offer online courses. Another financial resource might be a loan attached to some level of volunteerism or community service upon completion of your degree. You will need to look at different levels of graduate programs – while you need an accredited program, you may not need to go to an Ivy League school. From the standpoint of time, you may realize that you don't have time to go to class every day but you're not disciplined enough to do all your work from home via an online program. If this is the case, you can find an interactive online degree program which allows you that level of interaction along with some flexibility.

## GOOD ASSOCIATION AND NETWORKING

The importance of having the right people in your inner circle cannot be emphasized enough for those hoping to attain great goals. We have discussed a number of ways to obtain these relationships from Female Fusion, identifying mentors, and relationships with individuals in our personal and professional networks. The development of a personal accountability team can also be useful in moving toward your goal at a healthy pace.

A personal accountability team is a group of individuals (at least two) that you've shared your vision with and asked to hold you accountable. The chairman of your personal accountability team is YOU, thus your team will have a minimum of three people. Keep a journal with a table that shows your goals to share regularly with your accountability partner. Your accountability team should consist of individuals locally and remotely who you trust to help you achieve your goals. Social media resources such as Facebook can be extremely valuable in facilitating interaction with your accountability team. Use Figure 8.3 below to develop your ideal Accountability Team.

Your accountability peer is a person with whom you will share your goals, your plan, and your schedule to obtain those goals. You can have a digital accountability partner – you can even make your smart phone an electronic accountability partner! Have it send you reminders or ask for your status a week to 10 days in advance.

To make sure those that you're asking to serve on your accountability team understand just how important their support is to you, I recommend the use of a formal invitation to serve as your accountability partner. Invitation is used

| Goal: _____ | | |
|---|---|---|
| | Communication Plan | Meeting Plan |
| Chairman | | |
| Peer A.P. | | |
| Senior A.P. | | |
| Personal A.P. | | |
| Electronic | | |

**FIGURE 8.3**  Your accountability team

because if you are serious about achieving your goal this will be an exciting and worthwhile endeavor for someone who cares about you to participate in – it will ultimately be a celebration upon the attainment of your goal! A sample invitation is provided in Figure 8.4 and should be adapted to meet the needs you have in securing your accountability team.

Finally, when it comes to good association, take time to be a "good friend" or associate to yourself. Most of us are better friends to others than we are to ourselves. For instance, when we make a mistake we recount it over and over again in our minds, telling ourselves how stupid it was, wondering how we could have possibly done something like this, and even calling ourselves names. This is not at all how we would treat a friend. We must be a good friend to ourselves, as often we will be the only one available to provide the encouragement. So make it a habit to speak positively to yourself, to think healthy, empowering thoughts about yourself and be sure to give yourself a pat on the back with even the small successes.

## NOW THAT YOU'VE DONE IT!

Success is a lifestyle. Whatever success is to you, it is something that will likely grow and adapt though the years. The point is to always be pursuing it – keep your passion strong and you will achieve it. The key is to know it, say it, do it, don't quit on it, and celebrate it! Once you have achieved your goals, this should give you additional confidence to achieve even more. Take time to relish your victory, celebrate it, and then it's time to move on to the next big dream! Also, be sure to take time and help another person in the attainment of her dream. This will keep the passion burning in you and give you the fuel to be productive, be impactful, and live your dream for decades.

Dear _____,

I am working toward a goal in my life and I am requesting your support as an accountability partner in the achievement of my goal. I know that you have many demands on your schedule and should you be unavailable to support this request, I certainly understand.

I will be respectful of your time as my accountability partner and will take the lead in suggesting meetings, keeping you updated on my progress.

As my accountability partner, you can expect me to fully commit to my goals and do the things I have said are required for the attainment of my goals. I ask that you challenge me to reach my goals, keep on schedule for completion of all action items, and engage in regular meetings with me. I propose the following as a communication and interaction process.

- Initial meeting to discuss my goal(s)

    o I will send you my personal vision, goals, and plans at least one week prior to our

       meeting

- Monthly Status meetings (via Skype, phone, or in person as is convenient for you)

    o I will provide updates to my progress on each goal at least a week prior to our

       monthly meeting

- Annual goal evaluation

If you are willing to be my accountability partner, I agree to accept your open, honest, and sincere feedback. I also pledge to uphold my part of this relationship and fully commit to the attainment of the goals.

Sincerely,

_____

**FIGURE 8.4**    Sample accountability partner invitation

Never quit dreaming! Always believe in the next vision! We need you and are celebrating your success and passion today! In other words, it's time to do it again!

Your mentor can act as an accountability partner as well. As a mentor, if I have a mentee who doesn't seem to be moving toward her goals after a certain period of time, I will have a conversation with her to make sure those are still her goals. I would encourage you not to put your mentor in that situation because it can be hard for him/her to address. I suggest that you instead consider your mentor a back-up accountability plan in case your initial accountability peer fails you. Another place to find accountability partners is within professional organizations. These are great venues for finding like-minded people who will support you and help you move towards your goals. The Institute of Industrial Engineers (IIE) is an example of an organization where you can find account-ability partners, mentors, and like-minded individuals.

Sometimes all it takes is this power circle to encourage you to keep work-ing on attaining your goal. In Dale Carnegie's book, *How to Win Friends and Influence People* [5], Carnegie talks about having a small group of friends or associates that you meet with on a regular basis to share your goals and ambi-tions. Although this book is dated in terms of its political correctness, many of his points are still valuable, and I'm calling this group he discusses a *power circle* because this group is establishing goals, they have ambition, and plans, and they hold each other accountable. Knowing you're going to meet with that power circle can be motivating and can help you find resources and establish relationships that can be beneficial in the future.

## ALWAYS BELIEVE IN YOURSELF AND YOUR VISION

No one who is successful became that way without encountering obstacles in her professional and personal life. These problems are a part of the process and can come from the people, our environments, finances, or ourselves. The key is to recognize the source of the obstacle, determine how you will handle it, and know that you can make it to your goal, despite this obstacle. There are a number of ways to handle obstacles which vary by the issue. These approaches should be weighed and can range from ignoring it (if thinking about it is the largest challenge) to removing or even destroying it. An eight-step principle for overcoming obstacles has been adapted from Gilberd [6] and is as follows:

1. Address the source of your obstacle
2. Quickly develop a plan to eliminate it and minimize the impact it has on you
3. Keep your sense of humor
4. Completely ignore the naysayers
5. Follow your passion with conviction
6. Remember your past successes
7. Vividly visualize yourself overcoming this obstacle and how you "feel" when it's over
8. Visualize that you have already attained your goal every time this obstacle comes to mind

Even in the down times, the slow times, when we don't feel we're making progress, we must accept that challenges are a part of a successful life! Just because you face a difficulty, fail, or don't reach a goal this does not mean you won't reach your ultimate goal. Goal achievement is an iterative process: you do it once, attain your goal, and do it again to attain your next goal. But the more you do it the better you get, and always remember, don't quit. When I was a student, I committed a poem to memory that I would recite whenever I needed to hang on to my dream in the midst of an obstacle. I encourage you to consider doing the same.

*When things go wrong, as they sometimes will,*
*When the road you're trudging seems all uphill,*
*When the funds are low and the debts are high,*
*And you want to smile, but you have to sigh,*
*When care is pressing you down a bit,*
*Rest, if you must, but don't you quit.*

*Life is queer with its twists and turns,*
*As every one of us sometimes learns,*
*And many a failure turns about,*
*When he might have won had he stuck it out;*
*Don't give up though the pace seems slow –*
*You may succeed with another blow.*

*Often the goal is nearer than,*
*It seems to a faint and faltering man,*
*Often the struggler has given up,*
*When he might have captured the victor's cup,*
*And he learned too late when the night slipped down,*
*How close he was to the golden crown.*

*Success is failure turned inside out –*
*The silver tint of the clouds of doubt,*
*And you never can tell how close you are,*
*It may be near when it seems so far,*
*So stick to the fight when you're hardest hit –*
*It's when things seem worst that you must not quit.*

*Author unknown*
**Source: www.thedontquitpoem.com/thePoem.html**

If you don't quit, you will reach your leadership and innovation goals. Here's to you and the attainment of your greatest dreams, ambitions, and innovations!

## REFERENCES

[1] Weaver VJ, Hill JC. Smart Women, Smart Moves. New York, NY: American Management Association; 1994.

[2] Evans G. Play Like a Man, Win Like a Woman. New York, NY: Broadway Books; 2000.

[3] Hereford Z. 9 Essential Life Skills: A Guide for Personal Development and Self-realization. Canada: Mandz Publishers; 2007, p. 97.

[4] Matthews G, Dominican University http://cdn.sidsavara.com/wp-content/uploads/2008/09/researchsummary2.pdf (accessed June 28, 2012).

[5] Carnegie D. How to Win Friends and Influence People. Audio Book. An Adaptation of How to Win Friends and Influence People (1936) New York, NY: Simon & Schuster; 1999.

[6] Gilberd PB. The Eleven Commandments of Wildly Successful Women. New York, NY: Macmillan Spectrum; 1998.

# Index

Page numbers followed by *f,* indicate figure and *t,* indicate table.